CW00403817

BECOMING A

PRACTITIONER
RESEARCHER

First published in 2006 by Middlesex University Press

Copyright © Paul Barber

ISBN 1 904750 53 2

All rights reserved. No part of this publication may be reproduced, stored in any retrieval system or transmitted in any form or by any means, electronic, mechanical, photocopying, recording or otherwise, without the prior written permission of the copyright holder for which application should be addressed in the first instance to the publishers. No liability shall be attached to the author, the copyright holder or the publishers for loss or damage of any nature suffered as a result of reliance on the reproduction of any of the contents of this publication or any errors or omissions in its contents.

A CIP catalogue record for this book is available from
The British Library

Design by Helen Taylor

Cover from an original photograph by Joanne de Nobriga
www.spiritheartphotography.com

Printed in the UK by Cambridge Printing

Middlesex University Press
North London Business Park
Oakleigh Road South
London N11 1QS

Tel: +44 (0)20 8411 5734: +44 (0)20 8411 4162
Fax: +44 (0)20 8411 5736

www.mupress.co.uk

BECOMING A

PRACTITIONER
RESEARCHER

A **GESTALT** APPROACH TO HOLISTIC INQUIRY

PAUL BARBER

Middlesex
University
PRESS

ACKNOWLEDGEMENTS

I would like to express appreciation to those who helped me become a practitioner-researcher: Professor Annie Altschul; Professor Ruth Schrock; John Heron; Dr. James Kilty; Professor Petruska Clarkson; Professor Malcolm Parlett; plus my cats Pi and Nyssia and Chen who taught me presence and patience.

To my fellow travellers upon masters and doctorate programmes and within the various courses, consultancies and groups it has been my privilege to facilitate.

To Dr Peter Critten for his interest, general midwifery and kind suggestions as to how to deliver this creation, plus Paul Jervis who had sufficient faith in me to publish this work.

Especially to my partner Anna Lai Fong who encouraged me to write and my son Marc who keeps my interest in moment-to-moment inquiry and the transpersonal vital and alive.

ITHACA

When setting out upon your way to Ithaca,

Wish always that your journey be long,

Full of adventure, full of discovery.

Of the Laestrygones and of the Cyclopes,

Of an irate Poseidon never be afraid;

Such things along your way you will not find,

As long as you keep your thoughts raised high,

As long as a rare excitement

Stirs your spirit and your body...

Konstantinos P. Kavafis, Alexandria, Egypt 1911

*Your duty as a Gestalt-informed practitioner-researcher
is to be; not to be this or that.*

Contents

Choosing a Method and Practising the Skills *(Exploration)*

Exploring Experience and Illuminating Data *(Exploration)*

Towards an Integrated Whole (Resolution)

Chapter 5
Towards a Holistic Model of Facilitative Inquiry – Mapping a Multiple Reality

Tai chi is zen is meditation is yoga is gestalt is awareness is tai chi is zen
— and I have to put them all in a circle and start anywhere to know that...

Stevens 1984 p.73

Introduction

pre-contact

i.   Preamble – Researching Holistically and Experientially

This text is designed to help you 'think' and 'act' in the manner of a qualitative researcher and will attempt to brainstorm you with options and challenges in a Zen-like way towards fresh insight. Indeed Zen, 'holistic research' and Gestalt all encourage you to expand and raise your awareness, attend to everything, dismiss nothing and to establish a robust and intimate dialogue with what is unfolding in your immediate environment – right now. In this way, similar to a student of Zen you will also be encouraged to bracket-off belief and disbelief, to cultivate an open mind and to experientially inquire into what is before you. But first, I offer you a working definition of Gestalt as a researching method.

Gestalt – a German word meaning pattern or constellation – describes a phenomenological and whole-field approach that works primarily with direct perception and what a person is sensing, feeling and projecting out upon the world, rather than what they are thinking or interpreting. To this end a Gestalt-informed practitioner-researcher (someone who engages in inquiry as part of their professional role) cultivates an authentic relationship and accompanying dialogue through which to explore how an individual or community's 'awareness' is being constellated in their immediate environment. Central to this process is a researcher's ability to embody a genuine, interested and non-judgemental presence. Underpinning this approach are humanistic values (see 1.4) plus the suggestion that the people, experiences and understandings we inquire into are co-created, self-regulating and best understood experientially. Indeed Woldt and Tolman (2005) have suggested that 'if a picture is worth a thousand words – in Gestalt terms an experience is worth a thousand pictures'! In this context 'raising awareness' is both a research method and an educational outcome, and the researchers themselves are akin to data on a journey of discovery.

How you use the insights of this text remain entirely up to you but, presuming you want to perform hands-on practitioner-research at some time, it will be useful to carry through your reading a 'focus of inquiry'. Granted, this will change once you enter 'the research field'; nevertheless I encourage you to hold a general 'research question' in mind when you read. In this way, I hope the dialogue I build with you will provoke a dialogue between you and your practice.

As to how you might begin to inquire into your own practice once you've chosen an initial theme (say a desire to explore what your clients or colleagues 'most value about the service you provide'), you might keep a reflective diary in which to pool observations – chunks of chronological observation alongside subsequent reflections from which you can perhaps later extrapolate appreciative statements. Following this initial sweep you might choose to form a group to inquire into the 'best experiences' of those working with you. This book will help you understand the directions you can take when commencing practitioner-research such as this while alerting you to: where and on what to focus; the effect of your facilitation style; the developmental nature of groups; how to account for differing levels of influence; the authority of conscious and unconscious phenomena; and the research methods available to support you. It will also provide models through which to shape the information you surface and, last but not least, will enable you to cultivate the mind-set of a practitioner-researcher.

I feel I cannot stress too strongly the need for you to describe the mental-set and the position you are starting out from, for changes to this will provide evidence of how the research field is impacting you. Bear in mind that research of quality investigates the method as much as the theme and, as the researcher is the most important inquiry tool in Gestalt-informed research, then 'you' become a subject worthy of research!

By way of practical encouragement, periodically throughout the text examples of entries within an ongoing practitioner-research journal are provided in response to the reflections and questions raised. There are also mini case studies to illuminate salient points, plus three extended case studies designed to illuminate the real-life drama of being a researcher. To support you in your research process we also introduce the research-supervisor, someone who listens to your problems and helps craft solutions, coaches you in research and mirrors your wisdoms back to you. This is a qualitatively different person to that of the traditional academic supervisor who merely monitors standards and polices the research method.

As to its origins, this book grew out of some thirty years of inquiry as a group facilitator and organisational consultant; some twenty-five years preparing group facilitators and clinicians – notably upon an MSc in Change; some twenty years as a Gestalt-informed psychotherapist and coach; and some fifteen years teaching research on doctorate programmes. It is therefore a product of my own ongoing and continually evolving practitioner-research.

As a holistic stance to inquiry is taken in this text and Gestalt is used to service this aim, my Gestalt colleagues may feel I am 'not Gestalt enough'! As I have long felt that Gestalt was too important an influence to restrict to therapy and have spent many years dovetailing its wisdoms to holistic education, organisational consultancy, group facilitation and personal development and coaching – I make no apologies for this. For me Gestalt is the fluid cement that holds everything else together.

In summary, this work argues that social inquiry needs to account for inner experience of life where intuition and symbolic meanings are given form, for it is suggested that fantasy and feelings are as strong – if not stronger –

determinants of behaviour and meaning than what is conceptualised and intellectually planned. Simply, it is proposed that to capture the complexity of individuals and groups, researchers need to: be aware of the whole holistic field; appreciate 'what happens when it happens' and 'how' it happens; incorporate sensory perceptions and imaginative visions; engage with the situation in an experiential, humanistic, vibrant and authentic way; and account for macro scales of society and micro influences of the person. So, are you up for this challenge?

Reflections

To help you begin your research journey and dialogue with this text, you might consider writing up in a reflective journal the 'ideas and feelings stimulated by this opening preamble', as well as 'what interests you' and 'what you would like to explore in your practice'. You might also consider issues and problems you think you will be encountering and addressing. As over the course of your reading it is very likely this initial picture will change, I suggest you date your entry and as your views change you return to update changes to this, your original perspective. Here is an example of the first entry in the journal of a practitioner-researcher whose journey of inquiry we will be sharing with you throughout this book. All you need to know is that the practitioner-researcher in question works in an academic institution and that following a suggested trigger for reflection, a research journal entry in response will appear in italics:

(August) Having read this first preamble I'm beginning to suspect that Gestalt and holism might be about being open to all influences – NOW, plus creating a field within which to examine my own practice. I get a sense of a landscape that will be forever changing and populated by different issues and people, and of me 'recording everything', what I'm seeing and hearing as well as what I'm thinking and imagining for fear of missing something which becomes important later on in my study. At the moment my field of 'inquiry' encompasses a Department of Educational Studies and all who sail in her, and my 'task' – to increase awareness of all members of staff (which includes admin and support staff as well as academics) to what has been called 'work-based learning' (something I'm initiating) but which I prefer to call 'practitioner research' and to document/describe and learn from the journey.

ii. Learning Intentions of this Work – Facilitating Growth and Development

This text's experiential approach to learning is designed to:

- Develop an appreciation of researching and learning as integral to living
- Expand your interpersonal sensitivity, inquiry skills and personal awareness
- Inspire you to reflect upon the laminated character of reality and the nature of truth
- Identify facilitative strategies and inquiry tools for illumination of the human condition
- Stimulate your powers of critical reflection, imagination, courage and curiosity
- Illustrate a way of researching that enhances awareness and is educational for organisations, groups, the facilitator of inquiry and their subjects alike
- Foster a dialogue between yourself, case study examples, models and methods that support a Gestalt-inspired holistic vision of inquiry
- Illuminate a model of holistic inquiry that addresses multiple levels of reality inclusive of emotional and intuitive levels of experience which, though primarily focused on the present, describes a practitioner-researcher relationship that develops through time (see iv below).

iii. Reading as Reflective Inquiry – This Text as Dialogical Research

This work is designed to be active rather than passive and partial rather than impartial. At various times I will ask you to reflect on what you are reading and to apply its insights to experiences of your own. As you read through the text it is hoped you will be *'developed'* as much as educated to inquiry, and challenged towards consideration of how *'the personal'* dances with *'the transpersonal'* in holistic inquiry. Hopefully you will enter the fruit of these reflective exercises within your research journal focused upon an inquiry that interests you.

In order to honour 'direct experience' and to enter a dialogue with you I have written this book in the first person, for fear that if I censored what I thought or felt, or disguised myself and my bias behind feigned objectivity, you might be lulled into accepting my opinion as if it were some kind of unquestionable truth. I wish to avoid this conspiracy and would far rather you spit out what I say than swallow it partly chewed and undigested. Within the text you will also be invited to consider how a researcher's perceptive style and beliefs about reality affect their inquiry.

You will be asked to explore for yourself how the quality of a hard edged '*I-It*' *relationship* focused on task and boundaries, an '*I-I*' *relationship* preoccupied with personal interpretation, and a Gestalt (see 1.2) informed '*I-Thou*' *relationship* respectful of self and others. Each solicit very different influences and data.

Primarily, as this text is written for a practitioner-researcher, i.e. someone who performs inquiry as part of their professional duties, this work is of value to teachers and trainers, therapists and counsellors, consultants and change agents, managers and trainers, nurses and social workers, indeed all who facilitate qualitative social inquiry as part of their job.

In the Gestalt vein this text adopts – where we retain a focus upon whatever phenomenon is unfolding – you will not be allowed to settle into any one position, but rather encouraged to stay in dialogue with each and every position, inclusive of physical, social, emotional, imagined and transpersonal phenomena.

> Think 'structure' and you'll see structure. Think 'culture', and you'll see all kinds of cultural dimensions. Think 'politics' and you'll find politics. Think in terms of system patterns and loops, and you'll find a whole range of them.
>
> *Morgan 1997 p.349*

In the final analysis, this text invites you to experiment, to explore and to form your own conclusions. In research and facilitative inquiry, as in life, the quality of the journey rather than the arrival is the most important thing.

> Not knowing that one knows is best;
> Thinking that one knows when one does not know is sickness.
> Only when one becomes sick of this sickness can one be
> free from sickness.
>
> *Tao Te Ching*

Indeed, I have found the cultivation of 'uncertainty' essential to my practice as a practitioner-researcher, whether I'm within the role of teacher, group facilitator, organisational consultant or therapist; for nothing kills my interest, de-energises my experience nor deadens my curiosity in others more than 'certainty' carried aloft by an ends-driven outcome!

iv. The Developmental Models of this Text – Capturing Flow and Depth

Throughout this work two perspectives interplay. The first plots the development of a practitioner-researcher's relational movement through time within four evolving phases:

1   **Orientation** (initial meeting): a client/collaborator/stakeholder-centred phase where the researcher and client (be this an individual, group or organisation) meet, sketch an initial relational contract, orientate to each other's world-view and emotional presence, and begin to form a working alliance;

2   **Identification** (planning): a problem-centred phase where the researcher and client identify problem areas and prospective strategies, refine the initial research contract, raise to awareness the purposes and tasks of inquiry and the nature of the researcher-client relationship in which they will engage;

3   **Exploration** (implementing): a strategy-centred phase where the researcher and client work together to implement the strategies they chose earlier, modify these in the light of feedback and decide the next and future steps the research might take;

4   **Resolution** (debriefing): a quality-centred phase where the researcher and client evaluate outcomes, review what sort of publication of findings and follow-up is necessary, and complete the present research contract while working towards a positive ending of their relationship.

This model was originally derived from a study of the therapeutic relationship (Peplau 1952) and refined through doctoral study (Barber 1990b); it has been applied to facilitation in education (Barber 1996b) and consultancy (Barber 1999b), and constitutes a developmental and strategic map of the facilitative relationship a practitioner-researcher engages with their client/co-researchers. At various times two further phases may also be drawn into this frame, *Pre-engagement and Post-engagement*.

The second influential model of this text is a holistic one which maps multiple levels of influence. I have applied this model to many things: levels of experience and learning; modes of perception and making sense of the world; ways of perceiving and inquiring. It originally arose from doctoral study (Barber 1990b) into the lens through which various therapies seemed to facilitate inquiry, which I distilled down to physical, social, emotional, imagined and intuitive levels of engagement wherein you employ:

* Observational and interpretative skills at the physical/sensory level to collect information so as to create a working hypothesis

* Boundary setting and culture-building skills at the social/cultural level to enable collaborative inquiry and data born of genuine and authentic communication

* Person sensitivity and empathy so as to appreciate the emotional/transferential (biographical) level of experience

* Imaginative insight and metaphor so as to raise awareness to the fantasised/projective (imagined) level so as to illuminate the effect of unconscious influence

- Envisioning and intuition to speculate upon the unknown and unknowable influences at the transpersonal/spiritual level that may be facilitating you!

Although in reality the above influences run together, I have teased them out in this way so we might appreciate the facets of experience that contribute to our holistic reality. But be warned, in 'the real world' beyond our thoughts and senses there are no levels or developmental relational phases, merely energies waiting to be formed, as I hope the case studies illuminating this text will verify.

Reflections

Now that you have a more detailed list of the 'learning intentions' of this work, reflect upon your own practice – what stands out for you, what excites you, what concerns arise and what reservations, if any, come to mind?

(August) Wow! My first thought is 'Am I up to all this?' but I am intrigued how I can adopt and be seen by others as adopting 'a Gestalt-inspired holistic vision of inquiry'. I guess my question is: how different is that from my approach to research now? I'm also a little scared that I'm being invited to 'change' in some subtle and as yet un-clarified way.

Having been introduced to the key themes of this book, what view do you have as to how the four phases or stages – orientation, identification, exploration, resolution – can be used as a framework for your own research.

(August) I guess it helps me put a structure on what I am doing and could be linked with planning, so may use it when I come to write up my research proposition. In contrast to other research plans – the pace will be determined by the players, my stakeholders – we will evolve and change the plan together. I'm also aware of how the above levels go from the more mundane and observable 'physical level' to a more subtle and intuitive 'transpersonal level', and am intrigued with how I might capture such wide-ranging influences.

It would also be useful before moving on to the next chapter, where you will be applying principles and techniques to your specific field of inquiry, for you to consider the co-researchers-cum-stakeholders you will be working with. It might help if you thought of all these people gathered in one room and imagined having a dialogue with them; you might record the results of this imaginary dialogue in your reflective-journal.

(August) OK... I now need to consider these questions in relation not to an abstract Department of Educational Studies, but particular individuals representing different departments and interests, as well as how I will gain support and sponsorship for my inquiry.

Approaching Gestalt and Holistic Inquiry

orientation

Don't try to force anything.
Let life be a deep let-go.
See God opening millions of flowers
everyday without forcing the buds…

Bhagwan Shree Rajneesh in Hayward 1990

Chapter one

Researching Holistically –
Doing 'Less' and 'Being' More

1. Researching Holistically –
Doing 'Less' and 'Being' More

Research is akin to a tree: the roots draw from metaphysics and philosophy; the trunk is formed from observation and experience; the branches are shaped from interest, experiential engagement and imaginative speculation and the fruits are further questions.

Preamble

This chapter is designed to orientate you with the aims, style and content of this text. To encourage your reflection upon how Gestalt and holistic facilitation may be integrated in an approach to research, you will be invited to consider how what is on offer here compliments the world view that is gaining ascendance in the twenty-first century, which is suggested to be rapidly moving towards an ecologically informed holistic position. I also attempt to illuminate the core concepts that underpin this work. The definitions provided should not be taken to be truly definitive but rather as starting-points of your own research. We will also survey what holistic inquiry might focus upon, along with poetic aspects of inquiry in this vein. Hopefully, by the close of this chapter you will have begun to reflect upon your own world-view plus the bias and values you operate by.

1.1 Illuminating a Holistic and Transpersonal World – The Universe as a Dancing Gestalt

One of the great shocks of the twentieth century came about when Science began to realise – largely from insights born from the study of ecological systems and quantum physics – that it could not reach an understanding of the physical world merely by collecting ever more quantitative data or statistical analysis. This was especially brought home when physicists discovered that solid matter started to dissolve at the sub-atomic level into wave-like patterns of probabilities. There were therefore no *'things'* to be studied, but rather *sequences of dancing gestalt-like patterns* that inter-connected with everything else:

> The final net result is a whole-making universe, that it is the fundamental character of this universe to be active in the production of wholes, of ever more complete and advanced wholes, and that the Evolution of the universe, inorganic and organic, is nothing but the record of this whole-making activity in its progressive development.
>
> *Smuts quoted in Clarkson 1993 p.5*

Periodic leaps in awareness which questioned established *'scientific paradigms'*, the world-view of the scientific community used to define legitimate problems and solutions (Kuhn 1962), were termed by Kuhn *'paradigm shifts'*, times when the dominant world-view underwent a revolutionary break from tradition. At the dawn of the twenty-first century the 'old paradigm' that has been on the wane for some time appears to be one that venerates:

- The universe as a mechanical system composed of rudimentary building-blocks
- The human body as a machine
- The view of society as a competitive struggle for existence
- The belief in unlimited material progress achievable via economic and technical growth
- The belief that the female is subordinate to the male as a basic law of nature.

After Capra 1997

Conversely, the 'new paradigm' that has already begun to take hold:

- Is holistic and sees the world as integrated rather than a collection of dislocated parts
- Fosters a gestalt-like appreciation of the interdependence of the individual and their socio-cultural field
- Is deeply ecological (see Devall and Sessions 1985) to the degree that it includes spiritual awareness
- Views the world as a network of phenomena that are fundamentally interconnected and interdependent
- Recognises the intrinsic worth of all living things and sees human beings as merely a part of the web of life.

After Capra 1997

Evidence for this shift is not just confined to physics (Capra 1991) but is also discernible in the emergence of such new disciplines as 'transpersonal ecology' (Fox 1983 and 1990) and 'eco-psychology' (Roszak 1992), where *'the whole'* rather than *'the parts'* are emphasised. As our postmodern world looks to the non-physical sciences and metaphysics, a holistic Gestalt-inspired stance to the facilitation of research, one which is alive to the transpersonal, is not just for now – but something of the future.

The deep ecological and holistic awareness fostered by eco-psychology where care for *'the whole'* is expressed, in a Taoist-like way stresses man's place in the natural world while honouring the 'oneness' and interdependency of his existence and being. Note how this influence is expressed in the quote below:

Care flows naturally if the 'self' is widened and deepened so that protection of free Nature is felt and conceived as protection of ourselves... You care for yourself without feeling any moral pressure to do it... If reality is like it is experienced by the ecological self, our behaviour naturally and beautifully follows the norms of strict environmental ethics.

Fox 1990 pp.246-7

In a Gestalt and transpersonal approach to human inquiry, as with quantum physics, you don't end up with solids so much as phenomenological patterns determined and shaped by a greater whole. At the simplest level, a facilitator cum practitioner-researcher – be they a teacher, researcher or counsellor – who attempts to account for influences of 'the whole', must automatically take note of the transpersonal, for their search understanding of the larger picture leads them naturally to consider influences above and beyond the self:

> God is day and night, winter and summer, war and peace, surfeit and hunger: but he takes various shapes, just as fire, when it is mingled with spices, is named according to the savour of each... Men do not know that what is at variance agrees with itself.

Zohar quoted in Clarkson 1991

But Gestaltists don't jump to the conclusion that nature is the *'hand of god'* nor indeed ascribe properties to deities or theories; they rather keep the question alive and, in a postmodern sense, shun big narratives in favour of more local and situational events (Flick 1998). In this way, though alive to 'the whole', they keep the holographic germ of individual experience firmly in focus. Interestingly, the quantum physics notion of an innate non-personal intelligence holding fields of influence together (Capra 1991), again comes uncommonly close to the Taoist concept of the 'natural mind':

> Tao, when put in use for its hollowness, is not likely to be filled.
> In its profundity it seems to be the origin of all things.
> In its depth it seems ever to remain.
> I do not know whose offspring it is;
> But it looks like the predecessor of nature.

Tao Te Ching

Taoism extends and moves Gestalt notions of the 'field', 'interrelatedness' and the 'fertile void', into transpersonal territory. It also cautions us to consider the 'unknown' and 'unknowable', and to be alive to metaphor and paradox, while raising our awareness to a kind of knowing which extends beyond the intellect and senses. When quantum physics and Eastern philosophy start to converge in this way, it is wise for us to reappraise our world-view.

> All the world is working together. It is all one living whole, with one soul through it. And, as a matter of fact, no single part of it can either rejoice or suffer without all the rest being affected. The man who does not see

that the good of every living creature is his good, the hurt of every living creature is his hurt, is one who wilfully makes himself a kind of outlaw or exile: he is blind, or a fool.

Murrey quoted in Clarkson 1991 p.31

1.2 Gestalt – Illuminating Patterns within a Contextual Whole

Gestalt, through the cultivation and development of an aware and respectful relationship, inquires into the unique patterning of forces that shape perception and behaviour. It stresses that within every person and relationship we meet with a quality that we have never encountered before nor can ever meet again – for all is in flux. In this context, any conclusions we come to are current and temporary (Frank 1939), situational and relative:

> One cannot step into the same river twice nor grasp any mortal substance in a stable condition, but it scatters and again gathers: it forms and dissolves, and approaches and departs.
>
> *Heraclitus quoted in Staemmler 1997 p.46*

Framed by such unique influences, the present is approached as a wondrously never-to-be-repeated moment.

For us to appreciate uniqueness and immediacy to this degree, three components must come together. First, a practitioner-researcher facilitating inquiry in the Gestalt mode needs to practise what Buber (1951) calls *'inclusion'*: an existential position which is open and sensitive to novelty, curious about the human condition, suspending of judgement and alive to uncertainty:

> Cultivating my uncertainty to me means two things: First, I have to stay aware all the time that I am uncertain in regard to my attribution of meaning; I deal with a positive, desirable and delightful feeling that reminds me of the interpersonal reality of which I am a part. On another level, this can provide me with a feeling of security, for it tells me I am in touch with reality. My uncertainty becomes an aspect of my internal support system. It warns me not to attribute meanings one-sidedly and reinforces me to regard my client as a partner in the therapeutic process.
>
> *Staemmler 1997 p.45*

Here practitioner-researchers pay attention to what is *'becoming'* as much as to what is obvious – hence the title of this work. Second, in order to encourage 'whole-hearted' and meaningful inquiry, they convey understanding through the cultivation of a genuine, congruent and authentic presence founded on interest and concern. Third, they develop a transpersonal communication style which is:

17

...committed to dialogue, surrendering to the between. This is a form of contact without aiming, with truth and healing emerging from the interaction rather than from what is already known...

Yontef 1996 p.94

Inquiry of this nature is best performed through the medium of a transparent relationship which emphasises 'existence' while bracketing-off abstract theoretical explanations and 'cause and effect thinking'. For instance, although existential and witnessing, Gestalt does not represent a philosophical discourse but rather a philosophy for living:

> Existentialism wants to do away with concepts, and to work on the awareness principle, on phenomenology. The set-back with the present existentialist philosophies is that they need their support from somewhere else. If you look at the existentialists, they say they are non-conceptual but if you look at the people, they all borrow concepts from other sources. Buber from Judaism, Tillich from Protestantism, Satre from Socialism, Heidegger from language, Binswanger from psychoanalysis, and so on. A rich heritage, indeed. Gestalt therapy is a philosophy that tries to be in harmony, in alignment with everything else, with medicine, with science, with the universe, with what is. Gestalt therapy has its support in its own formation because the gestalt formation, the emergence of needs, is a primary biological phenomenon.
>
> *Perls 1969 pp.15-6*

Being both inter-relational and holistic, Gestalt is a close cousin of field theory which attends to what Lewin (1952 p.150) calls: 'the constellation (the structure and forces) of the specific field as a whole'. This view represents a sort of social Taoism, in that it suggests a person cannot be understood in isolation from their dynamic cultural, social and physiological network – their total field:

> Now what is first to be considered is that the organism always works as a whole. We **have** not a liver or a heart. We **are** liver and heart and brain and so on, and even this is wrong. We are not a summation of parts, but a **co-ordination** – a very subtle co-ordination of all these different bits that go into making the organism. The old philosophy always thought that the world consisted of the sum of particles. You know yourself it's not true. We consist originally out of one cell.
>
> *Perls quoted in Clarkson 1993 p.5*

At root, in its approach to inquiry, Gestalt stands for creativity, contact and experiential wisdom founded upon the authority of the 'lived experience':

> The therapeutic process is therapeutic in itself because it allows us to express and examine the content and dimensions of our internal lives. We live full lives to the degree to which we find a full range of vehicles

which concretise, symbolise, and otherwise give expression to our experiences. The depth, duration, and extent of cultivating each medium of expression are the other significant factors in defining the fullness of life. I have known many people who have spread themselves so thin that their lives took on a shallow, translucent, and sadly contrived quality. In the frantic flight to touch all we can in life, we wind up feeling like hurried tourists, snapping pictures of everything and seeing nothing.

Zinker 1978 p.8

Gestalt-inspired inquiry emphasises not just intercommunication – but *'contact'*. By attending to the inferences, assumptions and values exerting influence over current behaviour, and to distortions and limitations of awareness, it creates an organismic picture of a person or group's immediate experience, as they move within reach of the contact-zone or boundary of others:

> People regulate themselves organismically through the actions or processes called the contact boundary. The contact boundary is a function or organ of the entire organism/environment field. The individual components of boundary processes comprise awareness (what one is in contact with); motor behaviour (what one does); and feeling (affect). The contact boundary differentiates the field and has the dual functions of joining the individual with others and also maintaining separation. (…) But it is only by active exchange with the rest of the field that life and growth are possible.
>
> *Yontef 1996 p.91*

Just as 'action', 'contact' and 'choice' are seen to signify health, so rigidity, stasis and control – characteristics that interrupt our organismic flow and cause boundary disturbance – are taken to be symptomatic of a person, group or organisation's state of dis-at-ease.

We see from the above discussion that a Gestalt-informed researcher is more concerned with what is actually experienced and being felt, seen and heard in the immediate environment, than what is thought or interpreted. By following the movement of a person or community's 'continuum of awareness' – moment-to-moment focus – we then begin to appreciate what is of greatest need or interest (being brought to the fore) and what is contextual (left to melt into the background). This is not to say intellect, theory and interpretation are forgotten, but rather that they play second fiddle when we endeavour to refine 'immediate experience', to develop a 'felt sense' of the world and to build a 'picture of awareness' (Yontef 1996). Awareness is then stalked by attending to the individual's 'personal psychological process', plus exploration of the 'immediate experience of the person embedded in her or his environment' (Smith 1996 p.3). In this context, 'raising awareness' to how we co-construct our world becomes a primary outcome:

Through a creative involvement in the Gestalt process, it is my hope that a person:

- Moves toward greater awareness of himself – his body, his feelings, his environment
- Learns to take ownership of his experiences, rather than projecting them on others
- Learns to be aware of his needs and to develop skills to satisfy himself without violating others
- Moves towards a fuller contact with his sensations, learning to smell, taste, touch, hear and see – to savour all aspects of himself
- Moves towards experience of his power and the ability to support himself, rather than relying on whining, blaming or guilt-making in order to mobilise support from the environment
- Becomes sensitive to his surroundings, yet at the same time wears a coat of armour for situations which are potentially destructive or poisonous
- Learns to take responsibility for his actions and their consequences
- Feels comfortable with the awareness of his fantasy life and its expression.

As the work progresses, the person flows more comfortably in the experience of his energy and uses it in a way which allows his completeness of functioning.

Zinker 1978 pp.96-7

In the last analysis, though eclectic and drawing from a multitude of sources – field theory, Zen, perception psychology, biology – Gestalt is nevertheless a distinct system that represents 'process' rather than 'content':

I consider this blend of existential and Zen philosophy, this organismic personality theory, and this phenomenological experiential style of working to be the necessary and sufficient conditions to define the Gestalt approach. I don't define the Gestalt approach by techniques.

Smith 1978 p.74, quoted in Smith 1996

1.3 Innate and Tacit Intelligence – Transpersonal Influences over and above the Self

My understanding of the 'transpersonal' and the innate intelligence that works through, around and beyond ourselves is informed in part by Taoist philosophy – that suggests we are intimately connected to Nature, and Gestalt – which emphasises that we are interrelated to everything else, which together lead me to propose that:

- We emanate from and live within a dynamically interrelating and intelligent universal field – which suggests the cosmos is innately intelligent

- Intelligence is generalised as well as localised throughout the cosmos, which has physical as well as transpersonal manifestations – as above so below in ourselves

- As human beings we are not separate from the unified field but rather focal points within it, where consciousness peaks to create and witness a changing scenery – we are therefore intimately and energetically related to everything and everybody else

- From this perspective we are not our bodies or our ego, nor our personality, but multi-dimensional beings connected to a unified multi-dimensional field – who are this moment focused within a physical-social-emotional-projective-intuitive experience

- Within this context, matter is a phenomenon of consciousness and reality is a phenomenological creation we have constructed from perception – we perceive that which we have first learned to conceive.

Taking the above points each in turn, it may be suggested that:

- If we take the stance that 'the cosmos is innately intelligent', then everything has meaning and purpose and nothing ever happens by accident – even though we may not be able to perceive this from an individual vantage-point

- As practitioner-researchers, we need therefore to consider how the innate intelligence of an organisational or relational system might be worked with

- As we are 'intimately and energetically related to everything and everybody else', our respect should extend to reverence of all we are, all that we meet, and all that surrounds us

- Because we 'are at this moment concentrated and focused within a physical-social-emotional-projective-intuitive experience', we need to attend to this, our multi-faceted nature, in our address of client-systems and research

- As 'we perceive that which we have first learnt to conceive', we need to realise that we are dealing with a symbolically co-created reality rather than a cause-and-effect series of tangible facts; in the 'real world', the quantum one beyond our senses, there are no colours, no shapes and no smells, just stimuli waiting for organisation.

In this context, the *I-Thou relationship* a practitioner-researcher shares with their client becomes a reverential one, wherein both parties meet aspects of themselves while exploring the divine nature of life. Sanctified by a shared authentic presence, facilitative inquiry now becomes both a service and an act of celebration.

21

When I experience the other fully, acceptingly,
When I experience the flow of his feeling,
The beauty of movement, of expression, of longing,
Then I know the meaning of reverence, holiness,
And the presence of God.

Zinker 1978 p.17

1.4 Humanism – Ethics with a Human Face

Holistic researchers and educationalists, in a similar way to Gestalt practitioners attempt to account for the whole human system within its natural setting, inclusive of:

- Individual, social, cultural, symbolic and spiritual dynamics
- The phenomenological world we co-create
- Experientially derived wisdom and knowledge.

Philosophically, with its championing of open-mindedness and the veneration of experientially derived knowledge, humanism supports this stance. It also under-writes the transpersonal by supporting the wisdom of our hearts besides the development of our minds, while remaining mindful of more subtle ways of knowing:

No construction, however broadly based, will have an absolute authority; the indomitable freedom of life to be more, to be new, to be what it has not entered into the heart of man as yet to conceive, must always remain standing. With that freedom goes the modesty of reason that can lay claim only to partial knowledge, and to the ordering of a particular soul, or city, or civilisation.

Santayana quoted in Blackham 1968 p.11

By marrying holism with humanism, inquiry is also given an ethical base, which fosters personal growth and development.

To make more abundant and more secure and more developed what is already in our hands and in our hearts is the meaning and measure of the task, the source of our confidence, the guide of our hopes. The responsibility of the humanist is response before it is answerability. He has responded and tasted, and therefore he takes on responsibility and makes exertions, for himself and for others.

Blackham 1968 p.188

In this light, a humanistic value-base in service of educational and research ethics suggests:

- An individual's mind and body, as well as their intellectual, emotional and spiritual being are indivisibly related one to the other

- That given the resources, individuals have the potential to work towards resolving their own problems
- That it is important to meet life in an open, inquiring and creative way in order to maximise our growth as individuals
- That reason and democratic process should underpin all we do, individually and socially.

From this perspective, *you, your person-hood and humanity are most important tools of inquiry*, and relationships are the prime medium through which you conduct research.

To research the transpersonal you need to proceed imaginatively and intuitively, using symbols and metaphor to raise to attention the tacit human ways we relate to each other and the world. Indeed, you may have to employ a metaphor in order to compare and catch more appropriate metaphors:

> As we gain comfort in using the implications of different metaphors in this way, we quickly learn that the insights of one metaphor can often help us overcome the limitations of another.
>
> *Morgan 1997 p.353*

For example, as I write this passage I'm aware of identifying with the image of a monk, one who isolates himself from the mundane world to attune to the abstract and divine. This metaphor does not quite fit what I'm about, but it catches the dutiful side of writing. Dwelling upon the monk, another metaphor arises, that of the artist; seeing myself on a continuum with monasticism at one end and artistry at the other, feels much more comfortable and appropriate. When my writing flows I feel very much the creative artist, when the muse forsakes me the dutiful monk fits well enough. Alerted to humanistic values of democracy, experiential learning, autonomy and holism, while mindful of their own humanity, a facilitator cum practitioner-researcher is better able to:

- Experiment with their 'being' – as well as what they do
- Impact and be impacted by others
- Use facilitative and gestalt-based phenomenological inquiry as fitting and necessary
- Move with awareness to whatever new research position presents itself
- Question themselves and all before them.

Humanists, similar to Gestaltists, inquire from within a relationship. Because they do not consider themselves superior, they do not isolate themselves behind a facilitative, researcher or leadership role from the human race or those they study.

1.5 The Practitioner-Researcher – Life and Work as Research

A researcher systematically explores experience with a view to refining knowledge; a practitioner applies knowledge skilfully with a view to improving practice. As both must be integrated in real-life situations to affect excellence, we arrive at the notion of the practitioner-researcher. *Without research, practice becomes sterile*. Likewise, if practitioner-researchers in such professions as counselling and teaching fail to illuminate new knowledge within those involved, then something is drastically wrong.

As a practitioner-researcher, a human instrument who experiences alongside others, I regard myself as my primary facilitative and research tool and, because I am a social being constructed in the same way as those I study, I look within myself and to my own experience to glean a richer understanding of others.

As the reality we inhabit is a socially constructed one, where cultural 'meanings' rather than 'facts' predominate, to understand our world we must balance information which is intimate and experiential, with that which is interpretative and wide-ranging. In this context, the questions we form are more important than the results we defend, and knowledge becomes warm-blooded and tacit, rather than cold and factual in nature.

> Logical thinking cannot yield us any knowledge of the empirical world;
> all knowledge of reality starts from experience and ends in it.
> Propositions arrived at purely by logical means are completely empty of
> reality. I never came upon any of my discoveries through the process of
> rational thinking.
>
> *Albert Einstein*

1.6 The Researcher is the Primary Research Tool – Developing 'Mindfulness'

In this work, the researcher is seen to need sufficient social awareness as to enter, facilitate and shape the relational word they seek to inquire into alongside their co-researchers cum subjects. Though group workers especially come to mind, we all employ facilitation of one kind or another in our work.

As to what a researcher who facilitates a climate for inquiry may need to do, Rogers (Rogers 1967/83) suggests they may be best employed:

- Setting the initial culture and trust for exploration
- Helping to elicit and clarify purpose
- Acting as a flexible resource

- Responding to expressions, intellectual content and emotional attitudes while endeavouring to give to each individual the time and attention they warrant
- Taking the initiative in sharing themselves – both thoughts and feelings – in ways that do not impose, but rather represent a simple sharing others may take or leave
- Accepting and openly acknowledging their own limitations.

Honouring the human condition in the above way, a practitioner-researcher might draw from their personally acquired store of practical skill and intuitive wisdom to:

- Generate understanding
- Liberate and refine new knowledge
- Raise personal and social awareness
- Educate and empower those involved.

In this context, the facilitative skills of a practitioner-researcher dictate their investigative and social competence. But what exactly are they facilitating?

As a holistic researcher I seek to facilitate creativity alongside rigour and to educate those my inquiry involves. I want 'the process' of my inquiry as much as what 'results' to make a positive contribution. I reason that as life is developmental and growthful, and as humankind are by turns clear and chaotic, focused and defuse, I must respect these qualities in my facilitation and inquiry. This means I permit myself to be a researching artist as much as a researching scientist, for I am prepared to surrender myself to the expressive poetry of inquiry.

Artistic and Poetic Expression in Research – Inquiring with the Heart

In the passage below, by staying with my moment-to-moment awareness, a picture is produced of the sensory bombardment I experienced when wondering the streets of Kowloon the evening before my departure home to the UK:

> I'm still trying to soak up all the atmosphere around me, the colours, the people, the temple smells, the fascinating variance of street life: smart young children in uniforms; shabby old men playing mahjongg and dealing thin oblong cards in the parks; the burning of incense and red prayer sheets upon the temple walls; tiny knee-high shrines along the streets; huge brass urns shaped like dragons issuing forth tea at corner bars; giant leopard-spotted moray eels and bright multi-coloured fish of pinks and blues punctuated with crimson streaks in restaurant

aquariums opening to the street; fish markets with live lobsters, small
eels and fish of every size and hue; old traders pushing flat wooden
wheelbarrows through crowded alleys; the smell of steamed pork
dumplings and frying noodles; strings of red Chinese sausage; red taxis
hooting through the streets; herbalists with all manner of bone, antler
and dried fungi and roots stretching from floor to ceiling in small
square-compartmented old wooden shelving; and the people: small and
delicate with transparent skin, some round with flat noses, others
exquisitely delicate with fine lips and skin from olive to brown, more
often with serious expressions and downcast eyes.

Barber 1995

The above account portrays the 'poetic' flavour of coming back to sensory engagement – after task-completion and a phase of over-involvement and intellectual intensity. I had often heard of other facilitators experiencing a sensory rush, and now I was experiencing one at first hand. This 'deep description' puts the unfolding drama of research into context, while describing the swing from intellectual task to sensate process, a natural consequence of holding oneself in and being in a state of intense readiness for far too long. In this context, the researcher contacts their senses and the 'artist within' to convey the unique emotional climate they are living and working within.

Facilitative skills, when married to holistic inquiry and Gestalt, encourage you to relate in the same way that (hopefully) you relate to life, so that enjoyment, excitement and an openness to all join seamlessly together.

So, with earlier examples before us, how is facilitation actually practised? In **Figure 1,** we find an example of the 'qualitative' concerns a researcher inquiring in a holistic mode takes with them, namely, an attention to the interplay of:

1   Micro and Macro influences: how small- and large-scale influences of person, the group, culture and the cosmos affect inquiry

2   Perceptive functions: what we see and hear, imagine and think about

3   Conscious and unconscious processes: the known and the unknown

4   Bias: personal beliefs, values and givens

5   Methodology: how the investigation process affects inquiry

6   Growth: learning and other developmental effects

7   Differing levels of experience: keeping our senses and intuitions in dialogue

8   Personal politics: making, breaking, and maintaining rules.

The above will be returned to later in this work. To handle all perspectives at depth is impossible; rather, you stay respectful in the knowledge that there will always be more than you know or understand, can control or account for; you also research with love.

1.7 Existence as Life-long Research – A Concluding Summary

Gestalt, the transpersonal, humanism, the practitioner-researcher role, qualitative research and facilitation share much in common, for they support communion rather than isolation and holism in contrast to segmentation. When harnessed together, as you will discover in this text, these inputs make a powerful blend for mindful and educational 'real world' inquiry, where emphasis is upon:

- Solving problems rather than just gaining knowledge
- Predicting effects rather than finding causes
- Illuminating large effects rather than relationships between variables
- Concern for actionable results and testing programmes and interventions, rather than merely developing and testing theories
- Researching outside rather than within research institutions
- Multiple methods rather than single methods
- An orientation to clients and subjects rather than academic peers.

After Patton 1995

As for how 'real world' inquiry differs from 'artificial world' inquiry, Weick (1985) cites as an exemplar of artificial research a laboratory study into interpersonal attraction by anticipating interaction with a stranger whose traits are listed as more or less similar to one's own (Byrne 1961). He compares this with a study of 'fear and loathing' at a college social function where researchers actually took part in a college mixer (Schwartz and Lever 1976). He also cites an inquiry into 'reactions to fear' via anticipating electric shocks (Folkins 1970), in contrast with 'learning first hand how to work on high steel in a twenty-one story building' (Haas 1977). 'Real-life' research, therefore, looks not only 'upon' but 'within' the dynamics of events, and is performed in intimate relationship with the field. If your facilitation doesn't enact 'real world' research, what is it doing?

Holistic research, in the vein described here, thus extends 'real world' inquiry by looking not only 'within' but 'beyond' the self, to the transpersonal. It also fosters respect for the human condition through facilitation which is generative of personal development, empowerment and responsibility.

Figure 1 Concerns and Questions of Holistic Research

Micro and Macro Influences

Influences of the person, their relationship to the research field and with the researcher, the influence of their membership to various networks, groups, communities, organisations and other systems; cultural and social traditions that affect the research field; the inquiry's connection to life and the universe – ethnographic and transpersonal influences and micro and macro influences upon and within inquiry. *Questions generated:* How do I account for individuals and the effect of personal meaning? What social or group dynamics affect the field of inquiry? How do micro and macro influences interrelate?

Perceptive functions

Influences of thinking, feeling, sensing, imagining and intuiting – ways we perceive and construct the phenomenology of our personal everyday reality. *Questions generated:* What intellectual maps, theories or beliefs affect people's actions? What emotions energise and motivate behaviour? Are people more attuned to what they see or hear, or to what they actually do? What beliefs or dreams drive me and those I am researching?

Conscious and unconscious processes

Influences of socialisation, belief, transference, learning and the imagination; meanings we project out upon the world; mental defence mechanisms and idiosyncratic psychological interpretations; symbolic imagery that affects a study's psychodynamics. *Questions generated:* What unconscious processes shape events here? What may I be blind to in this setting? What do I miss as a researcher? What resistances or shadow dynamics affect people here?

Bias

Personal and group politics, 'isms', gender, class, racial and professional influences; assumptions and expected outcomes for the researcher and research – intrapersonal and interpersonal effects. *Questions generated:* What am I setting out to prove? What gender, class, racial, professional and cultural assumptions colour my vision? Are my values and hypotheses overt or covert? Which lines of inquiry do I choose? Which lines do I reject?

Methodology

Gains and costs of choosing a specific line of inquiry, focus, technique; the research approach and the effects of strategy and intentionality upon inquiry. *Questions generated:* How does my choice of research method limit me? How do I account for the unexpected? Is my research method suited to getting at the data I need? What skills do I need?

Growth

Educational and developmental outcomes; intrapersonal and transcendental influences that arise from critical reflection and meditation; tacit knowledge that illuminates deeper aspects of being. *Questions generated:* How am I growing and developing as a researcher? What do I need to develop to improve my research ability and skills? How does my research benefit or develop others? What difference does my inquiry make and what value might it add?

Differing levels of experience

Physiological, social, personal, spiritual – the many layered and laminated nature of multiple fields and realities that contend for our attention. ***Questions generated:*** Do I pay enough attention to physical evidence? Do I attend to social and relational pressures? Do I need to account for psychological influences within people and groups? Do people act from the stance of 'personal reality' or a culturally created 'group reality'?

Personal politics

What the researcher/research sets out to prove; overt and covert influences from those who fund the research; why the research was initiated in the first place; how research findings will be used – inquiry as an agent of change; what is seen as acceptable and/or unacceptable; who sets the rules and polices them. ***Questions generated:*** What cultural or political pressures and meanings have effect here? What do I seek to gain from this research? How are people socialised or controlled by the research process or the research field?

Adapted from Paul Barber 1999b

If a man will begin with certainties, he shall end in doubts: but if he will be content to begin with doubts, he shall end in certainties.

Bacon quoted in Clarkson 1991

Stand with humility before life – everything before you is a miracle. You cannot get everything 'right'; you do not have to be perfect; just share the range of your awareness at any time – what you 'see and hear without' and what you 'feel and imagine within'. Be aware of your limitations, do not judge yourself too severely for not finding the right answer – there isn't one to find.

Non-existence is called the antecedent of heaven and earth;
Existence is the mother of all things.
From eternal non-existence, therefore, we serenely observe
    the mysterious beginning of the Universe;
From eternal existence we clearly see apparent distinctions.
These two are the same in source and become different
    when manifested.
This sameness is called profundity.
Infinite profundity is the gate whence comes the beginning
    of all parts of the Universe.

Tao Te Ching

In this first chapter you have been introduced to a range of beliefs/principles/values that underpin a 'Gestalt approach to holistic inquiry'. Take some time out to write up in your reflective journal particular principles that have made an impact on you, as well as principles and values that you are less comfortable with.

(August) It's made me realise that research is not simply going out and imposing a questionnaire on others and writing up the results. It is about relationships – and there come with it personal and social responsibilities. My concern at moment is how all this squares with a very political and bureaucratic culture – the one I will be researching within, but I guess at least 'recognising' and naming this context is part of the process.

Acquaint yourself with the ideas and notions presented in **Figure 1**, then go on to using the categories and questions presented here to explore your own field of inquiry; i.e.:

(September) Application of **Figure 1**:

Micro and macro influences: *I am very conscious of how phrases like 'work-based learning' have been misrepresented, ill-judged. I am conscious also of my own very strong bias here that 'practitioner research' is a better descriptor of what we're trying to encourage. I intend to start by having a debate about what exactly everyone understands by 'work-based learning' and to explore examples of what this really means, at both the individual and systemic level.*

Perceptive functions: *I am again drawn to my own strong FEELINGS here – also the fact that being an INFJ in Myers Briggs terms – I am very strongly influenced by 'feelings'. I guess I need to listen more to what drives others.*

Conscious and unconscious processes: *Similar theme – what do I miss as a researcher? I need others and quality 'supervision' here.*

Bias: *My big problem – I'm not entering this inquiry with as much openness as I should.*

Methodology: *Will I be too dependent on an action-oriented approach to research?*

Growth: *How can I judge this? Will it be more personal than professional?*

Differing levels of experience: *Unravelling what has led colleagues to experience learning as they have, their differing styles of making sense, their* investment in intellectual sense-making and out-comes, the need to counterbalance this by raising awareness to other ways of 'knowing'.

Personal politics: What is it I really want from this? Conscious I've spent more time reflecting on the process and ignoring who this should benefit – potential students and the organisation in the long term.

In the course of your journey as a practitioner-researcher and your reading of various studies, as well as the case studies of this book, return to **Figure 1** periodically to critique and evaluate your practice.

Embodying Holism

identification

Life is a series of natural and spontaneous changes.
Don't resist them – that only creates sorrow.
Let reality be reality.
Let things flow naturally forward in
whatever way they like…

Lao-Tse in Hayward 1990

Chapter two

Appreciating the Energetic Whole –
Insights from Field Theory and Gestalt

2. Appreciating the Energetic Whole – Insights from Field Theory and Gestalt

What is true and authentic and genuine does not change, although your perception of it may vary or alter drastically depending upon your sense of belonging or alienation, internal ease or dis-ease; if you have not lived through something how can you believe it to be true?

Preamble

This chapter focuses upon how the fluidity, continuity and relational integrity of a team or organisation may be analysed as an integrated whole. We also explore the contribution that field theory makes to whole systems analysis, and survey models that enable causal relationships to be examined holistically. Within this section you will explore contractual, idealised, and authentic levels of relationship, and consider the effect each of these exert upon facilitation and data plus the researcher-client relationship. Questions and methods conducive to the illumination of tacit and subtle ways of knowing will be surveyed, and Gestalt psychotherapy is examined as an example of a holistic inquiry. By the close of this chapter you should have developed an appreciation of the various tasks that attend whole field analysis, and be better prepared to plan and facilitate holistic study of your own.

2.1 Dynamics of the Phenomenological Field – Influences of Emergence and Dissolution

Dynamic wholes, 'fields' if you will, exert an immense influence upon all we do and what we are. Although the Western scientific tradition emphasises biochemical and structural integrity, something else is energetically at play more akin to a common beat or pulse, something that has an ability to thread everything together. Indeed, scientific studies have themselves confirmed that cells have a natural cooperativeness that leads them into working together (Fox 1983):

> Living cells, separated from each other and pulsing to different beats, will eventually become synchronized in their pulsing. This phenomenon has also been observed in shops where they sell clocks - the clocks tend to synchronize their ticking. Even in women's dormitories and wards, women's menstrual cycles tend to coincide - see Leonard 1978. The emphasis here is on the modern scientific evidence for the interconnected-ness of all life on earth.
>
> *Clarkson 1991 p.31*

If synchronisation happens with people and with clocks, consider the implication for organisational and group behaviour. In this sense, 'fields' of influence are not merely intellectual conceptions but active, transpersonal and dynamic forces that bind us all to ever-greater living wholes. Consequently within a field perspective, instead of concentrating on singular causes, the practitioner-researcher would be well advised to look to external currents and patterns, or 'fields', within which 'specifics' tend to reside.

Malcolm Parlett (1993), in what has become a seminal paper on field theory, draws attention to the applicability of Gestalt principles to field analysis. In order to appreciate field relationships, Parlett suggests we attend to:

The Relationship of the Figure and Ground

The degree to which arising phenomena belong to either 'the figure' – what momentarily peaks and currently holds attention in the short-term – or 'the ground' – the background or cultural milieu and long-term structure from whence a phenomenon emerges. At the individual level this implies:

> ...attention to the whole field, to what lies in the background of peoples' lives as well as what is uppermost.
>
> *Parlett 1993 p.117*

Differentiation and Confluence

The degree to which a phenomenon is self-contained or has a tendency to merge with other phenomenon:

> Thus in one direction, there is the pull towards centralization, unification, submergence of differences, and the political advantages which stem from being bigger and more powerful. In the opposite direction, there is the pull towards separate identity, sectional distinctiveness, with the freedom from interference by others or the obligations of consensus politics.
>
> *Parlett 1993 pp.116–7*

Resilience and Reconfiguring

The degree a phenomenon resists merger (resilience) or has the ability 'to absorb change or disturbance' and to reconstitute itself (reconfiguration); a quality Pascale (1991) sees as far more valuable than stability in organisational life and culture.

> Seeking a new ground or context for a present event is, of course, to change the meaning of it – instead of thinking of a cancelled trip as a loss, it may be thought of instead as an opportunity to do something else even more satisfying.
>
> *Parlett 1993 p.118*

The Laminated Field

The degree of interrelation between differing layers and levels of experience, role engagement, fantasy, emotional process, symbolic and imaginal influences and the physical environment.

> We can switch from reality to role play, from experiencing something at a physical bodily level, to visual fantasy, searching for metaphor, to telling the story.
>
> *Parlett 1993 p.119*

Putting the above concepts together, a new cosmology begins to take shape, one where diagnosis and analysis of the whole becomes possible. For example, a practitioner-researcher in a facilitative role, focusing upon the emergence of a current social event *(figure)* from its contextual frame and/or chronological timeline *(ground)*, may now begin to analyse a social phenomenon in terms of its ability to resist systemic pressures *(resilience)*, tendency to stand alone *(differentiation)*, become absorbed (confluence), or to absorb influence and to change *(reconfigure)*. In this context, relationships may be compared to an organismic social dance where qualities of 'awareness' and 'sense of self' peak – from out of a richly woven, multi-layered ground *(laminated field)*.

Unlike systems theory, that tends to look to the communicative flow, field theory looks to organismic wholes. Note that from a Gestalt perspective each person is an organismic whole; a relationship between two or more people may also be viewed as a whole, and organisations likewise. All fields interrelate to ever-greater wholes; where you draw the boundary of your facilitative vision and inquiry defines 'the field' you have chosen to study.

When studying the *field* or *organismic whole* that constitutes a particular person, relationship, role, team, community or organisation, a researcher asks:

- What is happening currently in this phenomenon/organisation/ person's life? *(Figure)*
- What are the longer-term structures of this person/phenomenon/ organisation's life? *(Ground)*
- In what ways does this phenomenon/organisation/person seek to be distinct and separate from other structures/persons it/they meet? *(Differentiation)*
- In what ways does this organisation/person seek to merge or unify with structures/others they/it meets? *(Confluence)*
- How resistant to change is this person/phenomenon/organisation? *(Resilience)*
- How willing and able is this person/phenomenon/organisation to change? *(Reconfiguring)*
- Which levels of functioning – sensory/physical, social/cultural, emotional/transferential, imaginal/projective, symbolic/transpersonal – does this person/phenomenon/organisation characteristically move between? *(Laminated field)*

38

Reflect on yourself as a subject for research, and ponder the above questions. Very quickly you will become aware of your own dynamic complexity; that is, the ecology of your organismic being.

In relational terms, it may be suggested that individuals in the peak of relating, when they are fully contacting and connecting to others, are at their most aware and are most differentiated from others; and that following such active involvement, as they withdraw attention and energy, self-awareness recedes and a person fades back into the socio-cultural field they originally emerged from. That is, until their next re-stimulation into individualised action and movement through another contact-withdrawal cycle:

> ...contact extends into interaction with inanimate as well as animate objects; to see a tree or a sunset or to hear a waterfall or a cave's silence is contact. Contact can also be made with memories and images, experiencing them sharply and fully...
>
> *Polster & Polster 1974 p.102*

Most of us, I suggest, spend many of our days in a grey social soup because we have forgotten or fear the disturbance of how it feels to be truly alive and truly in contact. In this inactivated state we become background, part of the social scenery. Merging with our social background we let our social definitions and norms do our thinking for us; we risk nothing and check out nothing:

> Over the years I have found that most people suffer from functional blindness. Not only do we not notice the subtle visual aspects of our world; we often overlook the obvious. In my work I use my eyes a lot; sometimes they help me scratch out what the person's language does not tell me.
>
> *Zinker 1978 p.257*

Gestalt, as an organiser and facilitator of holistic inquiry, strives to wake us from this sleep, for it supports the view that:

> ...far from becoming a self as an organism that takes in what it wants from the environment, we become a self only through meeting other selves in an I-Thou relationship... I become a self with others.
>
> *Friedman 1989*

This causes me to speculate upon how different in quality and kind the information a practitioner-researcher acquires from a subject they share a trusted relationship with might be to that of a subject with whom they are merely acquainted. A facilitator or other practitioner-researcher's propensity to acquire sound data, I am suggesting here, is proportionate to their ability to develop and sustain an 'authentic relationship'.

Take a community, organisation, team or group you have experienced or currently work within, and consider:

- How are people and events organised into a whole here?
- What current influences affect behaviour?
- What is unique about the group or its culture?
- What is the group in the process of creating, on its present course?
- What are the stated goals of this group?
- What are its hidden, un-stated goals?

(September) The above questions make me think about just what the goals are of this 'group' I am working with, and whether I need to deal with sub-groups (as each academic group has different goals). I'm also aware of current financial restraints and the need to optimise our efficiency without incurring extra costs, and of how the formally appointed senior managers are not always the main movers-and-shapers or group leaders; that our culture is often shaped by charismatic junior players.

In terms of the dynamic influences within a relational field:

Figure . . . . Ground

Resilience . . . . Reconfiguring

Differentiation . . . . Confluence

- Where on the three continuums cited above would you place the issue you wish to research?
- As a practitioner-researcher are you more usually nearer the figure and distinct, or in danger of merging with your client group?
- Are you resistant to change or absorbing of it?
- Do you take a high or low profile as a practitioner-researcher?

(September) There is something here about my being prepared to move from 'ground' to become 'figure'; about 'profile', transparency and my need as a researcher and change agent to be more resilient and differentiated in this system, if I am to challenge it and to make a difference. Here the research becomes a stimulant for personal growth! I also note a bias within me, namely, that I want to change things in the work-place. I wonder what implications this might have for the research study I design.

Bear in mind that field theory is not just a method of inquiry, but may be used to shape and represent the information you surface, as well as help to analyse data.

2.2 Differing Dimensions of the Facilitative Relationship – Towards Authenticity

Throughout each phase of a facilitative relationship, from its orientation through to its resolution phase, three levels of relating run concurrently (Barber & Mulligan 1998 after Greenson 1967):

The **contractual level of relationship** houses a relationship's formally stated purpose, its working alliance, the social and research contract you forge with the subjects of your inquiry, the skill mix you represent and for which your clients seek you out. At this level the professional-to-client relationship unfolds and your professional ethics and training exert influence. All the conceptual, strategic and practical knowledge you bring inform this dimension, as well as:

- The objectives and tasks of the formal contractual relationship and research service
- Your understanding of the baseline you are starting out from plus the client's criteria for success (includes results plus relationship)
- The level of social and intellectual agreement that underpins the service offered
- The scope, values, boundaries and rules of professional engagement.

Here we find influences of this text coming to light, namely the researchers' handling of the orientation, identification, exploration and resolution phases of the researcher-subject relationship; their facilitation style; how they manage the research variables and their own researcher bias; their characteristic perception and sense-making style; their ability to identify blocks to an inquiry's movement and to resolve the same by timely intervention. All these, contractually, both deepen and move a facilitative inquiry further on.

The **idealised level of relationship** encapsulates emotional and imaginal levels of engagement and communication, and represents the shadow side of the contractual relationship where transference, unaware prior learning and idealisation are carried into the present. At this level we find the unconscious influences you bring, your ingrained fixed values and gestalts, plus the mental defences that drive you. Here facilitative aspects of the researcher-client relationship may echo parent-child, teacher-student or boss-subordinate dynamics, plus sexual game-play, along with:

- Traces of unconscious familial and educational conditioning
- The unaware acting out of unrecognised needs, i.e. to be loved, needed, valued, parented or loved by others
- Behaviours associated with heroes and heroines brought to life in your imagination

41

- Role modelling of earlier influential teachers and gurus
- Enactment of symbolic/archetype fantasy figures.

Here we find the influence of transference, counter-transference and resistance, the interplay of mental defence mechanisms and other subconscious influences.

The **authentic level of relationship** is more about who you are at core – the real you from the driver's seat stripped of all social denial, defence and artifice. This, your effective use of self, is dependent upon how aware you are of your real motives and how appropriately you share these in your work. It would not be appropriate to share your inner fears or to burden your clients with your own self-doubt and personal problems, but it is crucial for you to at least recognise what is going on inside yourself. Unless you know what drives you, how will you be able to self-assess, or to make informed decisions about what is appropriate to share or is best left unsaid. This level of real relationship, which is based on accurate perceptions and a willingness to be open, honest, and authentic with yourself and others, incorporates:

- Your core beliefs and values
- Your true self in contrast to your professionalized self
- Your root motives (good and bad)
- Your ability to witness and to critique yourself
- Your spiritual aspirations and your life's higher purpose.

Here a practitioner-researcher's store of personal development and awareness plus their presence, facilitative authority and ability to create a culture of open and honest inquiry and to exert influence come to the fore. While the contractual relationship is hard-edged and scientific, and while the idealised relationship is impulsive and expressive, the authentic relationship serves to stimulate an internal witnessing of the relational whole. A practitioner-researcher, who operates primarily at the *contractual level* informed by professional values and cultural norms, may observe and record what happens, but at best they will tend to collect data that merely narrates social action and common sense rationales. At worst, they may collude with untested 'basic assumptions' (Bion 1960) to the extent that their inquiry and investigations merely describe superficialities while remaining low in real meaning.

A practitioner-researcher who attends to the *idealised level* of a relationship informed by transference and projection, is likely to pick up the symbolic meaning of events and the emotional undertone, but their work – though creative – will tend to feel ungrounded. If they go the whole hog and act from this level, though they may emotionally impact their clients, their presence is likely to skew the information they receive towards a 'transferential' or 'gamey' nature.

By attending to the *authentic relationship* a facilitator or practitioner-researcher adds a further dimension, one informed by honesty and truth, at least to the degree that each person feels permitted and encouraged to communicate their own subjective truth.

Combine clarity around the task of inquiry, as emanates from the *contractual relationship*, with an appreciation of the emotional triggers and symbolic interaction involved; features of the *idealised relationship*, with honesty, as found in the *authentic relationship* and your research and its facilitation will acquire the potential 'to make a difference'. Facilitated inquiry in this vein is consultative, educative and generates authentic I-Thou meetings:

> So there is this new phenomenon coming, the We which is different from the I and the You. The We doesn't exist, but consists of I and You, is an ever-changing boundary where two people meet.
>
> *Perls 1969*

A Gestalt approach to inquiry, in the sense described here, fosters authenticity and enrichment of the contact boundary while setting out to inquire into the authority of the whole lived experience.

Reflections

When you consider contractual, idealised and authentic levels of relationship, at which level do you usually live, and what implication might this have for you as a researcher?

(September) I tend at times, due to my tendency to be emotionally influenced, to be in 'idealised' relationships with others, but think I need to be more 'honest'. To get at 'authentic' data, I guess as researchers we must court authenticity within ourselves. I'm getting a sense of 'the change' this research may be soliciting of me; research as teacher!

As you start to engage with your clients/stakeholders/co-researchers what kind of 'relationship' do you think you will be demonstrating: contractual, idealised or authentic, and how might you seek to balance all three?

(September) I am aware that it is important as a group to move to a more contractual, professional relationship where progress can be made and sustained in the longer term. I am also aware of holding back from sharing my own agenda; I guess a clearer professional-cum-contractual and more authentic relationship is desirable.

2.3 Gestalt-informed Communication and Contact – A Dialogical Example of Collaborative Inquiry

When you become truly aware, your behaviour changes and the constellation of your personality shifts, for awareness acts as a catalyst. Indeed, in seeking to increase personal awareness and to foster a potential for change, Gestalt-informed dialogue has been suggested to enact a co-operative inquiry within the framework of an authentic relationship through the application of a process akin to action research (Barber 1997a).

Below, developmental phases of a Gestalt relationship are combined with dimensions of collaborative inquiry to illuminate the research-minded nature of a Gestalt-informed dialogue in a therapeutic or coaching setting:

a) A contract is identified – **orientation** and **identification** (planning):
   - Rapport is established and rules of engagement are negotiated
   - Problems and tasks are identified
   - Working hypotheses are posed
   - Inquiry approaches are suggested and agreed upon.

   *(Here the **contractual level** of relationship is engaged.)*

b) Experience is engaged and experiments performed – **exploration** (acting/observing):
   - Boundaries are laid and a safe environment is created
   - Awareness is raised towards a developing theme
   - Practical experiments are undertaken
   - Support is mobilised
   - Fantasies are checked out and awareness of the moment is heightened
   - Patterns of the past are brought to awareness in the present.

   *(Here the **idealised level** of the relationship begins to be illuminated.)*

c) Findings are evaluated – **resolution** (reflecting):
   - Earlier working hypotheses are appraised
   - Reactions of the therapist as a co-researcher are shared
   - A debriefing of events and their prospective meaning is illuminated
   - Mapping of the inquiry to date is made
   - Future routes of inquiry are suggested.

   *(Here the **authentic level** of the relationship is strengthened.)*

In Gestalt coaching or therapy, the above cycle is repeated until sufficient awareness, re-integration and understanding are produced to enable a client to meet their current needs. When these needs are eventually met, the therapeutic/educational journey moves on to another cycle or is brought to an end. Here we have an example of a research design that facilitates personal change through the illumination of tacit knowledge. But having described the process and its infrastructure, what exactly does a facilitator cum practitioner-researcher working in the Gestalt tradition actually do? Simply, they attend to dialogue; describe what is in their awareness plus the perceptions in ascendance; illuminate interrelationships; and share their authentic presence whilst raising awareness to the various influences that shape the immediate relational field.

Regarding the questions a Gestalt practitioner keeps to the fore while coaching individuals or facilitating client-systems, a practitioner-researcher here seeks to clarify and raise attention to:

- The relationship of the presenting figure to its historical background (e.g. how the client-facilitator relationship interrelates to the father-daughter one)
- The effects of differentiation and confluence (how the facilitator's experience differs and coincides with the client's)
- Exploring resilience while inviting a reconfiguration (raising the difference between past relationships and current ones)
- Recognition of the laminated field and differing layers and levels of experience (the coexistence of past and imaginative influences upon the present).

To enable authentic exploration, qualities of acceptance, empathy and care need to be cultivated; what is more, your client or co-researchers need to believe that you are working for their common good.

As to the goals a researcher facilitating in the Gestalt tradition works towards, Zinker (1978) notes a need for Gestaltists to:

- Expand a person's repertoire of behaviour
- Create conditions under which a person can see his life as his own creation
- Stimulate experiential learning and the creations of new self-concepts
- Complete unfinished situations and to undo blocks to awareness
- Integrate intellectual understanding with sensory motor expressions
- Discover polarisations out of awareness
- Integrate misplaced feelings, ideas and actions back within the personality
- Stimulate conditions under which the person can feel and act more strongly, more competently, while becoming more explorative and responsible to himself.

From Zinker 1978 p.126

Note the attentiveness and alertness of focus implied in the above, the need persistently to check out and deepen the relationship, the striving to catch the undertone and to enhance authentic communication. Here we see a collaborative inquiry enacted by a therapist and client, where there is a sharing of insights – in a take-it-or-leave-it way, and the illumination of a working hypothesis – that is allowed to emerge from the mirror of a relationship. Intrinsically, what arises is seen to generate meaning. When working in this way, forming a hypothesis is secondary to 'staying attuned to the field' and 'keeping quality dialogue' alive, and evidence is allowed to organically arise and to speak for itself in the manner of grounded theory.

A holistic researcher would be well advised to account for the above areas of investigation and analysis, plus the sense of collaboration and ethos of care, in their own inquiry.

2.4 Staying with the Unbroken Wave of Moment-to-Moment Experience – 'Now'

Whether as facilitator, therapist, consultant or researcher, staying with my confusion while being led by what is emergent in the field always gets me somewhere in the end. For example, in the account below, I share from the driver's seat what it is like to operate in a field-led fashion. In the study herein described, I was contracted as a consultant to explore community dynamics with a view to facilitating personal and relational awareness as a first step in building a foundation for a peer-learning community.

Case Study

Inquiring into Moment-to-Moment Awareness:

The much-condensed sessions described here were of two hours duration and contained some twenty-five individuals. Hopefully something of the involvement necessary for field-attuned practitioner-research in a consultancy setting comes across.

Session 1

I take a seat, draw myself into the circle and wait. I glance around, orientating myself to the room I am in. One participant looks at me fixedly. A silence of fifteen minutes ensues. This interlude is finally broken by a participant observing how uncomfortable the silence has become. I express interest in how some participants seemingly kept themselves comfortable and how others became uncomfortable: 'After all, we had shared the same silence – so what might have been happening?' Some acknowledge that they were 'waiting for me to start', others note 'they were enjoying the silence' and, others that they 'had begun to relax' and to 'put down all that was troubling them'. A participant who had kept her eyes closed for most of the silence says 'what a waste of time it all is', and asks 'what can we learn from such an experience?' She goes on to remark upon the 'futility of the session', and the 'lack of activity of the facilitator'. I suggest that 'possibly the lack of structure has unleashed something a structured beginning might have missed?' I draw attention to the 'inner peace some found', the assumption that 'I would lead and make things happen', and the 'anger from some when I did not conform to expectations'. Two members own up to having initially labelled me as 'analysing and judging them during the silence', though in hindsight, they now see that they were doing this very thing themselves. I voice the hypothesis that 'perhaps in the absence of data we tend to project out meaning to fill gaps in our knowledge?' In the following discussion we come to a consensus that 'unless we check out all that happens, the group will run wild with ungrounded fantasy'. We agree as a ground rule: 'to risk checking things out – in future.' I observe that 'this is our first community ground rule', and ask 'what other rules would you like to further support yourselves here?' Confidentiality arises, is discussed, defined, dissected, and also agreed upon. I draw attention to 'the arising energy and how this contrasts with the start of the group, when energy appeared to be held within'. Attention is now focused upon how 'we block ourselves off from our emotional energy during our beginnings'. Energy is observed to 'be there – but denied'. 'Do we always start like this?' someone asks. This is seen to be a reoccurring pattern of the community, a sort of 'dependence upon someone else to start.' Looking back on today's beginning, members note how 'childlike' and 'dependent' they felt, plus how threatening 'unstructured time' felt for them. We end this first session exploring how 'dependence and rebellion' manifest within the group; the 'social scripts we enact that keep us helpless', and determine to 'use the group to inquire how this tends to happen' and to 'try out new assertive ways' in future sessions.

Session 2

A more active facilitative style develops this time from out of a similar non-directive start. Participants share here-and-now awareness while simultaneously offering their thoughts and feelings to the group. A good deal of one-to-one checking out of perceptions occurs, with group attention focusing upon first one, and then another pair of interactors. Reluctant contributors are gently encouraged to venture opinions, and inquiry is made to the underlying thoughts and feelings behind their quietness and seeming un-involvement. I for the most part role-model a reflective and inquiring stance: 'How do you feel about what is happening now?' 'Is there some fear or uncertainty here for you?' 'What is the worst thing that might happen?' 'What purpose does your present behaviour serve for you?' 'What are the gains and costs of acting in this way?' This role has arisen naturally from the culture of the group, been extended and refined a little by me, and has now been adopted by others in this group.

Session 3

The contracted purpose of the group is reviewed: 'What do participants now want from this group in light of their current awareness and needs?' An *agenda of possible themes surfaces, and strategies to meet these themes. We agree to periodically review our needs and, for the rest of the time, rigorously debate the rules we want the group to operate by. Members seem now to be considering the group their own, investing their energy within it, refining its purpose and boundaries, and using me more as a resource than as a leader to depend upon.*

Session 4

As the large circle of chairs forms, a theme of 'wanting to be seen' but also 'wishing to stay hidden' arises. This is interpreted as a tension between risking and staying safe. An experiment is suggested where volunteers walk into the centre of the group to answer questions put to them by the others. As we have a rule which stipulates that individuals can withdraw when something feels wrong for them, the exercise is perceived as safe. In this exercise, it is suggested that individuals experiment with what it feels like to answer, and to refuse to answer questions, while they are within the glare of group attention. This is at core an exercise in assertion, where an individual practices maintaining and exercising personal boundaries, while experimenting with openness in a scene subject to group pressure. Initially, questioning is supportive and gentle. As the exercise continues, more sensitive and personal issues are raised. Gradually, more challenging inquiry is enacted as trust builds. I relate this observation to the group, and we spend some time reflecting upon the dynamics we are experiencing, what we are unconsciously co-creating in the group, and the nature of what we are learning. By the end of this session, trust is recognised to be high in the community, and it is suggested that for trust to build, risks must be taken.

Barber 1986

My strategy, when facilitating in a holistic-field informed way, is to trust to the unfolding social process to guide me – and to remain flexible so as to follow the dynamic lifeline of a group. For this to happen I must refrain from imposing my own agenda, while noticing what I am withholding and the influence this 'withholding' has upon me and others. Though a leader, I must persevere not to compromise myself as a fully participating and authentic being in my own right, for my role modelling of an authentic relationship does much to set the tone for others. Remember, in non-authentic relationships you get non-authentic data.

Apply a Gestalt and field theory frame of reference to the above case study, and we have a means of analysing the whole energetic pattern. As for the ethics of facilitative inquiry such as this, though it is challenging and in-your-face, its tough-love relational style nevertheless endeavours to put into action such humanistic values as:

- A person is a whole and is (rather than has) a body, emotions, thoughts, sensations and perceptions – all of which function together and in relationship, one with the other

48

- A person is part of his or her environment and cannot be understood apart from it
- People are proactive rather than reactive and determine their own responses to the world
- People are capable of being aware of their sensations, thoughts, emotions and perceptions
- People, through self-awareness, are capable of choice and are therefore responsible for their behaviour
- People possess the potential and resources to live effectively
- People can experience themselves only in the present
- The past and future can be experienced only in the now through remembering and anticipating
- People are neither intrinsically good nor bad.

After Passons 1975 quoted by Clarkson 1989

'Care' need not be collusive nor mushy – it can be tough, but is always authentic.

In the next section we will elucidate holistic currents of a research field in greater depth.

Reflections

In regard to the group inquiry described above, what do you think might be going on in terms of 'role' and 'power'? For instance, when reviewing your own role as a researcher you might consider how the authority and presence you convey influences the type of data that emerges. If you hold a position of authority within the system you are researching, especially if you are seeking to enact change or to add value, just imagine the political influences at play.

(October) I am aware that as a practitioner-researcher, one who intends to use research as an agent of change, I'm a walking politician as much as a researcher! I think I will need to counterbalance this influence in my research design, perhaps by getting my co-researchers to analyse the data as well as myself, and/or by using a more collaborative approach to investigation than I first intended; I could even get someone to interview me!

2.5 Researching 'Here' and 'Now' –
Some Questions to Pose to Yourself and Others

Parlett (1991) suggests that five principles characterise a field theory approach, namely, a search for *organisation, contemporaneity, singularity, changing process* and *possible relevance*, aspects which are suggested to fluidly cement and bond social dynamics together. From the aforesaid principles, the following foci and practical research questions are caused to arise:

1. **The Principle of Organisation** = *'How are people and events organised here?'*

Here, as a facilitator conducting practitioner research, I explore how the tasks and social processes that shape individual behaviour are constellated by a group, or inform organisational culture as a whole. Essentially, I seek to examine how the 'structure' and the 'function' of a social network dovetail together, through voicing aloud such reflections and questions as:

'What is the fluid cement that holds us together?'

'What mutual needs are being met within this setting?'

'Who are the power-holders here who maintain the rules?'

'If this were a family, who would be the parents?'

2. **The Principle of Contemporaneity** = *'What influences of the present field explain current behaviour?'*

Here my focus is upon what is actually happening. Psychological perceptions of the past and speculations upon the future no doubt affect the present, but my primary concern stays with the 'here' and the 'now'; e.g.

'How are you feeling right now?'

'What catches your attention at this moment?'

'What needs of yours are being met here?'

'How are you supporting yourself at this moment?'

3. **The Principle of Singularity** = *'What is unique about the current situation?'*

Here my focus is upon the specific rather than upon the general as I attempt to raise awareness to unique events at the exact time of their happening. I also endeavour to illuminate what is especially to the fore of a group or community's attention, and to identify its unique character, idiosyncratic social pattern and communication. Current individual and group needs, plus the relative urgency of such needs, are examined by questions such as:

'What is different this time compared to when similar things happened before?'

'How do you see me as influencing you, the group and the current situation?'

'How do you behave differently here to other group settings in your life?'

'What feelings are particularly evoked in this setting?'

4. The Principle of Changing Process = *'What is in the process of becoming?'*

This focus, which honours the principle that everything is in flow, mutating from second to second and subject to constant change, keeps me wary to my tendency to systematise or fixate on categories and definitions, and causes my questioning to take the following form:

'If things go on as they are what do you believe will happen?'

'What are we co-creating or contributing to here?'

'If this team/group/organisation were a seed what would it grow into?'

'If this team/group/organisation were a family what kind of children would it rear?'

5. The Principle of Possible Relevance = *'What am I blind to or excluding at this time?'*

This principle alerts me to the fact that everything has potential meaning and is of relative importance to the whole. It keeps me alive to the need for openness, alert to the cost of adopting one framework to the exclusion of others and to the dangers of sticking to a prearranged agenda. It also prevents me from falling into the trap of mistaking the map for the territory. This raising to mind of potential blind spots leads to such questions as:

'How might a Martian describe what is happening to us now?'

'What would be the opposite stance to the one you are taking right now?'

'Is there somebody or something we frequently miss or exclude in this group?'

'What feelings never get expressed and what is never said here?'

Field theory provides us with a model of how we might facilitate, shape and phenomenologically appreciate the totality of experience, while simultaneously honouring its integrity. It also gives us an idea of where we might begin to focus our facilitative practitioner-researcher eye, namely upon how the field is organised *(organisation)*, its current influences *(contemporaneity)*, uniqueness *(singularity)*, organic development *(changing process)* and blind spots *(possible relevance)*.

Field analysis within the context of our earlier case study (session 4 of the case study entitled *Inquiring into Moment-to-Moment Awareness* shared in 2.4) is performed below to demonstrate how field theory might be applied to effect dynamic whole-field analysis.

51

An Illustrative Field Analysis

Session 4

As the large circle of chairs forms, a theme of 'wanting to be seen' but also 'wishing to stay hidden' arises. This is interpreted as a tension between risking and staying safe. An experiment is suggested where volunteers walk into the centre of the group to answer questions put to them by the others. As we have a rule which stipulates that individuals can withdraw when something feels wrong for them, the exercise is perceived as safe. In this exercise, it is suggested that individuals experiment with what it feels like to answer, and to refuse to answer questions, while they are within the glare of group attention. This is at core an exercise in assertion, where an individual practices maintaining and exercising personal boundaries, while experimenting with openness in a scene subject to group pressure. Initially, questioning is supportive and gentle. As the exercise continues, more sensitive and personal issues are raised. Gradually, more challenging inquiry is enacted as trust builds. I relate this observation to the group, and we spend some time reflecting upon the dynamics we are experiencing, what we are unconsciously co-creating in the group, and the nature of what we are learning. By the end of this session, trust is recognised to be high in the community, and it is suggested that for trust to build, risks must be taken.

Barber 1986

Applying the aforementioned criteria of field analysis, the following insights emerge:

Re **Organisation:** 'How are events and people organised here?'

The course frame and developing community dynamic appears to organise and energetically cement the group together. The facilitator acts as a culture carrier and symbol of leadership, partly supported by his status and nomination as a group facilitator, and possibly by the prior exposure of individuals to teacher-student conditioning in earlier classroom settings. Looking closer at the impact of transference and prior learning, we may speculate that exposure to the parent-child relationship may support the teacher-student relationship described here, as well as the subject's own professional enculturalisation; note, all were mental nurses who had received training within a large hospital setting, which could be suggested to foster some degree of institutionalisation.

Re **Contemporaneity:** 'What influences of the present field explain current behaviour?'

The developing culture of the group, in the context of its recent history, is seemingly beginning to take shape and have influence over what emerges. Individuals are starting to experiment with risk-taking, and there is an excitement and expectation about what is happening.

Re **Singularity:** 'What is unique about the present field?'

52

This is a multi-racial group on a professional update programme never to be repeated; it is also the first time participants have been willing to take risks to the degree they are doing so today.

Re **Changing Process:** 'What is in the process of becoming?'

A new level of engagement is flowering; the risks people have taken today will impact group culture and change its historically derived profile. This may bring them closer together or cause them to be even more cautious in future. One thing seems obvious: the social world they have hidden behind for so long is starting to disintegrate and a new authenticity is seemingly emerging.

Re **Possible Relevance:** 'What am I blind to or excluding at this time?'

I am aware the course is in its final stages, and wonder if I am excluding my own irritation with how slow this group was to bond and get going, or my own sense of personal or professional failure in having taken so long to get to this more productive phase? I am also aware that although racial issues were raised, sexual issues were never brought to attention nor addressed in this group.

When facilitating an inquiry into 'the whole of what is experienced', I try to bracket-off my personal agenda so as to let the field's dynamics guide me. I also endeavour to observe the effect my withholding has upon others – and indeed myself. As a practitioner-researcher enrolled as a facilitative leader, I attempt to serve the group and its process while taking care not to compromise my own authenticity – for my being in touch with my own authenticity does much to set a 'mindful' relational tone. Within this context, the above analysis captures the flavour of a research-minded journey where the end product or task achievement of the group, is seen as far less important than the character and rhythms of its movement and organic being. 'Mindfulness' and 'beingness' do much to promote excellence in facilitation, and make an immense contribution to the quality of a social inquiry.

Reflections

In your reflective journal comment on how Parlett's five principles might be applied to research with your co-researchers cum stakeholders.

(October) **Principle of organisation:** *Makes me realise how little 'cements us together' as a department. It looks like I will need to develop a more robust 'culture of inquiry' and might need to look at specific interventions to address this when my research groups begin.*

Principle of Contemporaneity: *I notice right now in my pre-research interest groups how much energy I am expending getting THEM to work together – how can WE make it work together?*

Principle of Singularity: *There is, however, something unique my department is developing – a willingness to review its core values and of sense of needing to 'integrate' a lot of stuff.*

Principle of Changing Process: *I wonder if left to themselves – without my research intervention – this group would develop and what it might it grow into.*

Principle of Possible Relevance: *I'm aware how 'obnoxious' I'm becoming as the deadline to start the research proper and to get going draws nearer.*

Again I am aware here of the potential of field analysis to further my data analysis. For instance, I could review information surfaced via transcripts of interviews or group inquiry while asking myself: 'How do events seem to be organised here?' 'What current influences seem to be shaping us?' 'What appears to be unique here? etc., and from this surface, tentative hypotheses as to the influences that shape and mould the department.'

2.6 Developmental Tasks in Holistic Inquiry – Setting some Conditions and Boundaries

In a holistic approach to inquiry, though an attempt is made to honour the whole ecology, an awareness of 'task' nevertheless remains essential – the baby must not be thrown out with the bath water! 'Tasks' provide a structure and a focus. They can also keep the intellect busy with a strategy so that your emotions and intuition might roam more freely. Without task boundaries, perceptions may merge. When there is a great deal of uncertainty, for instance at the beginning of a facilitative enterprise before a theme has started to emerge, an anchor in task may be imperative for role security. Though it is my preferred style as a Gestaltist and researcher to facilitate intuitively and holistically, I do not, therefore, let my preference blind me to the strategic acts an inquiry demands. Below, again within the framework of a developing facilitative relationship, numerous tasks are suggested as necessary to give shape to inquiry and to focus the mind:

Pre-Entry Tasks *(prior to and during the orientation and identification phases):*

- Identifying the skills and qualities you bring to the inquiry
- Surfacing the bias and transference that clouds your vision
- Reflecting upon your interests and motivations for the study and forming a speculative plan

- Seeking clarity regarding the ethical and political implications involved
- Negotiating a contract appropriate to your expertise and skills and your client's needs
- Appointing a Devil's advocate or supervisor to rattle and shake your blind spots.

Self-Supervision Tasks within the Field *(within the exploration phase):*

- Modifying the design of your inquiry in light of field experiences
- Observing how the inquiry begins to manifest itself
- Noticing how you are drawn to certain themes and issues
- Surfacing and recording what happens within the field and within yourself
- Remaining alert to the appropriateness of your actions and judgements
- Noticing the effectiveness of the inquiry as it unfolds
- Evaluating the presenting needs of individuals within the field
- Being alert to the inquiry's developmental flow
- Staying flexible and prioritising the most useful issues to pursue
- Policing group behaviours and ethical boundaries to maintain relational health.

Post-Operational and Review Tasks *(within the phase of resolution):*

- Reviewing the effect of research at individual and group levels
- Reviewing what you and others have learnt en route
- Noticing how you might better your approach next time
- Reflecting upon the gains and costs of the approach you have used
- Raising awareness of what is worth celebrating
- Considering what you need to do to improve your practice
- Feeding your impressions back to the field for commentary
- Deciding the most useful way of presenting or summarising the information before you
- Giving voice in your report to the different views of those within the field
- Formally communicating your findings
- Speculating upon where future developments might proceed.

Hopefully the above tasks flow naturally out from your facilitation, rather than being imposed upon it. This said, at the meta-level, task-clusters serve the following developmental purpose:

In the above division, **'pre-entry tasks'** relate to the facilitator's need to identify their skill base, and by implication, evaluate their suitability for the job at hand. This input is essential in the negotiation of a suitable facilitative, consulting and/or research contract, when you contemplate the strategies you might engage. At this stage you should also consider the ground rules and principles you wish to employ; the research methods you favour; the theoretical models you might use to illuminate meaning; and the strategic design most suited to your purpose. In sum, you need to develop an appropriate mind-set and a speculative plan of action in order to build a trust-inducing social container, conducive to inquiry.

'**Self-supervisory tasks within the field**' relate to a facilitator's on-the-job evaluation and quality control. This includes monitoring how 'what is found' differs to 'what was expected', how judgements form and are acted upon, and how coping strategies are chosen and put to use. These tasks open a facilitator to feedback while raising their awareness of how they are evaluating their facilitation and its impact upon the field.

Finally, '**post-operational and review tasks**' relate to assessing the wider effects of the facilitative inquiry undertaken, its influence upon the researcher, effects on participants and within the wider community wherein the study was performed. Here pros and cons of the study are appraised, learning is evaluated, and reports and recommendations considered.

Taken all at once, the above tasks may appear too much and too many to handle; but broken down into a series of relational phases, an appreciation of the actions a facilitator needs to consider, and possibly to engage, is illuminated. To this end, in our later chapters, strategic inquiry cycles similar to the one above are further refined and developed with a view to enhancing whole-field inquiry and holistic learning.

Qualitative inquiry is not for the faint-hearted. Both Gestalt and Tibetan Buddhism are agreed, that if you begin something you should then go all the way with it, because if you begin and quit, the unfinished and incomplete business you have left behind will haunt you for all of time. Trungpa Rinpoche describes the experiential path – which is life – as 'like getting into a train that you cannot get off. You ride on and on'. (Trungpa Rinpoche in Hayward & Cohen 1988)

Reflections

You have now reached the end of the 'identification' phase of inquiry where you have hopefully raised awareness of what interests you and contemplated an issue or research question to be addressed. As a result of this, you and your colleagues/stakeholders should have begun to surface some key issues for joint exploration. For example:

(October) So where are we now? I had a meeting where we decided upon an initial focus, looked at how we might record and surface data, and agreed tentative future dates. As for the research tasks expected of the orientation and identification phase, the tentative research group I have in mind has begun to identify the skills and qualities we bring to the inquiry, surfaced our interests and motivations and formed a speculative plan as to the way forward. I have also considered the prior learning (transference) that clouds my own vision, but barely begun to consider the ethical and political implications involved, nor as yet found a supervisor to rattle and shake my blind spots.

Choosing a Method and Practising the Skills

exploration

*Each person must accept the cards life
deals him or her.
But once they are in hand,
He or she alone must decide how to play the
cards in order to win the game...*

Voltaire in Hayward 1990

Chapter three

Moving from Awareness into Practice –
The Researcher as the Primary Research Tool

3. Moving from Awareness into Practice – The Researcher as the Primary Research Tool

'Pay heed to nourishing what is right, and with what one seeks to nourish oneself' (I Ching); therefore strive to research and explore that which best supports your Dharma – your own unique gift and personal contribution to humankind.

Preamble

This chapter aims to further develop your understanding and appreciation of qualitative inquiry, by a review of its origins and traditions. To this end naturalistic inquiry and ethnography are described, through to case study and field theory, and more recent developments of heuristic inquiry and chaos theory. You will be invited to consider the mind-set that qualitative research supports, and to consider how your own values may impact or skew facilitative inquiry. Discussion of the art and science of inquiry is further developed, and Yin and Yang influences within inquiry are appraised. Within the following chapter you will be encouraged to critically reflect upon the relationship between research and knowledge, and to consider the role partiality and passion play in 'real world' research. Criteria relating to the development of a qualitative approach to inquiry are examined, as are the first steps you might take to get a study underway. A developmental model of the practitioner-researcher relationship is suggested and, by the close of this chapter, it is hoped that the case studies provided will have furthered your insight into the practicalities of quality facilitative inquiry.

3.1 'Becoming' and 'Being' the Research – Traditions of Qualitative Inquiry

Having touched on notions of 'new paradigm' and 'old paradigm' thinking, it is well to familiarise ourselves with the tradition within which facilitated qualitative inquiry is located:

> The epistemological basis for research could be said to have two extremes. One can be described as the position where it is assumed that knowledge and understanding are tangible, to be acquired by a researcher as observer, the positivist. The other maintains that knowledge is something to be personally experienced, compelling the researcher to be involved with their subjects, the anti-positivist.
>
> *Black & Holford 1999*

Though qualitative inquiry is not so radical these days as it was in the Sixties, just consider the scientific paradigm it set out to challenge:

> Scientific knowledge is proven knowledge. Scientific theories are derived in some rigorous way from the facts of experience acquired by

observation and experiment. Science is based upon what we can see and touch etc. Personal opinion or preference and speculative imaginings have no place in science. Science is objective.

Chalmers 1982

Science believes in the tangible, provable, sensate, received, objective world, and attempts to define laws which support this, its proposed world view. What cannot be seen, objectified and statistically recorded, from this perspective, is rejected. The grand lie that rational positivism sought to perpetuate, is that life and reality can only be studied objectively via the senses and intellect. But just how sound is this common sense premise? Chalmers (1982), in reviewing the scientific approach to research was eventually forced to conclude that:

- Ultimately there was no such thing as proven scientific knowledge
- There was no foolproof way of devising theory from factual experience
- Science bases its assumptions on far more than observable phenomena
- Personal opinion and prejudice colour scientific theory
- Objectivity can never be guaranteed.

The holistic and facilitative perspective of this work, with its Gestalt and humanistic flavours, is essentially anti-positivist and supports a position where:

The evaluator searches for totality – the unifying nature of particular settings... It also assumes that description and understanding of a person's social environment or an organisation's political context is essential for overall understanding of what is observed.

Patton 1995 p.49

But this said, though standing closer to the qualitative end of the spectrum, as a holistic facilitator-cum-researcher I do not dismiss positivism, but rather facilitate dialogue between both perspectives.

In the case study overleaf, an example is provided of a mixed method approach to inquiry.

Researching from Within an Experience –
The Researcher as the Research

The following passages are extracted from a study of hospital care, by a researcher who underwent post-operative care as a hospital patient. In this study, the researcher was both the subject and the method of inquiry:

Nights on the ward felt interminably long and encouraged the negatives within me to surface. In the early hours, with nothing to divert me, I would often question my state and future. At my most despondent I would reflect: 'Will the pain ever end'; 'Will I ever get near to the health I enjoyed before?' When more hopeful, I would reflect on: 'What is the usual amount of pain to have following an operation such as mine?'; and 'How might I facilitate my own advancement to a healthy recovery?'

I also pondered my sexuality. I had no sex drive: 'Would it return?'; 'Would Anna ever find my scarred body sexually attractive?'; and 'How much of a burden would I represent as a dependent, painfully preoccupied entity who could not care for himself let alone for her?' Depersonalisation and anomie were highly charged issues for me at this time. My life seemed purposeless and I felt myself slipping further into apathy. Anna broke this with a simple intervention on her next visit; she brought a note pad and pens. I was accustomed to writing and researching and now had tools for this. I had also begun to realise that I would have to self-facilitate myself to health.

Over the next few days I examined the major focus of my hospital life, 'pain', and kept a journal to this end. Every so often I would appraise my situation by attending to my 'thoughts', 'feelings', 'senses' and 'intuitions' [...] As I continued to shift through my perceptions a five-point scale emerged:

Level 1

Moderate discomfort, dull aching, attention can be displaced via concentration on sensory stimuli such as TV, with the effect that renewed energy emerges.

Level 2

Constant discomfort thwarts concentration; displaced attention helps but does not solicit more energy or override residual feelings of dull heaviness; lost creativity; thinking an effort.

Level 3

Greatly interferes with perception, continually drains energy and interferes with other activities; attention drawn inward; begins to consume consciousness making thinking impossible.

Level 4

Sharp focused pain overwhelms the individual's sense of self; little attention available for external world; fleeting glimpses of objective reality; disorientation and absorption in pain; responses instinctive.

▶ **Level 5**

Powerless to communicate as in grip of painful stimuli; no contact with external world as consciousness replaced by a twilight state attuned to pain-inducing stimuli.

When in Level 1 I could still work, write, and watch television with a degree of enjoyment; this was my baseline, a point at which I could doze, think, feel and fantasise.

At Level 2, via concentrated effort, I could switch attention from pain to visual stimuli, that is, override one sensory stimulus with another.

At Level 3 my thoughts, feelings and imagination were drawn into the field of pain.

At Level 4 painful sensation permeated the whole and perception of reality came only in fleeting glimpses.

At Level 5 there was non-appreciation of everything; it was as if pain filled the universe. Level 2 pain was tolerable, but if I let it develop to Level 3 life felt pointless. With this scale to hand I knew when to request painkillers.

I speculated upon relaxation as a means by which pain might be reduced, and to this end experimented with prolonged hot baths. These I found relaxed the muscle spasms I associated with stimuli at level 3 and above, and if persevered with could reverse the pain spiral and cause Level 3 pain to transmute back to Level 2. With this information to hand my environment felt less muddled and helpless. I had used my research-mindedness to provide me with purpose and power, and was beginning to exorcise the apathy within me.

Barber 1991/98 pp.250–2

A focus upon the dynamics and nature of experience is central to the above account. Here we see a researcher employing introspection in order to champion the authority of what is being experienced – 'now'. Though a scale of pain is suggested, this emanates 'out of experience' in an organic qualitative way. This does not tell you about pain in the positivist scientific sense, from the outside, but Gestalt-like invites you to experience 'what pain is'. There is no fragmentation of experience to reduce it to 'a single truth', but rather a portrayal of truth from within an authentic relationship, where the researcher 'is' the research, in contrast to merely 'doing' it.

In the above way, the 'whole' of experience comes across through the 'being' of the researcher and person involved. Interestingly, this research was not contracted nor funded by an external body, nor did the researcher plan their study, rather it emerged from 'contact' with an unforeseen life experience, which in turn became a vehicle for growth and learning.

The emphasis on contact is central. Contact between organism and environment is seen as the vehicle for personal growth. Growth occurs at the 'place' where organism and environment meet, i.e. the contact boundary – which authors sometimes describe as 'the organ of growth'.

Perls et al. 1951 quoted in Harris 1999

Contact, the growing edge of all experience, is the beginning and the end of Gestalt and qualitative inquiry.

Reflections

The aforementioned case study is a vivid account of research 'from the inside'. Looking at your own role as researcher within your professional group, can you identify ways of exploring 'who you are' and your sense of 'being' as you engage with your group?

(November) I want to find a way of bringing myself back to the experience, to the confusion of the moment and not seeking for cognitive closure. How do I do that and who can help me? I guess I'll just have to 'do' less and 'be' more! I think when I restrict myself from fully contacting others I similarly seem to restrict them. Possibly they are taking their cue from me and I'm a more important culture carrier in the research group than I realised? Again, I think sometimes I get into 'role' and lose contact with my own authentic base, which has the knock-on effect of my being rather more 'I-It' than 'I-Thou' than I consciously intend myself to be. I need a research supervisor to help me here?

3.2 Maintaining Fluidity and Flexibility – Following the Energetic Flow

Qualitative inquiry is not a single thing with a singular subject matter. [...] All of the major social sciences have drawn on and contributed to qualitative methods, but each in a somewhat different way depending on the theoretical interests of a particular discipline.

Patton 1995 p.65

While scientific researchers reduce their perspective and limit their appreciation so as to produce repeatable results that conform to 'scientific facts', qualitative researchers bring humanity, subjectivity and creativity back into focus. Only when we are open to everything, the visible and the invisible, are we able to contemplate and to be informed by an unknown.

Qualitative inquiry, like life, can sometimes evolve in directions unforeseen or unplanned for. This, its organic nature, is what makes it intellectually frustrating to the pure scientist and freeing to the social scientist. As opposed to refining a specific research question or setting out to prove an established hypothesis, as in the case study below, you find yourself led by what emerges within the field.

Case Study

Keeping a Fluidity of Intention – Letting the Field be your Guide

Initially, I entered the host organisation with the intention of studying the effect of personal development, within the context of a commercially cited master's programme, upon individual working practice. But, as the study progressed, it became increasingly obvious that the dynamics of the peer-research group were themselves beginning to exert a far greater impact than the educational content of the programme. At this point I revised my working title: 'The effects of personal development upon work-based practice' in favour of 'The influence of a peer-research group within the workplace'. As time progressed, this title in turn became redundant, as the peer-researching community in question now started to have an effect on the organisation. Over the next eighteen months, what had originally begun as a study of the individual transformed into a study of the organisation, and what was intended to address the effect of learning within the workplace became an investigation into how collaborative inquiry, in the shape of a peer-learning and researching group, helped to bring about organisational change. As one line of inquiry became spent or changed route, I reorientated the direction of study to the direction of prime relevance and the research field's energetic flow. If I had stuck with my original intention at all costs, what grew into a major two-year research project could easily have petered out or been aborted in the first three months.

In summary, we may say that qualitative inquiry leads a practitioner-researcher in the Gestalt tradition towards a facilitative style which encourages them to:

- Adopt an eclectic multi-dimensional stance
- Show interest in the quality and subtlety of experience
- Generate knowledge through dialogue, self reflection and social involvement
- Champion the authority of what is being experienced – now
- Look to the interrelatedness of everything
- Inquire within the framework of an authentic and intimate relationship
- 'Be' a researcher rather than to merely 'do' research

- Expand awareness and to raise consciousness through question and dialogue
- Emphasise the authority of the person and their phenomenological experience
- Retain a flexibility of inquiry and focus able to follow new avenues of inquiry.

The various qualitative traditions emphasise differing aspects of the above, but all value the subtlety and 'authority of experience' and court an adaptable and responsive inquiry style. Add to this Gestalt, and living and loving may be seen as ways of researching. Dogs do research with their noses, babies their mouths and adults arrive at a holistic whole-field 'knowing'.

Reflections

In terms of the ways of engaging in the 'Gestalt' way described above, reflect in your log what phrases catch your attention and which you might follow up.

(November) Should title of this book be 'Growing into Practitioner-Research', as I am conscious more of the growing 'authority' of my group – in fact at times as a researcher I feel I'm following them! I have to get used to this, or rather to examine where it is leading, and if it is serving my research purpose.

3.3 Objective Subjectivity – Differing Perspectives of Qualitative Inquiry

Robin Shohet (2005) reminds us of the internal logic of objectivism, namely, that if we distance ourselves from something we turn it into an object, a thing without energy to impact or life to transform us. In this way *emotions* lose their transformative power through being reduced to 'sentiment', *creative insight* runs the risk of being seen as 'chaotic', and *intuition* is derided as 'irrational'; in short, the myopia of the pure sciences where so much is bracketed-off that reality is distorted. In research terms, the world of everyday experience becomes a grey 'objective' place and the researchers themselves are alienated from the richest of their inquiry tools – the power of experience and the impact upon them of holistic influence. This is the legacy that qualitative inquiry sought to redress.

As there are many shades and flavours of qualitative inquiry, it will serve you well to cultivate an understanding of what each emphasises and implies. Just as a painter depends upon a rich palette to represent what they experience, so holistic researchers and educators need to draw from an extensive range of facilitative tools. The art is in selecting the best tool for the job. As differing research methods illuminate differing kinds of data, it is important to know the pros and cons of each approach. There is also another reason why you must account for the origin and ancestry of your method: if you fail to establish its pedigree or to locate yourself in a specific tradition of inquiry, your facilitative inquiry is likely to be undervalued. To help you here, some orientations to qualitative social inquiry are listed below. These are arranged chronologically, in order of their evolution and development. Some are more of a philosophy than a method, but all provide a framework for collecting and analysing data. It is my contention that an appreciation of qualitative research has much to offer Gestalt and other therapeutic approaches, and that Gestalt and other humanistic approaches to therapy have much to contribute to qualitative inquiry. Indeed, I would suggest Gestalt's legacy has done much to shape the investigative methods and facilitative perspectives portrayed below.

a) Naturalistic Inquiry – Research within a Natural Setting

Naturalistic inquiry grew from a recognition of the difficulty of using a positive scientific approach for studying human beings (Susman & Evered 1978). What worked well enough with objects and differing species was seen to be severely limited when applied to people and social settings, areas where *'values'* and *'attitudes'* prevailed. This should not surprise us, for treating people as objects ignores their ability to reflect on problems, to be emotionally involved and to act symbolically. In short, everything that typifies humanity and social engagement. As qualitative approaches to research originally grew from the tradition of naturalistic inquiry, this is explored in some detail.

Lincoln and Guba (1985 pp.39–45) identified the following as characteristic of naturalist inquiry:

- Research is carried out in a natural setting
- The inquirer and subjects are seen as primary data-gathering instruments
- Tacit knowledge, intuition and feelings are seen to be legitimate data
- Qualitative methods of sensitivity and flexibility are favoured
- Purposeful sampling rather than random sampling is used to extend the data range
- Inductive analysis is used to describe settings and relationships
- There is a preference for theory to emerge from data in a grounded way
- Meanings and interpretations are negotiated with respondents

- A case study reporting mode predominates
- Data is idiographically interpreted with attention to uniqueness of the field
- A tentative approach to data is taken and broad generalisations are employed
- Boundaries of the study emerge from the focus of inquiry
- Internal field-criteria of reliability, validity and objectivity are devised within the field.

In sharp contrast to positivist research, naturalistic inquiry encourages the generation of hypotheses, focus and research design, to emerge organically out of the research field – rather than imposing these upon it. Research of this type, because we do not know the precise form of data to be collected nor the research outcome, causes the adaptability and flexibility of the human instrument to come into its own (Robson 1995).

In naturalistic inquiry, because knowledge and data is seen to be relative and tacit, and because uniqueness is emphasised, the generalisation of findings and application to other settings remains tentative. Inquiry in this mode removes the filters scientists and classical researchers have traditionally used to hide inadvertently from the real-life drama of their work, with its emotional investments and intuitive flashes, its stop-go dynamics, blind alleys and failures, confusions and extensive recycling of earlier concepts and models.

Naturalistic inquiry supports Gestalt and holistic inquiry's search for experiential wisdom born from engagement with real world events, and especially informs the case studies cited in this work.

b) Ethnography and the Case Study – Walking in the Shoes of Others

Ethnography looks for the ways culture, tradition and idiosyncratic meaning shape individual and collective behaviour.

> In the tradition of anthropologists, the primary method of enquiry is participant observation, involving intensive fieldwork. Culture is meant in its broadest sense when applied to a setting, where it is assumed that any group will establish its own standards of behaviour, decision making and action.
>
> *Black & Holford 1999 p.1.9*

The main focus in ethnographic study is upon the relationships and motivations of those involved. Joining with subjects within the field, the researcher seeks to provide a written description of the implicit rules and traditions of the studied group, while attempting to generate a working hypothesis as to the underlying motives that shape behaviour. Generally, the researcher sets about to produce a *'rich'* or *'thick'* description 'which interprets the experiences of people in the group from their own perspective' (Patton 1995 p.148).

In design, ethnographic research is loose and emergent and sets out to link *'research questions'* to *'data'* and to *'conclusions'*. The ethnographic tradition, especially in a case study form, has been widely used to research groups, communities, organisations, roles and relationships.

Although ethnographic approaches are flexible in the field, a good deal of pre-inquiry planning is necessary. For instance, prior to engagement you will usually need:

- A conceptual framework
- A set of research questions
- A sampling strategy
- To decide on methods and instruments for data collection.

Patton 1995

Nor does planning cease with preparation, for the above continue to undergo refinement throughout the study. As to what case studies study, this tends to include an in-depth review of:

- Settings: the venue and site of the study
- Actors: who is involved, their origins and behaviours
- Events: what happens and when it happens
- Processes: the roles and relationships that define a situation.

Miles & Huberman 1984

All of this data is then addressed through an array of participant observation, interviews, document and record review. Grounded theory, an approach that gives preference to data that arises from the field, rather than from theoretical positions, emanates from out of this ethnographic tradition.

Ethnography keeps holistic inquiry alerted to individual and unique perspectives and is discernible in the Gestalt approach and in the case studies of this text.

c) Action Research – Spiralling towards Change

The term 'action research' was coined by Kurt Lewin (1946) – the originator of field theory – to describe an approach to research which involved the refining of data and knowledge through several cycles of *'planning'*, *'acting'*, *'observing'* and *'reflecting'*. You start with a general idea, define a focus and objective, and devise a plan of action. If this stage is successful, you emerge with an overall plan of how to reach the objective you have in mind, and a notion of the first step you need to take. Next, you take this first step and execute another cycle of planning, action and fact finding to evaluate the effects of this second step. This prepares you for the third step of modifying the overall plan and engaging the research cycle once more.

Action research is concerned both with *'action'* – solving concrete problems in real life situations – and fostering *'change'* (Rapoport 1970). Because of this, emphasis is usually upon real situations and small-scale investigation which enable a more intimate monitoring of effects (Cohen & Manion 1994). Focusing upon a specific situation and event the researcher intervenes within the client-system or research field with the expressed aim of diagnosing and resolving its associated problems.

As *'re-education'* and *'researching for change'* are often central to this approach, collaboration with subjects is generally expected, as is a focus on what is unique.

> While the approach is 'scientific' in that it has an intended outcome and variables are controlled to test the veracity of the intervention, it does not aim to study a large number of cases with the intention of generalising to a large population.
>
> *Black & Holford 1999 p.1.5*

The action research cycle with its developmental movement through interconnected stages of planning, acting, observing, and reflecting focused upon problem-solving, has been widely adapted to organisational consultancy (Paul & Lipham 1976) to effect:

- Dialogue about issues and problems
- Deciding what to focus on and how to act
- Strategically acting to address problems identified earlier
- Evaluating the effectiveness of the action taken.

Goodlad 1975

What Mead did for ethnography Lewin did for humanistic psychology. He took a movement and developed it into a method. Working just after the Second World War when rigid social systems were being questioned, Lewin used action research to facilitate democracy. Subsequent exponents of action research have called for the furtherance of democratic principles through the direct involvement of subjects in the design, direction, development, analysis and use of research (Carr & Kemmis 1986). A similar case has been made for management consultancy (Barber & Mulligan 1998).

Collaborative and co-operative inquiry, and the experiential learning cycle (Kolb & Fry 1975; Heron 1988) have all been derived from action research. Sadly, action research seems of late to have lost its way. What began as a lively 'action orientated' collaborative process is now so often reduced to a series of managerial tasks, largely as a consequence of a drive towards simplification (Hopkins 1985) and re-interpretation (Elliot 1992). The need for an alive, action-centred, collaborative and dynamic way of researching – one which honours experience as a whole – thus still remains. Hopefully, this text will help to fill this vacancy.

Action research keeps holistic inquiry and facilitation alive to the cyclic rhythms of investigation and change, and may be used to complement Lewin's other contribution to qualitative inquiry, field theory (Lewin 1952). It has also been used to illuminate the process of Gestalt psychotherapy (Barber 1997a & 1997b). Chapter 5 develops this theme further.

d) Field Theory – Attending to the Dynamic Whole

Field theory, according to its originator, Lewin (1952), is not so much a theory as a 'way of thinking' and of 'looking at the total situation'. The field theory way of 'looking' attends to the whole pattern of what is perceived, the 'organised, interconnected, interdependent, interactive nature of human phenomena' (Parlett 1991). A researcher in the field theory tradition does not seek to interpret or label, so much as to raise awareness to the 'relational whole'. Here 'meaning', as in naturalistic inquiry, is largely left to the focus of study or 'field' to dictate. From this perspective, what the field produces is seen to have intrinsic meaning and worth in itself.

Parlett (1993) makes the point that Lewin drew upon Maxwellian field theory from physics – which states that unity is not due to mass, but rather to a 'field of force' (Wheelan, Pepitone & Abt 1990) or dynamic relationship which cements everything together. An obvious question arises here: what does a researcher attend to in order to address 'the field'? Four fluid and inter-flowing dimensions are suggested by Parlett (1993) as worthy of attention within any given field:

- The degree to which phenomena are **figure** (i.e. stand out) or ground (i.e. constitute the background out of which other phenomena emerge)
- The degree to which phenomena are self-contained or merge: **differentiation and confluence**
- The degree to which phenomena show resilience to merging and are able to reconstitute themselves (**reconfiguration**)
- The interrelationship of different layers and levels of experience: **the laminated field.**

Practically, a Gestaltist inquiring through a field theory perspective in therapy endeavours to:

- Treat the individual or group as a systemic whole
- Let dynamic conditions in the field emerge and lead them (as participants) within the field to share their own reactions and responses

- Support their subjects' capacity to be self-determining
- Raise to awareness conditions within the relational field
- Encourage individuals and groups to identify and label their own experiences
- Put field-generated hypotheses forward for investigation
- Offer maps to enable sense making
- Work from within the framework of an authentic I-Thou relationship.

Field theory supports Gestalt's notion of the energetic nature of relational wholes, which are discussed further and at greater facilitative depth in Chapters 2 and 5.

e) Grounded Theory – Letting Data Speak for Itself

Grounded theory, like naturalistic inquiry and ethnography, focuses upon unravelling experience with a view to creating an integrated theory to explain the relationships and meanings that events manifest for subjects within the research field (Glaser & Strauss 1967). As with naturalistic inquiry, procedures for data collection, methodology, theory and verification, arise from the information that is made available in the field (Struass 1987).

Addison (1989) draws attention to the following contributions that grounded theory makes to social inquiry. It:

- Continually questions gaps in data, inconsistencies and incomplete understandings
- Stresses open processes of investigation
- Emphasises the context and social structure
- Generates theory and data from interviewing rather than observation
- Ensures that data collection, coding and analysis occur simultaneously and in relation to one another
- Grows its theories out of the data so they remain grounded in that data.

The Gestalt approach to holism outlined in this text, though standing close to grounded theory, departs from it through an emphasis on facilitation and in-depth examination of the self (See section 1.2 above).

Grounded theory keeps holistic inquiry and education attentive to details while anchoring them to the interactive field. Like Gestalt, it draws attention to what is present 'now', and creates a felt sense by a deep description of events.

f) Holistic Inquiry – Looking to the Phenomenological Whole

Holistic thinking is central to the systems and field theory perspectives and is close kin to Gestalt, in that it suggests that the whole is greater than the sum of its parts:

74

> ...a system cannot validly be divided into independent parts as discrete entities of inquiry because the effects of the behaviours of the parts on the whole depend on what is happening to the other parts.
>
> *Patton 1995 p.79*

Holistic research essentially attempts to encompass many dimensions and variations of scale, and obvious happenings in the external world, as well as inner events which give shape to individual truth. Nothing is purposefully denied. If something happens or floats into consciousness it becomes a legitimate part of 'the field' and, as such, must be accounted for. Retaining an observation of the inner, subjective world along with the outer, objective one presents us with a valuable way for getting at the complexity inherent to real life. This 'holistic' way of observing the world is not merely an act of 'looking', but rather the generation of a mindful watchfulness; an in-depth – at times transpersonal – alertness inclusive of seeing, listening, meditating and reflecting deeply upon experience.

The above form of 'active involved observation', which includes the heart as well as the eye, moves the researcher towards an appreciation of, and inquiry into:

Reality as physically evidenced by our senses (physical-sensory):

- Attending to sensory data and what we see and hear
- Focusing upon the physical environment and what actually happens
- Being aware of physiological responses and energies in the here-and-now.

(Here a holistic researcher/facilitator employs focusing and interpretative skills.)

Reality as socially taught and intellectually constructed (socio-cultural):

- Defining the purpose and task
- Applying cultural norms and playing an appropriate role
- Exploring strategy, prescribing action and generating feedback.

(Here a holistic researcher/facilitator employs boundary and culture-setting skills.)

Reality as emotionally experienced in relation to the past (emotional-transferential):

- Orientating ourselves to where we have come from and where we are now
- Understanding the emotional patterns that drive us
- Re-writing our emotional scripts.

(Here a holistic researcher/facilitator employs motivating and counselling skills.)

Reality as imagined by projections from the self (projective-imaginal):

- Understanding how we become trapped in our own fantasies
- Raising awareness to the symbolic and archetypal roles we play
- Moving beyond egotistically driven behaviour.

(Here a holistic researcher/facilitator employs challenging and processing skills.)

Reality as an intuitive journey of the soul (transpersonal-symbolic):

- Exploring deeper yearnings and aspirations
- Meeting with creative and life-enhancing influences
- Visualising and creating a future.

(Here a holistic researcher/facilitator employs envisioning and valuing skills.)

Holistic inquiry in its mixing and matching of methods cements all other approaches to inquiry together. In particularly, Chapter 5 takes this notion further.

g) Phenomenology – Exploring Experiential Ways of Knowing

In phenomenology, behaviour is seen as determined by personal experience rather than by an external objective reality (Cohen & Manion 1994). Consequently, emphasis is placed upon direct experiential engagement:

> The most significant understandings that I have come to I have not achieved from books or others, but initially, at least, from my own direct perceptions, observations, and intuitions... from transcendental places of imagination and reflection.
>
> *Moustakas 1994 p.41*

As what appear in consciousness are phenomena – something 'as perceived' rather than 'as it really is' – phenomenology stands in the Descartesian tradition (see Knockelmanns 1967) of looking within ourselves to discover the essential nature and meaning of things. Indeed the self to Descartes was an 'intuitive-thinking being who doubts, understands, affirms, denies, wishes for and against, senses, imagines' (Moustakas 1994 p.32); a holistic being if you will, who acquires knowledge through an intuitive-reflective process by impressions formed within the mind of a living self (Descartes 1977 p.202). Phenomenological inquiry, field theory and Gestalt are very close kin indeed.

Though there are many schools and approaches to phenomenological inquiry:

> There are three aspects of their viewpoint on which most phenomenologists would agree: – the importance and primacy of subjective experience – consciousness is active and meaning bestowed

- a certain kind of reflection allows us to gain knowledge of certain essential structures of consciousness.

Black & Holford p.1.2 1999

Phenomenology keeps holistic inquiry mindful of the ways individuals uniquely construct their world and underpins the Gestalt and the holistic approach of this work.

h) Postmodernism – Putting all to Question

Philosophically, postmodernism says we have lost our 'belief in emancipation and progress through knowledge and scientific research' (Kvale 1992), and suggests that we are now moving to a position which supports heterogeneous local contexts defined by flexibility and change. Postmodern approaches to inquiry are in essence existential and de-constructive, take a position of advocacy and social relativism, and draw attention to the aesthetics and ethics of research.

> A postmodern approach to research does not seek to overthrow and replace existing research paradigms and traditions but it does seek to critique them and to thus call attention to aspects which are neglected or ignored.
>
> *Scott & Usher 1999 p.56*

A researcher in the postmodern tradition is appreciative of each and every influence – while simultaneously critical of the same. They are not interested in whether something is right or wrong, but more – in a facilitative sense – of 'what works for clients' (Black & Holford 1999), 'why it works' for them and, 'what they consciously and unconsciously are choosing to ignore'.

> Postmodernism blows the whistle on scientific intellectualism as one more form of Victorian morality which inappropriately tries to establish itself in relation to people. One then has to move the parameters of science beyond the quantifiable to the qualitative. This is not intellectual and rational, but rather ethical in a new tradition which is yet to really emerge. The science of quality would regard the ethical as arbiter – it is the well-being for one's fellow person/humanity.
>
> *Loewenthal 1996 p.377*

The holistic thread of this text (which is not interested in right or wrong, but more in the facilitative sense of what works) has considerable postmodern sympathies. Postmodernism fuels a questioning of all phenomena, and has a considerable sympathy with Gestalt and the critical thrust of this text.

i) Heuristic Research – Searching Within to Understand what is Without

In heuristic inquiry attention is placed upon developing:

77

...interpretative understanding or meaning, with special attention to context and purpose.

Patton 1995 p.84

This approach draws attention to the tradition and contextual frame in which meaning is given and where interpretation is formed. It encourages an opening of the self in order to reveal ever deepening levels of personal inquiry and self questioning, in an attempt to explore the researcher's own unique situation and inner depth of experiential knowing.

In heuristic inquiry, autobiographical and 'meditative' reflections come especially to the fore (Douglas & Moustakas 1984), as the researcher questions 'What is my experience of this phenomenon?' and 'What is the essential experience of others who share a similar experience to my own?' Indeed, the researcher's effort to travel ever deeper into his/her inner experiencing of a specific theme surrenders him/her to an experiential journey sign-posted by six interrelating phases:

- **Initial engagement:** the researcher immerses his/herself in a deep personal questioning of what precisely he/she wishes to research, in order to discover and awaken an intense interest, relationship and passion in the research subject

- **Immersion:** the researcher begins to live, sleep, dream and merge with the research question to the extent that he/she becomes it, so as to appreciate its intimate effects from the inside

- **Incubation:** the researcher allows the inner workings of intuition to clarify and extend his/her understanding of the question, while awaiting the tacit knowing that percolates to consciousness from a deep well of subconscious inner experience

- **Illumination:** the researcher reviews all of the data acquired from his/her experience and that of co-researchers, in order to identify tacit hidden meanings and an integrating framework that might be further tested and refined until it forms a comprehensive fit with experience

- **Explication:** the researcher attempts to examine fully what has awakened in consciousness, in an attempt to familiarise him/herself with the layers of meaning that surround the phenomenon being studied, inclusive of its universal qualities and deeper meanings so as to create an appreciation of its phenomenological whole

- **Creative synthesis:** the researcher forms a creative synthesis of the research theme (inclusive of opposing ideas and arguments for and against a particular proposition) with a view appreciating the real significance of what people actually experience (inclusive of knowledge, passion and presence) (Moustakas 1990). This process is not dissimilar to the Gestalt one of 'focusing'. Where Gestalt differs from 'phenomenological inquiry' and 'heuristic research' is essentially in its effort to keep a dialogue going within the context of a robust social relationship.

Heuristic inquiry, similar to Gestalt, facilitates holistic attention towards the authority of inner experience and, as such, flavours much of this text.

j) Appreciative Inquiry – Illuminating Change

Appreciative inquiry is closely aligned with heuristic inquiry, and seeks through reflection to illuminate the essential nature of a person's (or group's) experience, through the recovery and revitalised remembering of 'key' or 'most meaningful' events. As with a case study approach, the researcher enters with a theme for investigation, along with a prearranged method which proceeds in the following way:

- First, members of an inquiring group are usually asked to recall an experience relating to a negotiated theme
- Second, they are each asked to describe and share a 'best experience' of this theme
- Third, each member of the group is encouraged to be curious and to engage in dialogue with the person who is sharing
- Forth, the facilitator of the inquiry encourages members to set aside their preconceptions in order to get firmly in touch with their memories of an experience similar to the one being shared, and to fully explore what it was about themselves, and the situation under discussion, that made this a 'peak experience' for them
- Fifth, once members have exhausted their reports and pooled the available data, the facilitator asks the group to list and to develop a consensus – on the basis of their discussion – with regard to the core attributes of the inquiry theme
- Lastly, the facilitator invites members to acknowledge anything they have observed in the group, which has especially helped them become more aware of attributes connected to the research theme.

Appreciative inquiry has been described as a powerful tool for organisational change:

> Creating new and better theories/ideas/images is, therefore, a powerful way of changing organisations. Appreciative inquiry seeks these new images in and among people's best intentions and noblest aspirations, attempting a collaborative envisioning of what the group could be at its very best. From the practical standpoint the problem is how do we get people to dream alternative futures together, to envision new patterns of social organisation that are better than what they currently have or may ever have individually experienced.
>
> *Bushe 1998 p.2*

This dialogical and illuminative approach, similarly to action research, aims to bring about change, but through effect upon the organisation's inner dialogue. If you change the stories people tell to justify past events and present circumstances, it is suggested you will change their construction of reality and in turn their relationship to the world. *'Nothing the "rational mind" decides it wants will actually happen if the "inner dialogue" is resistant to it'* (Bushe 1998 p.4). In principle, appreciative inquiry owes much to Cooperrider's (1990) review of research on sports psychology, which suggests you get more of whatever you put your attention on and apply your mind to. In this regard, appreciative inquiry pays especial attention to *'tracking'* – a state of mind where one actively engages in looking out for what one wants more of, and *'fanning'* – amplifying and encouraging actions that help you get more of whatever you are looking for.

Appreciative inquiry supports Gestalt and holistic inquiry's notion that active engagement and qualitative contact is necessary for inquiry into, and an illumination of, personal meaning.

k) Complexity and Chaos Theory – Listening to the Fertile Void

Complexity theory and chaos theory have recently been adopted as lenses of qualitative inquiry (Reason & Goodwin 1999), in order to account for non-linear and non-cause-and-effect influences within larger eco and social systems. Chaos theory, derived from the study of global weather patterns (Lorentz 1991), akin to field theory, draws our attention to the interrelationship of micro and macro effects. Complexity theory, akin to holistic inquiry, asks us to attend to the whole while honouring emergent processes that arise on the edge of what is often seen as chaos:

> The science of complexity takes us to the threshold of a new relationship with the complex processes that define the context of our lives: the weather, the ecological systems on which we depend for clean air and food, organizations and economies within which we live and try to manage.
>
> *Reason & Goodwin 1999 p.291*

From this perspective, emergent and irregular phenomena that do not fit into the overall pattern are accorded as much respect as frequent and ordered phenomena. For example, medical diagnosis depends on fine observation and the correct assimilation of physical symptoms and facts; but intuition and the generation of a felt sense, born of wider holistic judgement, are just as important for success. That is to say, fluctuations are as important as systemic influences. We are hereby cautioned not to believe that everything of importance is already in existence, and that there is much more 'unknown' than is 'known' about the world.

80

Chaos theory and complexity theory awake us to non-linear self-organising processes of the field, and say something about how we, as holistic and Gestalt-aware researchers, may explore the fertile void and all that is obscured and hidden from view.

Reflections

Of the methods introduced, which ones would you like to explore further? Which impacts on you most? More importantly, which do you see as best illuminating the kind of data you need to address to answer your research question or to illuminate your field of interest?

(November) As I'm looking at how people, staff and students perceive 'work-based learning' and wish to implement change, I feel reaffirmed that action research is a most appropriate method, but will now dovetail to this aspects of collaborative inquiry. I would like to do some phenomenological interviewing. So perhaps a mixed-method study might best suit my purpose.

3.4 Applications to Life – Exploring and Experiencing the Whole

Hopefully by now, you can see the relevance of Gestalt to holistic inquiry and qualitative research and you are beginning to glean how Gestalt has influenced a whole family of research methods and may even claim to be a phenomenological research method in its own right.

> If you begin then go all the way, because if you begin and quit the unfinished business you have left behind will haunt you for all of time… The path is like getting into a train that you cannot get off. You ride on and on.
>
> *Trungpa Rinpoche in Hayward & Cohen 1988*

Qualitative research, framed by Gestalt and holistic inquiry, encourages an approach to research in which many of the above methods can coexist. For example, in the account below, several perspectives are interwoven to get at the complexity and 'laminated feel' of real experience.

A 'Deep Description' and 'Multi-dimensional' Approach to the Study of Human Experience and Organisational Behaviour

Below is an extended analysis of a study cited earlier (see section 3.1) which explores the effects and influences of awaiting and undergoing major surgery, and was conducted by a researcher from the vantage-point of the 'patient role'. It interweaves naturalistic, anthropological and heuristic inquiry to a holistic, phenomenological and Gestalt-inspired frame where data is allowed to speak for itself in a raw, grounded-theory way.

The Context

At the socio-cultural level this was a contentious piece of research for several reasons:

- The nursing profession was at this time in the midst of patting itself on the back for being modern, and was in the process of developing Project 2000 – nursing for the twenty-first century; it seemed to believe that it had evolved beyond its mistakes of the Fifties.

- At the time, the researcher was a senior lecturer in the professionally prestigious Institute of Advanced Nursing Education at the Royal College of Nursing, and so could not easily be ignored.

- The study was conducted from the opposite side of the professional fence – as a client, in the role of a patient on a surgical ward.

The Researcher Bias

Professionally, the researcher was out to prove a point that unless nursing paid attention to its nurse-patient relationship, any amount of technological improvement, revamping of mission statements and professional reorganisation would be to little avail. Personally, as a post-operative patient in a hospital bed, the researcher needed a project and focus through which to empower himself and to provide a sense of purpose.

The Client and the Research Contract

The client was the nursing profession and the health service. However, as the research/consultancy was unsolicited and the inquiry would also ultimately benefit the researcher, he was also in one sense a client! As for the contract, as a senior lecturer at the Royal College of Nursing he was professionally contracted to represent the interests of the nursing profession at home and overseas, and to research and promote excellence of practice.

The Methods

In character this was a multi-method holistic study, with case study, heuristic reflection, phenomenological and ethnographic elements.

The Tools

- A diary was kept of everyday events, including what was personally experienced and its times and dates.

- Having acquired several weeks of data from a participant-observer position, the researcher compared and contrasted Izabel Menzies's (1960) findings of institutional routines as a defence against anxiety in hospitals in the 1950s, with that of his experience in the late 1980s.

- Qualitative and quantitative methods of data analysis were employed to explain how often things happened and what it was like to be on the receiving end of a supposed therapeutic relationship.

Findings

In one sense, the findings were personal, but at another level they illuminated the human condition and institutionalised professional practices. This research into the experience of life and near-death has more than a touch of the transpersonal within it. For example, prior to surgery the researcher recorded:

Now I prepared myself for the worst – surgery. The physician gave way to the surgeon. I was informed that, as my stomach was pushing up through my diaphragm to embarrass my lung, an operation would have to be performed. This information, delivered in a matter of fact way left little to discuss. Before this information had sunk in, or I was able to make inquiry, people had gone.

As evening fell I was wheeled into the surgical ward and my body was shaved and prepared for the operation. The premedication stopped my retching and relieved most of my discomfort. I was alert and able to relay my medical history when asked.

A consultant anaesthetist now came to my bed. He was gentle, softly spoken, and for the first time I felt the busyness around me start to subside. His voice was slow and I felt supported and listened to.

I saw Anna and mother again at this time, and stayed light and joked while they wished me the best. No need to 'make a drama out of a crisis' I felt. I was resigned to what had to be. As there was no real choice to make, I felt little anxiety. I felt detached, a witness to events, and determined not to give in to hopelessness. In the pre-operative room I met the anaesthetist again. His voice remained soft and unhurried and I felt myself relax. I remember saying to myself that if these were to be my final moments I was going to live them with dignity.

As the anaesthetic flowed into me and I drifted from consciousness, I caught snatches of a dream of a canal bridge I played under in childhood. I remembered I had dreamt this dream under dental gas at the age of four.

...My next conscious moment was filled with darkness. I tried to open my eyes and speak, nothing moved or came out. 'Am I dead?' I wondered. Resigning myself to powerlessness, I reasoned I would just have to make the best of it. I next heard a snatch of voices, seemingly far off, and felt myself being lifted and turned. I realised for the first time I was not dead. Many questions surfaced: 'Has the anaesthetic worn off?'; 'Is this before or after the operation?'; 'Will I feel the surgeons cutting into me?' This was all very matter of fact – I was not allowing myself the luxury of an emotion.

Gradually I explored my bodily sensations. I became aware it was not me breathing; something was inside doing this for me. I remembered a film, 'The Alien', where a parasitic entity invades a human host; I smiled to myself but nothing moved. Strange to say, I also felt free to take stock: 'I have had a full life – do I really want to go back?' I weighed things up for some time, remembering, reflecting on my life and relationships. Anna, and Marc my son, were foremost to my mind. I had lived a fatherless childhood, I would not inflict this on my own son. Similarly I was determined not to leave Anna in this way. In short, I contracted with myself to stay alive whatever it cost in terms of my personal resources. I never once during this time doubted it was in my power to live – or to die.

This state of suspended existence lasted for some hours. Eventually my consciousness became hazy; I thought I heard Anna's voice, but could not tell how much was real and how much imagined before floating into unconsciousness again.

My awakening to conventional reality was blurred, but recognisably on a ward with a cardiac monitor and tubes around me. I was aware of Anna and mother but could not focus upon them; as in a dream, the more I tried to focus the harder it was to see. I felt as if I was suspended in thick syrup – all my movements and senses were out of synchronisation and my thoughts formed in slow motion. Occasionally this slow other world of heavy haze would suddenly rip apart and pockets of alertness and clarity enter, to give way just as suddenly a little later to slow syrupy haze again. Even though my external world was fuzzy my internal one stayed clear. It was as if an internal 'other world' reality, one where I could witness myself (as in lucid dreaming), awoke and remained coherent and logical to its own laws, taking over to provide a venue where I could work things out in peace.

[...] Gradually cohesion returned and I was able to glue my sensations back into a recognisable social world where I could start to relate to others.

Barber 1991/98 pp.234–9

Besides illuminating insights through the authority of lived experience, this study also employed quantitative inquiry to analyse how long it took nurses to answer the call bell – an average of five, with a maximum of twenty-five minutes was recorded as waiting time. A record was also kept of nursing reactions and interventions.

A rudimentary analysis of nursing behaviours and interactions suggested that there was a highly significant fit between Menzies's study (1960) of the 1950s and current practice in the 1980s. A comparative study was therefore conducted to test the working hypothesis that: 'Nurses of the Eighties were as defensively bound and professionally distanced and damaged by the demands of clinical care, as their sisters of the Fifties'.

Menzies findings have significance for organisational life and serve as useful prompts to what to look for regarding institutionalisation, professional ritualization and other systemic defences against anxiety; below, the researcher lists the findings of Menzies earlier study of the 1950s, before sharing current observations of the late 1980s:

Splitting up of the nurse patient relationship

Here tasks are seen to demand more attention than individuals; patients are treated all the same, personal distinctions are reduced, clinical duties prescribed and listed. Little opportunity is afforded for development of one to one relationships; authentic practitioner-client relationships are strongly discouraged and professional distance strongly reinforced.

Example: The researcher observed that nurses were constantly on the lookout for physical jobs to do. This behaviour was strongly reinforced. For example, when a senior member of staff encountered juniors talking to clients, jobs were quickly found for them to do in areas distant from the individual they had engaged in conversation, i.e. they were exiled to the sluice room to clean up or the laundry cupboard to stack linen. In this way counselling never occurred, and ward maintenance jobs prevailed.

Depersonalisation, categorisation and denial of individual significance

Clients are referred to by their label rather than names. Uniformity of response and client management, attitude and performance are encouraged; individuality and personal uniqueness are discouraged, as are creative new ways of solving long-standing problems.

Example: The researcher's experience testified to the fact that patients were rarely referred to by name, but rather identified by diet, condition, or with reference to the consultant surgeon – 'Dr X's thorax in bed four'!

Detachment and denial of feelings

Staff are expected to exert strong control over their feelings; displays of emotion are discouraged; involvement is feared; juniors are disciplined rather than counselled and told what to do rather than listened to or heard. Clients' feelings are generally ignored, with the consequence that systems of control predominate over systems of care.

Example: Every nurse within the ward appeared to have two forms of presentation or communication style. To colleagues the tone of voice was generally feeling-less and businesslike, and to patients jollying, rather patronising in a playful way, and chiding. When a patient died, no time was set aside for appraisal or mourning. In consequence, nurses plunged themselves into ward tasks with increased energy and were seemingly even more desperate to keep themselves busy.

Decisions reduced and avoided via an adherence to ritual and routine

The anxiety of free choice is replaced with instrumental activity and institutionalised procedures; decisions are shelved until new policies are formed. Questioning is discouraged and new ideas resisted, in favour of the time-proven methods.

Example: To take night sedation at any other than the usual time or to request painkillers outside of the medicine round produced pronounced tension. Relatively simple requests from patients, such as to delay night sedation or to sleep through breakfast after a sleepless night, were referred by junior staff to seniors, such was the fear of employing one's own initiative or of breaking from routine.

Responsibility diluted by checks and counter checks

Individual action is actively discouraged, everything has a tendency to be obsessively recorded. Trust of others – and their skills – is a rarity; fear of failure a constant motivator.

Example: Even aspirin, a common enough drug in the home, was given out in a manner one would expect for a deadly poison. Temperature, pulse and respiration, observations the researcher as a trained nurse could easily have done for themselves, were performed for them, and what appeared on their observation chart, the record of their pulse and temperature, was given much more credence than those symptoms they personally reported. Blood pressures recorded by juniors were nearly always counter-checked by senior staff, and observations by patients given little weight.

Collusive redistribution of responsibility and irresponsibility

Trustworthiness and authority are allocated to seniors and irresponsibility and untrustworthiness to juniors; consequently, seniors end-up acting in a 'parent-like' way and juniors act in a dependent 'childlike' manner. Personal power is denied and professional autonomy and personal initiative are largely left under-used or become disused.

Example: It was commonplace to hear juniors being chastised for supposed errors openly in front of patients. Likewise deviations from routine – for whatever reason – brought a quick and sharp rebuke. Everything was seemingly directed at keeping the status quo.

Responsibility avoided by generalisation and role obscurity

Roles are unspecified, responsibilities blurred and boundaries largely undefined. Ample space is provided for excuses to be found, conflicts ignored and personal responsibilities disowned.

Example: Alongside the need to record things obsessively and to keep the routine operative was another, conflicting thread: practitioners would refer everything back to the next level of seniority. This seemed to be in part good sense (to avoid being told off for using initiative); but it also appeared to have the flavour of getting back at seniors and acting out passive anger at the system. Seniors in like manner tended to select those individuals who were less compliant, or whom they appeared to dislike, for the more tedious jobs. Open disagreements and dislikes were thus avoided, kept under wraps, and punitive power play was enacted with the professional veneer well and truly intact.

Delegation to superiors of professional and personal choice

Disclaimed responsibilities are forced upwards to seniors. Staff perform well below their level of competence and skills, and responsibility is shirked.

Example: Largely due to the aforementioned dynamics, seniors were forever overloaded with petty decisions. This in turn reaffirmed what appeared to be a personal need in themselves to be seen as a 'work hero', a person who gives his/her all and stays voluntarily after hours; the nurse as an all-giving, all-powerful, heavily idealised and indispensable being. Seniors here appeared dangerously close to burn out.

Idealisation of self and underestimation of the potential to develop

Homage is paid to the belief that 'practitioners are born rather than made', that selection of the 'right' people is more important than training or personal and professional development. Maturity and responsibility are allocated to rank rather than to individual merit.

Example: Personal and professional status within the clinical setting seemed to revolve around rank and rank ordering. This gave immense power to those who knew the routine and the system – the power holders of the hospital. By venerating those who had remained longest in the hospital – or the specialism concerned – routine was safeguarded and change all too successfully resisted.

Avoidance of change

The full consent of everyone is sought before change can take place, and so progresses at the speed of the slowest and most resistive team member involved. Problem confrontation is avoided, and change is avoided for fear of having to challenge the existing social structure, which keeps the status quo – and those who support it – firmly in place.

Example: Understandably, in the light of all the above restrictions, change all but failed to permeate throughout the clinical setting. Upon the wall of the nursing office was a chart of various nursing models, individualised Kardex reporting of patients occurred, but the researcher (as client) was never interviewed by a nurse in all of his/her stay – some six weeks – nor was a care plan produced. Things just went on as they always had done.

Implementation of Findings

This took the form of:

- Writing up the study interspersed with professional insights for nurse training and practice

- Publishing the findings in a major preparatory text for nurse training and preparation.

Measures of Success

The above study was recorded in a major work on nursing, and became essential reading for the professional preparation of nurses at a basic and a master's level. This study was therefore circulated widely, both nationally and internationally, and continues to influence entrants to the nursing profession into the twenty-first century. On the strength of this publication, the researcher was invited to consult and partake in the implementation of Project 2000, a governmental report which served to revolutionised nursing education. He/she then became an external examiner for several master's courses in nursing and was invited to facilitate several supervision and self-development groups within the nursing profession.

Real life, in essence, is experienced as a whole. This is so whether we carve it up into interrelating cycles (action research), focus upon a specific situation (case study), look within (heuristics) or look outwards from ourselves (positivism) – or look to the processes of perception (phenomenology) or the wider context (field). Experience, in the final analysis, is a flowing organismic whole, of which even the most sophisticated method of research captures merely a pale reflection.

Reflections

What lessons do you take from the case study described above and how might they be applied to your own research group?

(October) I'm aware of how rituals and systemic defences can influence behaviour, and wonder if similar dynamics will affect my study; after all, I am in an institutional setting within a conventional academic culture with set ways of doing things. But the really scary thing for me is the frequency, to my mind, that we appear already to have institutionalised such social defences as 'depersonalisation and denial of individual differences' and 'detachment and denial of feelings' in our culture; all of which will frustrate the implementation of change intended by my research. Possibly all organisations have the defences Menzies has attributed to hospitals? If so, organisations – whatever their form – will work in the interests of the status quo! What started off as a straightforward investigation is now becoming much more complex.

3.5 The Nature of Research and Knowledge – When a Fact is a Fiction

Inquiry is a natural consequence of day-to-day life; it arises as soon as we say 'What should I do now?' or 'How can I avoid this happening next time?'

> When an individual enters the presence of others, they commonly seek to acquire information about him already possessed. They will be interested in his general socio-economic status, his competence, his trustworthiness, etc. Although some of this information seems to be sought almost as an end in itself, there are usually quite practical reasons for acquiring it. Information about the individual helps to define the situation, enabling others to know in advance what he will expect of them and what they may expect of him .
>
> *Goffman 1978 p.13*

But what moves the naive inquiry we all perform on an everyday basis towards the status of *research*? Simply, to qualify as research, your inquiry must involve a careful searching, your method of collecting information must be located within a recognisable methodological tradition, and you must demonstrate systematic investigation and critical reflection upon both *what you are doing and how you are doing it*. You need also to illuminate your *motivation and rationale* and *what influences you at the time*. This criteria also differentiates naive facilitation from facilitation of excellence. Research, is a mindful process, where the tools of investigation are examined as rigorously as a study's theme. With rigorous investigation held in place by the frame of *research-design*, the information you acquire can better be bestowed with the status of *knowledge* – in contrast to opinion, supposition or personal bias. But then again, what exactly is knowledge?

Knowledge, is commonly believed to be objective, externally verifiable and supported by a background body of *factual* information. It is often seen as generated and acquired through a course of study and/or experimentation, which accords with the prevailing scientific paradigm in ascendance at this time. But as we live in a social world where we learn *how to perceive* and *how to label experience*, knowledge is socially created and culturally defined; and the objective perceptions we pride ourselves on are merely the creation of our physical and social organs of perception, not representations of a thing itself.

Faith plays its part here. For instance, no one has seen an atom – much less split one – yet we take atoms for granted. And facts, what are these but beliefs in which we are schooled to place our trust? In this context science, a major organiser and generator of factual knowledge in the Western world, may be compared to a prevailing purveyor of superstition, a social organ – somewhat similar to a religion – in which we are invited to place our faith. This process of cultural legitimisation throws up some interesting anomalies. For example, if a man talks to God we see this as prayer, but if a man reports God speaking back to him he runs a danger of being labelled psychotic and institutionalised!

A Comparative Example of Research and Knowledge

Consider a Buddhist monk inquiring into the nature of 'being', who meditates under guidance while systematically investigating and experimenting with differing meditative techniques. His systematic address of spiritual enlightenment can be as precise as that of a research scientist in the lab. In truth, both have much in common. Both are trained to a specific discipline, critically reflect upon what they experience, refer to knowledgeable texts and literature relating to their research theme, and perform rigorous investigation while putting to test the hypotheses they hold about their respective world views. But while Buddhist beliefs and bias are openly expressed, what science and scientists take for granted is often hidden. Scientific positivism, with a style of reporting that objectifies experience by speaking in the third person, would have us believe that personal, political and emotional influences do not affect the researcher. A humorous thought comes to mind: a person who splits-off their senses and intellect from their feelings and fantasies – in psychiatry – is likely to be diagnosed as schizophrenic, but a like-minded process employed in the pure sciences appears to masquerade as research excellence!

3.6 Aesthetics of Research – Bringing Partiality and Passion back to Life in Research

As I am a passionate being who is interested in people I bring this passion and interest to my research. In contrast to the pure scientist I put my biases out in the open so that you might appreciate just what I am selling. Surely, this is more ethical than presenting my work as factual unquestionable truth? Remember, unlike quantitative researchers, qualitative researchers do not so seek so much to triangulate data, that is explore from different perspectives and methods a phenomenon to establish its truth, so much as in a Gestalt way, to 'crystallise' meaning – as there is taken to be no 'fixed reality' to triangulate (Heron 1988).

As a holistic researcher, though I attempt to blend quantitative and qualitative approaches to inquiry, I am nevertheless aware that they represent very different creatures. *Qualitative research* I associate with the arts and experiential engagement, and see as conducive to capturing emotional expression and imaginative meaning. *Quantitative research*, conversely, I associate with the sciences – objective observation and the pursuit of knowledge through rigorous experiment, often in settings where wholes are dissected into component parts and statistical analysis carries the day. Though this distinction is less pronounced today than it was some ten or twenty years ago, the legacy of science has historically led to research supportive of such conventional norms as:

- Faith in rationality
- Emotional neutrality
- Disinterestedness
- Impartiality
- Suspension of judgement
- Absence of bias.

After Mitroff 1974

But new trends are afoot and expressive influences and counter-norms have begun to creep into social research over the last forty years in the shape of:

- Faith in non-rationality
- Emotional commitment
- Interestedness
- Partiality
- Exercise of judgement
- Presence of bias.

After Mitroff 1974 p.79

In this early movement, from impartiality to partiality, we see the beginnings of postmodernity:

> Postmodern thought has involved an expansion of reason, it has gone beyond the cognitive and scientific domains... in particular the de-humanising of power into anonymous structures.

Kvale 1992

In the context of the aforementioned research traditions, holistic research of the type identified in this text is qualitative, postmodern and aligned with Diesing's (1972) definition of holism as studying and accounting for the whole human system within its natural setting. This contrasts with Yin's (1989) use of holism as a term to describe studies which focus upon a single or global level – but ignore everything else. In this text, 'holism' in a field theory way (Lewin 1952) honours the dynamic interconnectedness of 'phenomenological experience' – our knowledge of the world as it appears in our consciousness when we attend to 'the totality of what lies before us in the light of day'. (Heidegger 1977 p.75)

In holistic inquiry of the kind I am advocating, science and art are not seen as diametrically opposed to each other, but are rather approached as aspects of the experiential whole. Indeed, science is seen as having expressive elements and art as encompassing scientific traits. Akin to Yin and Yang, science and art are appreciated as parts of a whole with dual possibilities that are constantly transforming one into the other. This relationship is further explored in examination of the practitioner-researcher relationship below.

91

The Nature of an Inquiring Relationship – Facilitating the Art and the Science of Inquiry

The model shared here was originally co-created within a doctoral study (Barber 1990b) into the facilitative relationship and processes of change, and has been applied to education (Barber 1995) and consultancy (Barber 1999b) prior to our current theme of research. In essence it describes the following four relational phases – for research to me is primarily relational:

1) **Orientation:** where a practitioner-researcher and their clients/co-researchers meet, sketch an initial contract, orientate to each other's world-view and begin to form a working alliance

2) **Identification:** where a practitioner-researcher and their clients/co-researchers identify problem areas and prospective strategies, refine the contract and raise to awareness the purposes and tasks of their inquiry

3) **Exploration:** where a practitioner-researcher and clients/co-researchers work together to implement the strategies they have chosen, modify these in the light of feedback and decide future steps

4) **Resolution:** where the practitioner-researcher and clients/co-researchers evaluate outcomes, review follow-up, complete the inquiry while working towards a positive ending of their relationship.

Though largely progressive, a researcher-client/co-researcher relationship may occasionally slip back to an earlier phase. This is especially the case when a crisis of trust occurs, when role relationships change or at times when the presenting problem or the research thrust re-focuses elsewhere and the identification phase needs to be re-engaged. Besides presenting a developmental model of the practitioner-researcher relationship, when we examine in more depth the above phases, a framework for understanding and mapping the interplay of the art and science of inquiry – as well as its relational politics – becomes apparent:

Orientation (an artistic phase?)

This is an artistic stage in my view, a period where the practitioner-researcher and/or facilitator and their clients meet to generate a working allegiance, form first impressions and orientate to each others attitudes and world view. This is a phase – when things go well – of developing trust and common language, where sharing and self-expression come to the fore as those involved begin to understand one another and start to feel understood. Sensitive relating and gentle adaptation characterise this stage, as the relational dance begins and social choreography starts to emerge. This phase is long and drawn out when people have little in common, short in long-standing relationships, and may be skipped over entirely in ritualised settings where habits and procedures set the scene and person-to-person contact is minimal. This phase needs to be a client-centred one where attention is directed to empathetically entering the client's world in an attempt to understand their relational requirements and needs, so that as much information as possible can be absorbed from the client-system.

Identification (a scientific phase?)

This is a more scientific stage, a time of clear observation and clarification, where diagnosis of the prevailing issues occurs, alongside the clarifying of intentions and the raising and refining of possible strategies for the way ahead. Here prospective hypotheses are formed and the expertise of the researcher comes to the fore. Especially important at this stage is the defining of 'Who is the real client in this facilitated inquiry'? This is of especial importance in organisation and consultancy settings, where a practitioner-researcher will have to differentiate between the relative needs of: the contact person; senior management; the managing director; those subjects directly involved; the shareholders; the organisation; other research funding bodies; and the business community itself. Also important here is the diagnosis and generation of a tentative working hypothesis as to what is required. This phase can be a protracted one when the core focus and nature of the research is not readily identifiable. From the researcher's perspective this is a problem-centred stage where attention is directed towards isolating possible problems in the researcher-client relationship as much as in the research field. Here relational supports, such as planning the frequency and method of debriefing, need to be seeded.

Exploration (an artistic phase informed by science?)

At this stage a chosen strategy is enacted and the field of interest engaged. Here skilful relational expression and acute observation meet in action. Constantly, the researcher has to keep a healthy dialogue between the unfolding relationship, the research field, and his or her intellectual constructs and mapping. The relational dance now moves into full swing as robust energies from the research field may put the relationship to test. The emotional cut and thrust of the relationship at this time demands an intuitive response from a practitioner-researcher. Issues of the orientation and identification phases do not so much vanish at this point, but are rather less to the fore as action inquiry and strategic intervention take priority. Maintaining the relational health and energy of the relationship is also an increasing concern now, as environmental pressures and problems are worked through. At best, the researcher learns to 'do less but to achieve more'. From the researcher's perspective this is a strategy-centred stage when working hypotheses about the nature of the unfolding researcher-researched relationship are put into action and refined in the light of experience. As the researcher is often seen more regularly and becomes trusted, he or she may now start to receive anger and frustrations earlier held from view. The real, rather than the imagined, research problem may also emerge at this time.

Resolution (a scientific phase informed by art?)

Here client and researcher debrief, evaluate and critically appraise the outcome of the inquiry they have performed; they work towards resolution of the current research/consulting contract and their researcher/facilitator-client relationship. Though they may meet again at a future time, they must now complete what the relationship was designed to achieve, analyse and evaluate the results and, if appropriate, write up the research for presentation to a wider audience. Celebration of achievements and reflection on the possibilities for future involvement should be raised here, along with evaluation of the value added to the researched area by the research already performed. This phase is one where you pool together the data you have amassed, critically reflect upon and analyse your findings, consider the implications of what has been surfaced and make recommendations.

A holistic researcher has a great flexibility of approach within the above relationship. During the life of a single study they might start as a non-participant observer but step into the ethnographic tradition (Mead 1928) to describe what unfolds culturally. A little later, they may enter more deeply into experience in the manner of a heuristic researcher to explore the effect of the inquiry upon themselves and, finally, facilitate group exploration in a co-operative inquiry mode (Reason 1988) to counterbalance their own interpretation of events. Depending upon the data they seek and the avenues of inquiry that open up in the research field, they mix-and-match approaches as differing phenomenon arise for investigation.

In the final analysis, holistic inquiry in the gestalt tradition integrates 'the science of researching' (concerned with methods, theory, exactness and the verification of data) with 'the art of researching' (concerned with expression, human growth and development, communication, aesthetics and the relational dance). As to how the science and art of facilitation feel from the driver's seat in facilitation, this is explored further below.

Practically, as a Gestaltist in the identification and resolution phases of the researcher/facilitator-client relationship, in the role of **researching scientist** I do the following:

- Listen to the whole of the person before me (their message, emotional tone, posture)
- Stay alert to the relational process (distance and closeness, objectivity and intimacy)
- Demonstrate alertness to what unfolds (nodding, repeating phrases, drawing closer)
- Focus upon the developing theme (listening to the intention and direction)
- Ask clarifying questions (reaffirm what has been said)
- Remain self-aware (attend to my emotional and intellectual reactions).

Conversely, in the role of **researching artist** within the orientation and exploration phases, I try to:

- Suspend my internal intellectual dialogue (hold my own process in check)
- Attune to my senses (what I see, hear, smell, touch)
- Allow myself to be emotionally impacted (note my energetic response to what is said)
- Meditate upon the other (stay with what unfolds rather than rehearse a response)
- Let the wider field inform me (stay mindful of the context and setting).

As a researching scientist I am less relaxed and more intellectually focused. As a researching artist I am more attuned to the relational dance and trusting of what unfolds. As this text is primarily about the art of research rather than its science, I will pursue this avenue a little more.

Holistic inquiry in its scientific aspects, seeks to provide knowledgeable information and models of understanding, but being a process-centred discipline its findings remain tacit and soft-edged. As an art, holistic inquiry expresses itself through acts of sensitive emotional exploration whereby new gestalts are illuminated. But because it is neither a pure science nor a pure art, a more subtle metaphor is needed, one that is less either-or. In this vein, a Yin and Yang model of inquiry is suggested below:

Yin = Researcher as artist	Yang = Researcher as scientist
Soft focus and wide ranging	Hard focused and narrow in range
Inner-world directed	Outer-world directed
Exploration through direct experience	Application of theories and hypotheses
Attuned to feelings and intuition	Attuned to thoughts and senses
Attending to the relational dance	Attuned to boundaries and rules
Concerned with being and becoming	Concerned with doing and achieving
Expresses and creates	Diagnoses and tabulates

Adapted from Barber & Mulligan 1998

Do not fall into the trap of perceiving Yin and Yang as if they were separate polarities: they are not. They might look stark when perceived in isolation each from the other, but remember that Yin and Yang is a 'complete concept with dual possibilities, inseparable and constantly striving to compliment and unify' (Huang 1989 p.23). Indeed, Huang offers a much more poetic rendition of the above:

Yin = Feminine, dark, passive, negative, yielding, falling, warm, night, moon, being.

Yang = Masculine, light, active, positive, firm, rising, cold, day, sun, doing.

95

Moving the above model beyond its metaphorical frame, Woldt and Ingersoll (1991) have used it as a guide to language analysis:

YIN	YANG
Mythic Language	Factual Language
Associative	Dissociative
Metaphorical	Literal
Connotative	Denotative
Non-linear	Linear
More right brain	More left brain
Speaks to a 'here and now' state which transcends time and space	Speaks to a 'there and then' state which denotes time and space

Woldt & Ingersoll 1991 p.96

Yang (nearer to science) puts us firmly in touch with sensate and intellectually constructed or taught aspects of the world. Yin (nearer art) awakens us to expressive, symbolic and intuitive aspects of existence. As a holistic practitioner-researcher I attempt to illuminate the journey I make with both my head (scientist?) and my heart (artist?), so as to do justice to the whole of what is experienced.

A practitioner-researcher inquiring in the Gestalt mode facilitates within the frame of an authentic relationship, giving themselves permission to experiment with their whole sense of being. They follow and flow with the energy, glide in or out of the field and relate or disengage with others while remaining mindful and raising questions to all that they do. Holism of this nature supports meditative reflection, facilitative and statistical inquiry and group encounter, for 'what you do' is far less important than 'how you do it' and the educative and growthful way in which you proceed. If you endeavour to 'stay with your experience', to share this with others and strive to do no harm, little should go wrong. But to help you to move with awareness to whatever new position presents itself, you need to develop towards a transparent rather than opaque communication style.

Case Study

Researching Transparently – A Lesson from Heuristic Inquiry

In the following record extracted from field notes under a heading entitled 'The drama of being a facilitator: What have I let myself in for now?' I describe how it felt to be alone and in a strange land, on the night before leading a workshop on 'Facilitating Change':

Back in my room I note that this is my most impatient time, the evening before a workshop when I am aware of what is to come but out of contact with the experience itself. My dreams echo this imaginative place I am in. I dream of being in a formal setting with royalty, drinking too much and feeling out of control, then journeying home on an extremely tall double-decker bus on top of a swaying ladder. No need to analyse this dream. These images are of disorientation, alienation and emotional tight-rope walking – everything I'm doing here. I awake and allow myself to feel my fears; in contacting them they disappear. I go back to sleep. I awake, a snatch of my last dream surfaces: I was in a small dark room with formally dressed people and 'the Principal', who is busily trying to get the environment perfect for me. Outside, drills upon a building site drown out our voices – she goes outside and stops this. I note people still sitting anxiously on chairs – I look at my watch, it is still one hour before the workshop – in dream-time – and very few people have arrived. In my waking state I recognise this to be a fear common to group facilitators, namely, that no one will turn up. Two other common fears are those of being overwhelmed by the emerging process, and/or meeting unmanageable resistance and having no influence. Planning does not allay these fears, for the cut-and-thrust of experiential learning tends to generate individual and group pressures you have to respond to intuitively – at the time. Still, this dream has served the useful purpose of purging me of my unconscious fears. Roll on tomorrow, reality can't be any worse than my dreams. It is dangerous for me to have time on my hands, I keep rewriting my intentions for the workshop and replaying what might happen. This rehearsal, is a sort of psychic preparation, continual and unconscious – occasionally surfacing to awareness. I jot down the facilitative options before me – as if to cover all eventualities. As I write I notice the bottled water I'm drinking has Arabic letters. I am reminded that Hong Kong receives it's water from China and beyond; this is a fragile world for all it's robustness. What securities have people here following 1997? All they are, have and own is at risk. What price reflective learning in this climate? Possibly I am projecting my own inner anxieties on the world without?

Barber 1995

You may find the above personal style of reporting unfamiliar, or judge it as self-indulgent, but why should not research have its own poetry? After all, many novels and films say more about the human condition and illuminate experience, far better than the average research study! So why not reverse this?

As can be seen from the above study, there is a fine line between *using the self as a research tool*, and *indulging yourself*. So what makes the difference? The contextual frame is all important in the above report. For instance, a lot is happening that specifically relates to 'change' – the core focus of this study. The researcher's experience parallels the workshop theme – facilitating change – and says masses about conscious and subconscious coping mechanisms that accompany individual change processes. In the context of this study, entitled 'The Trials and Tribulations of Pioneering Experiential Learning in Hong Kong', primary data of the study is being lived by the researcher and is thus worthwhile recording. Observations of this kind get at unique individual experience in the way a video or non-participant observer could never do.

On a continuum with 'marginal participant observation' at one end and 'full participant observation' at the other, there is a vast array of facilitative choice. Essentially, it boils down to how appropriately a practitioner-researcher positions his/herself and the inquiry in relation to:

Depth   *How deep within the fabric of experience is the data you seek?*

Necessity   *How necessary is it to become personally involved to acquire the data you need?*

Relevance   *How relevant is researcher involvement to what you want to study?*

Skill   *Do you have the necessary skills to facilitate an in-depth social inquiry?*

Resilience *Are you robust and resilient enough to cope with the interpersonal pressure?*

In terms of what you want to study, should you answer 'not very' to the first and second questions, 'not that relevant' to the third, and 'no' to the remainder, you might need to think again about becoming a participant and qualitative researcher! Perhaps a statistical approach would most suit your interests and you should close this text now? But, given that you decide an involved practitioner-researcher stance does justice to what you wish to examine, you will require a supervisor, someone who can help you explore your own values and perception style so that these don't inadvertently bias your judgement and vision. A supervisor, coach-cum-shadow-consultant of your research, essentially helps you to:

1) Remain centred and alert while social and emotional dynamics swirl around you

2) Tune in to what is happening now

3) Be in an experience while you simultaneously attempt to witness it

4) Be open to others in the manner of a true 'I-Thou' relationship

5) Give voice to your experience and what you are possibly missing in the moment

6) Read between the lines and raise awareness to the undertone of what is said

7) Engage as an authentic person rather than a 'role'

8) Crispen-up your rationale and use of an involved qualitative approach.

At root, supervision concerns the facilitation of self-examination. It raises to awareness potential blind spots so as to increase the range and depth of your research vision:

> If others examined themselves attentively, as I do, they would find themselves, as I do, full of insanity and nonsense. Get rid of it I cannot without getting rid of myself. We are all steeped in it, one as much as the other; but those who are aware of it are a little better off – though I don't know.
>
> *Khan 1983 p.13*

Aspects of self-supervision and facilitative criteria are littered periodically throughout this text.

Reflections

How do the art and science of inquiry, as described above, impact upon you and your role as a practitioner-researcher?

(October) Noting my own tendency to allocate meaning to events via how things 'feel', I suspect on a continuum with science at one end and art at the other, I'm more at the artistic end. I think it might be useful in my inquiry to work in a case-study way, building-up layers of thick description of how people experience 'work-based learning'; perhaps they might reflect upon the feelings and images that float to mind when they consider times they were most fulfilled at work. I'm also beginning to appreciate that if our view of the world is 'phenomenological', something created by the process of perception rather than having an objective separate existence, that a more 'artistic' and expressive process of information gathering might be the most appropriate route for me to take.

How useful do you consider Yin and Yang might be for the analysis of dialogue or as a model for literary analysis?

(October) It's interesting to consider how such a broad brush-stroke as this might be used to perform an initial sweep through the information I'm surfacing in my study. I can also see how Huang's model might be used to illuminate feminine/emotional and masculine/intellectual themes and undercurrents in my inquiry.

Rate yourself against criteria of Depth (how deeply the data you need is embedded in experience); Necessity (how personally involved you need to be to acquire the data you need); Relevance (how relevant researcher involvement is to your study); Skill (do you have the skills to facilitate an in-depth study). Consider how a supervisor could help you continue to pay attention to these issues and help make your research more transparent.

(October) This is getting more than a little complex now! But, as a thumb-nail appreciation of my theme, 'how people experience my work in the area of work-based learning', I note that as I'm exploring the department's culture, that my data is deeply embedded in the experiential field; that mining deeper into experience is a necessity for my study; that researcher involvement is essential, but that I will need to polish up on my appreciation of group facilitation, perhaps by attending a few courses if I am to take others deeper into a group's experiential territory. I'm also aware that I will need to talk to my research supervisor (now that I've got one) who is alert to both group facilitation and group dynamics; he is someone who can both challenge and support me to go deeper.

Human beings have deficiencies as research instruments, for example: tendencies for data overload, to magnify the impact of first impressions and to discount the novel and unusual; the trend towards over or under-reacting to new information; excessive confidence in their own judgement; repeated evaluations of the same data tend to differ; a tendency to ignore information that conflicts with existing hypotheses (Sadler 1981). How might you alert your supervisor to keep you on track?

(October) I'm aware of my own tendency to over-commit, to become overenthusiastic and to fail to break-off from something once I'm fully involved. I guess I should contract with my supervisor to watch out for any over-investment on my part in my research and to alert me to when I'm losing a sense of the wider picture.

3.7 If Deep Description is for You –
How Might you go About It?

Given that a holistic and qualitative approach to inquiry is best suited to your purpose, how might you go about it? Spradley (1980) cites the following as worthy of consideration:

Space: physical layout and setting - for instance, the effects of space and light, the limitations these impose and the messages they give;

Actors: the people involved - who they are, the roles ascribed to them formally and informally, their ages and nationality, country of origin, cultural heritage;

Activities: what actually happens - the actions undertaken and the effects produced, the reactions of those present;

Objects: the furniture - the setting and trappings within the physical environment, how these are placed and how they affect the dynamics that unfold;

Acts: specific individual behaviours - personal reactions and responses, who does what and when they do it;

Events: particular occasions and meetings - happenings and gatherings during a specified period, how these relate and contribute to the research as a whole;

Time: the sequence of events - what happens and when it happens, what it contributes to and what subsequently evolves in the time-span;

Goals: what the actors seek to accomplish - the aims, goals and desires of those present, and how they influence the research field and the relationships in view;

Feelings: emotions and their context - the communal energetic field and the emotional drivers brought into view by each individual, the emotional rapport established between the researcher and the researched.

In the description overleaf, we find example of the above criteria in action:

101

Applying Laminations of Deep Description to an Emerging Study

Start simply. First, record what you see and hear (Space; Objects; Actors):

As I enter the room I am aware of the buzz of conversation. There are twenty-five people in attendance seated in a circle in one corner of the room furthest from the door. Of those in attendance some three-quarters appear to be in their mid-thirties, the remaining quarter in their fifties, and the sexual ratio seems equally balanced. There are no desks nor tables in evidence, only the people and their chairs, plus an empty remaining chair for myself. The room is light and airy, and my eye is quickly drawn back to the empty chair that awaits me.

Second, record what happens and what unfolds chronologically (Acts; Events; Time):

As I walk to my chair the conversation dies down, all eyes turn to me as I sit. I rest in silence for some fifteen seconds. Acclimatising to the room I glance around to survey those who are present. After some thirty seconds, when I feel composed and orientated enough, I begin my presentation.

Third, reflect on what you and others feel and seek in the moment (Feelings; Goals):

I start by sharing the goals that I have brought for the day, and ask how these compare with those of others. Broadly my goals are supported by the group, but there appears to be an underlying anxiety that no matter what we say or do, things will revert back to how they have always been.

Fourth, go home and critically reflect on what you experienced (Activities), and look below the surface of what occurred to illuminate tentative working hypotheses, insights and questions:

As I write up my field-notes, after the day's events, recalling the various action-learning groups we engaged, I find myself reflecting back on the beginning of the day. I believe there was a great deal of intrepidation around my choice as a facilitator for this team building event because of my association with, and introduction into the organisation by, the managing director – who had earlier stated the need for downsizing. I guess some may have perceived me as a possible hatchet-man brought in to do the dirty. I must remember to check this out next time we meet together.

To go further, form a speculative theory or a tentative model of what is happening, and when you return to the field keep this hypothesis in mind and see if it is supported. Try also to catch the gestalt – the perceptive pattern that is evolving from the whole. After a few cycles of planning (raising hypotheses to test), acting (participating in the field) and reflecting (drawing conclusions from experience) – and reflecting upon the undertone and tacit communications you are perceiving in the field, in an action research fashion – you will be well on your journey to becoming awash with research data and speculative findings.

When I have collected sufficient data through diaries, personal journals, field notes, audio-tapes and group inquiries I settle down to write up an account of my facilitation and the results of inquiry:

- In the first draft I often find myself spilling everything out, emotions, reactions, sensory impacts and memories; here data piles on data as I let go, in a cathartic fashion of everything I've stored.

- In my second draft I tease out themes and structure and try to provide context and a chronological timeline, paying attention to what happened, when it happened, who was involved and what concerns me now.

- In my third draft I note down my reflections, critique my observations and offer tentative hypotheses, tailoring my presentation to the particular audience I am writing for while noting the opinions and observations I am beginning to evidence.

- By my forth draft I attend to my writing style, create a title and sub-titles, form an abstract, introduce myself and the methodological perspective, review the literature, share my experiences in the field, structure my findings, develop conclusions and recommendations and review what I have learnt from the study.

- In subsequent drafts – and there are many – I keep polishing and tweaking the emerging frame, taking care to distinguish between:

    - Findings: information and data about situations and events
    - Interpretations: explanations, hypotheses and models that arise from out of the data
    - Judgements: values I bring to bear on the data
    - Recommendations: suggested courses of future action.

I then put down my report for a while, a couple of days or so, before returning to read it afresh.

- When I am satisfied with the 'beast', for indeed by this time it feels beastly and a chore, I pass over my account to someone else to read – someone who has no knowledge of the field – with an eye to clarity and reader-friendliness.

The writing-up of a facilitative study always takes four or five times as long as I envisage, as new insights arise from the act of writing, which in turn demand assimilation. In the process of reporting my study and integrating my field notes, I begin a rudimentary analysis of what has happened, by reflecting upon what I've experienced through the lens of such questions as:

What is at issue?	What other methods might be used to test my hypotheses in the field (triangulation)?
How was my data obtained?	
What other evidence might there be?	How does my data confirm or challenge other studies or the literature?
How else might I make sense of data?	
What evidence supports my argument?	What flow charts or models might further illuminate my findings?
What themes or categories seem to be suggested?	Which are the main themes and which are minor themes?
How is my view of this situation undergoing change?	Who else can verify or confirm my observations?
Which theories or models challenge my interpretation?	How applicable are my findings to other areas?
What is the tacit working hypothesis am I entertaining?	What patterns are emerging for me – if any?
How much should I let the information speak for itself?	How has the study developed through time?
What levels of meaning shade into each other or cluster together here?	Are my findings repeatable or unique?
	What theories support my vision?

From this examination working hypotheses arise to be tested in later cycles of inquiry, or to be verified through discussion with co-researchers or clients in the field.

The models supplied in the following chapters provide an ample supply of ready-made theories with which to compare, contrast, elucidate and to analyse inquiries of your own.

In the next chapter we will examine the practicalities of building a research community and consider the group dynamics that influence the facilitation of team, community and organisational inquiry.

> What is ordinarily called 'security' is clinging to the unfelt, declining the risk of the unknown involved in any absorbing satisfaction.
>
> *Perls et al. 1951 p.233*

Reflections

In relation to the descriptors and effects of Space, Actors, Activities, Objects, Acts, Events, Time, Goals and Feelings, use these descriptors of 'Deep Description' to make sense of an encounter within your research group or two appraise how these orientations figure in your research field.

(November) I have in mind to review the culture of my research field. In terms of space, my action inquiry groups meet in a 1960s university environment within a somewhat cramped and dark teaching space. Although we exist within a basic classroom space, outside through the windows we have views of excellent landscaped gardens! In the buildings it feels akin to a technical college or 'knowledge factory' as some students have said, while outside is this enticing though under-used green space. We work in the most basic of environments though look out upon the best! I guess I'm thinking in terms of psychic as well as physical space here!

The **actors**, these are primarily students and staff within the Department of Educational Studies. Staff as a group, many of whom have differing agendas, personal ambitions and contrary intentions still appear to pull together for support and to play a political game when blame is in the air – possibly this is because they feel under-managed and without leadership; I'll need to check this out later. There are also differing levels of staff; senior professors appear remote and only tend to appear on political occasions to welcome new groups or to make key appearances; senior lecturers seem hungry for recognition and heading up the various projects and modules; lectures and staff-tutors appear closest to the student body and to share their concerns. Against this backdrop students appear to play a cue-seeking game, keeping on good terms with the lecturers and staff-tutors and showing due respect to the senior lecturers and professors; but unlike staff, they tend to fragment as a group when placed under pressure.

In relation to **activities**, lecturers seem under constant pressure to deliver and 'to be running to stand still', fitting more and more in, writing papers for publication, furthering research, while endeavouring to keep the admin going now that support staff have been reduced and forever trying to prepare on the hoof the lectures they are expected to deliver. I am struck in my account of the lack of loyalty to the system, from staff and student alike, both of whom seem to look to their own resources in order to survive.

Objects, these are possibly the uncomfortable chairs, the lack of air-conditioned rooms and failing computers that add to the competition for resources and general sense of uncared-for-ness that prevails.

The **events** that come to mind as I write this account are sharing in the joys of students who succeed in this climate, the celebration around surfacing new awareness, the kick I get from liberating students from their self-defeating beliefs, the free expression that arises from the experiential learning and action inquiry sessions I conduct within the department.

Being responsible for the above counter-cultural influence I feel as if it will only be a matter of **time** before the system catches up with me and my research is seen as threatening the status quo! Perhaps I'm being a little paranoid here, but new management has replaced those who initially supported my work, and what is more, the professor who was interested in this project has left and a new wave of influence is entering the department. I guess I'm feeling a little vulnerable and unsupported at this time; maybe I need to give a progress report and to educate the new managers to its benefits?

Goals have changed over the past year, especially departmentally, and that's possibly why I fear the foundation and support for my inquiry have slipped out of sight. Originally, changing the culture and delivery of work-based learning was a live issue, now, with the original initiators having moved on, I feel I've moved from being 'flavour of the month' to being a dinosaur – a relic of an earlier regime and past era. Again an update and a renewal of dialogue with the current power-holders might be in order, as the organisational stakeholders have changed.

Re **feelings**, as the more ambitious members of staff, those who appear to want to progress within the department, have distanced themselves from the inquiry groups I facilitate, I wonder if I am an embarrassment to the system. This said, students are very enthusiastic and committed, so there is much to encourage me to continue.

Having performed the above exercise, I'm amazed how jaundiced I come over on re-reading my relationship to 'the system'. It makes me wonder about the political motives I may have infused within my research, plus a need to counterbalance this bias for my research to be seen as valid. As to a way forward, it appears I need to widen my dialogue with prospective patrons and to cultivate a more informed staff culture.

EXTENDED CASE STUDY A

Letting Experience Speak for itself – An Action Inquiry/Learning Group Inquiry into Staff Perceptions of Work-Based Stress at a Cancer Centre

Preparatory Trigger Points. While reading this case study you might pause to consider:

- How the focus and direction of this inquiry was initially stimulated by a short appreciative inquiry (see 3.3j), but thereafter evolved in ways generated by its own volition, the interests of individuals and what peaked to awareness organically within the group

- The ongoing interplay between sensory (3.3b) and phenomenological (3.3g) observation

- The integration of education and personal/professional development alongside inquiry (1.6)

- Consider in terms of Spradley's (1980) field criterion, worthy of consideration in inquiry, how space, actors, activities, objects, acts, events, time, goals and feelings are addressed within the study

- How the contractual, idealised and authentic levels (see 2.2) of relationship clamour for attention and are handled by the researcher at various points of the inquiry.

Preamble: This case study shows how, by staying with the unfolding dialogue and experiences of those present, a researcher can illuminate the working conditions, experiential realities and stressors of organisational life. Besides representing 'an exploration and inquiry into staff stress' this inquiry was expected by its stakeholders and the client system to also provide personal support and professional development – see **Figure A1**. It unfolded following an initial three hour appreciative inquiry (note **Figure A2**) into 'the work experience', after which I met each fortnight with participants in an action learning set with a view to:

a) Illuminating and sharing 'the working experience'

b) Recording the themes and events that unfolded

c) Evaluating the success of strategies implemented in the workplace between meetings

d) Meeting the support and information needs of participants as and when requested.

Between meetings I circulated my notes and updated the same in light of feedback. In this way, a growing appreciation of the working environment and the issues that frustrated working practice permeated group awareness and prospective supports and solutions were discussed and crafted.

Themes and Work-based Examples – A Chronological Record

After a series of introductory contracting meetings with interested parties (senior managers of nursing, radiotherapy and multidisciplinary representatives of various grades) permission to begin this inquiry percolates down from the Clinical Director, finance is confirmed and dates are provided for us to begin. In terms of data

Figure A1   The Proposal

The working party's request: A wide-ranging multidisciplinary exercise which would offer staff support alongside personal and professional development.

The offering: An action-learning approach framed within an initial pilot study of eight to ten participants, extending over a six-month period, where members pilot and evaluate the effectiveness of action learning while shaping its form and use with other staff. In the longer term, should the pilot be successful, as skills in coaching and group facilitation are part of the learning input, it is envisaged that some participants may wish to be trained as facilitators so as to be able to offer a similar peer-learning input to the wider community.

The action-learning approach suggested is one designed to provide 'alongside' personal support, a learning culture wherein professional development will be fostered through:

a) Opportunities for participants to construct their own individually tailored learning contracts

b) A medium for personal sharing, growth and the transfer of relevant knowledge

c) Exposure to coaching and facilitation plus training to these approaches

d) Opportunity for skills practice and peer coaching

e) An illumination of current organisational needs and work-based issues

f) The generation of problem-solving strategies for the workplace

g) A qualitative inquiry into the current work situation and its opportunities.

Content: The content, though personally tailored to the needs of those within the group, could also be used (upon request) to provide such educational input as was felt to be appropriate concerning:

• Authoritative and facilitative styles of intervention

• Personal effectiveness and leadership styles

• Coaching individuals and developing teams

• Successful communication and team management

• Understanding group and organisational dynamics

• Facilitating groups and teams

• Researching and writing up projects

• Managing change.

The approach: Within the research-minded approach described here, participants will be expected to:

• Explore their individual and personal development needs

• Reflect on their interpersonal relationships, social skills and ability to manage themselves and others

• Rehearse various skills under supportive guidance in the action learning sets, with a view to applying the same in the workplace

• Give feedback and receive the same from peers

• Keep a record of their implementation of learning in the workplace

- Develop coaching and facilitative skills which can be used to further develop others within the peer community between action-learning sessions.

Via the above process, it is suggested that the senior management team might also acquire consultation and feedback as to its current and emerging needs.

On completion of the programme (the first full meeting of three hours and twelve action learning sets of one-and-a-half hours) participants will be encouraged to co-operate in the write up of a report outlining their learning to date and its application to the workplace. With consent, this may be circulated to colleagues beyond the group and to their senior managers for comment and practical appraisal.

Figure A2   About Appreciative Inquiry

Appreciative inquiry (Cooperrider 1990) seeks to foster an awareness of the conditions and motivators that maximise peak performance. This tried-and-tested method of consulting and training has been observed (Bushe 1998) to draw attention to new and better versions of the theories, ideas and images that people hold about themselves, whilst raising to mind their best intentions and noblest aspirations. This collaboratively envisions and anchors ideas about how people might give of their best. My adaptation of this approach emphasises Gestalt's insistence upon contact, authenticity, dialogue, our co-creation of reality, and those conditions that manifest an I-Thou relationship. I also have an interest in Dharma – what it is you personally have to offer to mankind at a soul level, that unique something you have within you to share that enriches yourself and others alike.

Appreciative inquiry translates into hands-on practice as follows:

- First, individuals are asked to give a general impression of what it feels like to work in their current workplace or community
- They are then each asked to describe, in turn, a personal 'best experience' of working, a time when they felt they were at their most effective and efficient
- While members share their 'best experiences', those who are listening are encouraged to remain curious and ask questions of the person sharing
- The facilitator encourages members to get in touch with their own memories of similar experiences to the one being shared, and to explore what it was about themselves and the situation they have in mind that made this time a peak experience for them
- Once members have each shared their reports, they pool together the information they have surfaced and, on the basis of ensuing discussion, list and develop a consensus of the core qualities they associate with their best working experiences, and identify what they need to learn to build upon and to integrate and re-create this experience further in their work
- Finally, the facilitator invites members of the learning group to acknowledge anything they have observed in the discussion/inquiry group that has specifically helped them to become more aware of their own practice, and how they might improve their own performance.

collection, I am contracted by the group to make notes during our sessions, to write these up after our meetings and to circulate the record to the following meeting for verification. Below I share in chronological order the fruits of this record – after the initial appreciative inquiry (see the report later in this account) – plus the resulting meetings, with headings that broadly capture the main themes and issues as they emerged.

Insensitive Management

(18th November) We spend time reviewing a situation where a manager seems blind, or possibly indifferent to the effect their behaviour is having upon others in their team. There is not so much a lack of skill as an absence of person sensitivity and an ability, or indeed incentive, to communicate. We discuss how to address this issue, especially when the person concerned ignores feedback, discourages dialogue and has the power to influence your future career. This theme strikes a chord common to all who are present. Raising awareness to the problem and getting a result, without denigrating 'the person' of the manager themselves (who may be suffering the same stresses as ourselves) seems to be a very live issue. This said, if a senior colleague fails the team, do you fall into the compassion-trap of sympathising with the pressures they are under and do nothing; do you confront them and risk retaliation; or do you blow the whistle and demand change? In the first option, it is felt the problem remains untouched and clients, staff and system continue to suffer; in the second and third options you run the risk of committing professional suicide. In situations like this a person's ability to function as an internal change agent seems fatally hampered, and the intervention of an external agent is desirable.

The Nature of Managerial Meetings

(9th December) Members report that decisions that affect them directly are often made without prior consultation or discussion. Even so-called Practice Review Meetings are all too often used to relay decisions rather than to reflect on practice or to report on the effects of policy. In many cases it is reported that meetings were experienced as a method of imposing managerial power and staff control, and that people feel unheard. Indeed, *'if you speak out, it's likely your card will be marked'*. Neither policy appraisal nor appreciation of the working conditions seems to take place, and one person who raised an important clinical point in a meeting was told unsympathetically by their manager *'that's life – now get on with it'*.

Overall, it appears as if there is little managerial accountability, with 'managers' and the 'managers of managers' being seen as 'too close' and bordering on the incestuous.

On Being Heard and Making a Difference

Following three ten-minute buzz groups where we discuss factors that have stopped people here from complaining about unsatisfactory working conditions, we highlight the following negative features:

- Retaliation by managers
- A sense of despondency that nothing will change
- Reflections on practice being sabotaged by managers hoisting their own agendas

- The presence of a non-listening manager who maintains an ongoing monologue and talks over you and others
- Evidence of critical incidents being subjectively evaluated with managers selecting out only those issues they wish to address at risk-assessment meetings
- Too much historical grievance and hurt influencing current practice, so that issues are rarely heard or approached with the objectivity they deserve
- Managers who treat criticism of their clinical area far too personally, so that 'clinical concerns' are heard as if they are 'personal complaints'.

We note that although most managers were satisfactory, some five per cent seemed to be problematic and unable to relate, thus tarnishing the image of managers as a whole. As to why feedback rarely makes a difference, we observe that 'trigger forms' – forms you fill to give clinical feedback – are not audited or objectively assessed, and consequently are open to manipulation by the hidden agendas of some problematic managers.

We break into threes in a ten-minute buzz group to surface ideas as to how we might give feedback in more effective ways and note that we:

- Need to feel taken seriously and that our opinion is valued, and to experience that we are being listened to
- Feel more able to give feedback when openly supported by colleagues
- Need a venue where issues are depersonalised and stand on their own merit
- Feel much more empowered in reflective practice meetings when real issues are discussed without managers giving the impression of feeling attacked or over-defensive.

Fearing to Make a Difference

Though some of us note that *'it doesn't pay to stick your neck out'* and cite incidents where we have felt personally victimised by managers, we nevertheless brainstorm the following routes to achieving improved bottom-up feedback:

- Anonymous feedback sheets
- Having one day a month or so allocated to managers working clinically
- Employing facilitated meetings with the whole team
- Instigating reflective practice meetings which also appraise managers and management.

Simply, clinical and managerial staff appear to be out of sync and unable to understand each other's priorities. So what's the way forward? Regular, facilitated reflective practice meetings seem to be most favoured by the group.

The Need for Clinical Feedback

(6th January) The group is concerned with how people progress upwards in this system, especially when their work record is poor. *'What criteria is the Trust using?'*; *'I've given up trying to make sense of appointments here'*; *'I just can't understand the logic behind some appointments!'* Such statements sum up the emotional tone of those present. Again, what especially rankles is the tendency for some management posts to be filled without interview, while more junior staff – even when applying for their own post – have to endure multi-interviews to secure their employment: *'It's not a fair nor an even playing field'*; *'One rule for them and another for us'*; *'Managerial accountability is invisible here'*; *'Posts are created without negotiation and the first we know is a new manager has been put in place over us'*; *'Managers have often been so long out of service, they can't appreciate our current demands. Indeed, I think they fear being exposed by clinical demands, so how can they represent us?'*

As discussion unfolds, the need for bottom-up feedback resurfaces because clinical staff feel poorly represented and isolated from management decisions. *'We don't want a bribe – we'd just appreciate a thank you or a person-to-person appreciation now and then'*. We note the them-and-us dynamic we are in danger of setting-up here, plus how the lack of appreciation of the differing demands placed on managers by clinicians (coupled with our perception of them as being clinically incompetent) further jaundices our opinion. We also note our own tendency to be passive, blaming and intolerant towards managers, and to represent ourselves as victims and managers as persecutors.

The Lack of Negotiation

(27th January) Again an alertness and sensitivity to the negatives surfaces: we note that things happen without negotiation or dialogue (for example, a new staff member materialised without the team having been informed or prepared so that orientation for both parties is hampered); and that a cloak-and-dagger mentality prevails in certain areas, holding information back and causing current issues and prospective changes to remain un-discussed (in one case, staff were given two minutes warning of the demonstration of new and essential equipment). In this meeting a series of confidential events are discussed but, by request, left unrecorded.

The Lack of Flexibility

(10th February) *'A lack of system flexibility; more work and less resources; the balance of skill mix and a lack of training time'*; *'Time at a premium and the lack of preparation, people aren't trained to standard, so can't cope or relax as seniors'*; *'Wider team not involved in decision making – just one or two leaders'*; *'We're not getting together to talk about things – in senior meetings, managers produce more checks and counter-checks, but other important things are not discussed, so that a distancing from the real problems results'*; *'Angry senior manager to manager relationships'*; *'I sometimes get so despondent when thinking about work as I get so frustrated'*; *'Confidentiality is not respected in this system, so reporting upwards feels dangerous'*; *'Sweeping promotions when all acting-up people were confirmed and swept into post, irrespective of quality'*; *'Personnel seems biased towards senior management, and are seen as no support to hands-on staff'*; *'No study-leave policy and allowable time – time owed as extra'*; *'Movable goals let alone goal-posts; so furious I looked for loads of jobs – though my speciality means few posts around'*.

Not feeling Listened To

'Seniors must be sold your ideas as theirs, or nothing happens; its all manipulation and you have to play the game'; *'When things go a level above they always seem to be bounced back'*; *'You say it again and again; writing it even doesn't even work,*

only if you threaten to resign – but how often can you do that? Always have to make a drama to be heard – but it's so exhausting'; money is found for the re-grading of some but not for others – no fair policy in place; years in post are paid for but not work-load or merit.

'Management has the power to allocate points if you're liked'; 'In this climate, even praise from managers comes as a shock and is mistrusted now!' A case study was shared to illustrate the above points, where the absence of an agreed policy concerning bed allocation was seen to breed chaos and lead to bad practice. The ways forward that people here suggest might be adopted to change policy:

- Placing concerns on paper and getting them included on the appropriate meeting agenda
- Investigating how the issue effects everyone and making a joint statement for action
- Asking for a meeting
- Going to the top – to the Clinical Director – to request a clarification and/or change of policy.

Over-Formalisation

(24th February) There seems to be no informal way to correct systemic or personal errors, everything has to be formalised here. Because of this, juniors are scared to speak out or, in some cases, even to approach seniors. The overall feeling people ended up with was expressed as: 'What's the point? There's no point, so it's just head down and carry on'; 'You're left to yourself'. Managers are in meetings or beyond the workplace, and so they naturally enough end up lacking current clinical knowledge and skills, and become out of touch. 'No wonder we have little respect for managers!' 'We'd have much more respect for managers if they were hands-on and role-modelled good practice'.

The above incestuous mismanagement culture is seen to be exacerbated by the isolated nature of the department: problems stay local and 'No one in the wider hospital seems to know – or care – what we do or what happens'. 'There's no confidentiality: an issue was raised confidentially with one manager and snowballed into a meeting with another!' The appointment of managers is seen as suspect and lacking quality control: 'Managers seem to be in position by default, with no external competition!' This is a recurring concern: by automatically promoting internal staff who had been temporarily 'acting up', without interview, management is seen to be missing a chance to weed out the least worthy.

Change – Will it ever Happen?

(23rd March) Our opening discussion poses the question 'Will change ever really happen here?' 'For example, peer reviews might happen upon the surface, but will things really change – I doubt it'. This said, it is recognised that an external facilitator might be needed to start things off and to a prevent slip-back into old patterns. Health and safety might also help. But there is 'the stigma of identifying yourself as "stressed" and being unable to cope'. 'Then again, if stress causes sickness and time-off work, perhaps managers might buy into trying to alleviate it?' 'The Trust has to hand the findings of a questionnaire they circulated relating to stress – I think it was last year, but we still haven't heard the results!' We hear from one member that although much-needed meetings are taking place, no minutes appear to be being taken and no points of action are being requested. *'This organisation is good at spin, but poor at action.'* *'For example, vacancies are not advertised or filled although three months warning of staff leaving is given beforehand, and what is more, the remaining staff are not trained-up to fill the skill gap. Such sloppiness saps your trust in management'.* *'Take for instance the exit interviews requested by the Clinical Director where managers dot the I's and cross the T's but don't pool the information nor carry this through to change things.'*

Though the hospital has new equipment, this is seen to come about more from the government's timely release of funds than any attempt to meet clinically voiced needs by a listening management. *'We suffer from "reactive change" rather than planned change'.* *'There is a general lack of cohesive unity and our methods of practice are a constant cause for concern'.*

As a case study example of positive and lasting change, we spend time unpacking what was necessary to get the Centre running. It took three years of championing the cause by sponsors, clients, interested parties, Macmillan funding and political pressure, plus the timely support of a Government directive to further cancer care within the NHS – all of which encouraged change. *'200k had to be raised to show we could cover three years running costs'.* *'When things go wrong we can't go to the Surrey Advertiser, but clients do, and this provokes change'.* As a negative case study of change we examine the car parking situation here, and how such a relatively minor thing as this can have a great effect as a stressor for clients and staff alike.

Factors that Limit Change

We raise awareness to those factors that frustrate change, namely:

- Time pressures which breed task fixation
- Managerial stress which doesn't support goodwill ('and when goodwill goes out the window we're all lost')
- Staff shortage that keeps us task-minded rather than client-centred or relationally aware
- The resistance of managers to a clinical voice being heard at senior policy meetings ('a nurse consultant would never be allowed here').

So How Might We Promote Change?

Support each other, especially across disciplinary boundaries; reduce territorial controls; cross-fertilise and communicate more regularly; build in time to meet and to reflect; keep up the pressure to enact regular practice meetings which discuss the quality of care and staff relationships as well as tasks; make recommendations such as this in light of our findings and meetings in this group. (Next time we will review a facilitative model of leadership/management).

Our Non-listening Culture

(6th April) As an illustration of our current non-listening culture and how we see ourselves as powerless to effect change, we hear of a manager who, on a new team member's first day in the clinical area, trapped her in the office and talked at her for some five hours non-stop. *'We have learnt never go in the office, for once caught by him you have to be quite rude to get out again. We rescue each other by bleeping one another when we see someone stuck in the office with him for too long'*. Others note *'He's always dashing around and not listening'* and that at *'formal dinners we put names in a hat to see who will have to sit by him'*; *'He is totally indiscreet and has no sense of boundaries'*; *'...we thought he'd retire at 60, and now he says he's staying on to 65'*. At this point, I'm driven to ask how an out of control, hypo-manic and chaotic manager such as the one described, one who fails to address his workload or manage his time, is never confronted and thus left unfettered to reap ever more harm? I then hear that *'he's very volatile and attacks people ruthlessly, so many are scared of him'*. *'Besides, he'd never listen or change'*. We hear *'the Director knows all about him'*, that *'most staff are at a loss with how to deal with him'* and that he causes more problems than he solves, yet remains in post! In this light, what price quality control or managerial supervision? Collusion such as this, to me as an outsider, appears to be a major problem at all levels in this culture and at times, like today, I challenge the group with the idea that they have got the management they deserve. *'But if senior staff ignore the problem and don't challenge him – how can we?'* *'It's so difficult when seniors say "it's you" not them at fault, or that it's "your problem" and you must solve it with the person concerned'*. Though I am sympathetic, it remains a fact that care providers have a professional duty to act as advocates on behalf of their clients and to foster efficient procedures that maintain the best possible quality of care. No matter how difficult it is to challenge the status quo – and even if we fear that complaining is professional suicide – by accepting the situation we collude with the problem and so fail ourselves, our profession and our clients.

Our Responsibility-avoiding, Blaming Culture

'You're fine here just as long as you learn to work with the system – otherwise it's always your fault'. *'Immersed in task and time demands there is little time or energy left to address management or to sort out relational problems'*. *'Management wears us down – rather than facilitates the work, and it's a rarity to feel supported.'* *'One girl asked where the annual leave board had gone, and was told it'd been moved into the office. It's only a small thing, but events like this keep happening and things are changed without explanation, even though the motive might be innocent'* – for example, in this case, a newly confirmed senior manager wanted to change the office dynamics. Now she was no longer acting up, she presumably chose the moment to impose her own ideas on how things were to be done from now on. In this way, weak managers are covered rather than confronted. We also hear that *'Managers seem to cover up for each other even though they don't support each other personally'*. In this light, it appears managers role-model collusion and others follow. *'Everything here is always so secretive, as if a conspiracy is taking place'*. *'For instance, policy documents are kept hidden in the office and clandestine motives and behaviors are commonplace'*. *'St X's is a secretive culture – saying you're supported by the Clinical Director is an absolute joke'*. For example, *'outpatients and ward staff remain isolated and don't know each other even by sight in some cases – there's no cross-fertilization, it's like a chasm.'* *'There are no common problems because problems don't get shared, so splits and divisions grow and remain – upstairs and downstairs don't mix'*.

Servant Leadership

We examine the concept of servant leadership by way of a contrasting managerial model. 'I don't think our lot has a model' says one. I raise the question, if managers aren't serving the team in their clinical role, who or what are they serving? *'Themselves and their own agenda'* someone observes. We divide into two groups to examine in detail the notion of the servant leader and where we ourselves model or fail to model the qualities it supports.

In discussion we note that person-centred or process-centred modes of management – qualities associated with the model under discussion – appear alien to seniors here. *'Yet patient-centred care we are told is how we ought to work, so surely management needs to role-model and to support this way of working by modelling a culture friendly to this approach, but it doesn't'.* Though we agree with the sentiments of servant leadership, for the most part it seems that the human and humane part of us gets overwhelmed by task pressures and the robot in us. In this way, it is suggested that we become 'human-doings' rather than 'human-beings', and the quality of our provision of care suffers in consequence.

Our Failing System

(20 April) *'The clerical helper and clinician share the same computer, and the clinician just has to wait'; 'Routinely we have to perform non-clinical duties you just do to keep the system going'. 'If you don't do the extra, at the end of the day the patient suffers. But there is a knock-on effect here, for staying back late to phone the patient then becomes a regular part of the job'.* Insensitive managerial attitudes don't help here, for example: *'On New Year's Eve we came in early, as the senior said we might start early and leave early when the work was done, but the manager came in and said we had to stay – over-ruling the senior. What's worse, she went off early herself and left us behind working'.* Such instances are seen to *'fragment any sense of goodwill, to lower morale and to undermine the authority of senior clinicians who try to give something back to staff'. 'On Friday I was busy working through my lunch hour, but there's a complete lack of appreciation – it's as if managers set themselves apart from those they manage'. 'When they get the title "manager" something happens to them, they go to pieces, they seem to feel there's more to this than they realised – and they freeze up'.* We consider the influence of the management culture. For instance, could a person-centred manager survive here? *'My new manager's trying to be person-centred and personable, but she's getting flak from other managers, as if she's letting the side down! When she first came, she was very dynamic and forceful – in a good way – and I was very pleased with her, but now she appears to be being ground down. It's happening already; she's off to meeting after meeting and has left us unmanaged at crucial times.'*

Negative Roles and their Internal Drivers

It is suggested that *'Management possibly feels as powerless as ourselves, and takes it out on us'* – as indeed we seem to do with them! Managers are seen to fall primarily into the persecutor, blamer and placator categories. *'Management culture is punitive, in that they fall out and go against each other regularly'.* But why should managers be this way? It is noted that authoritarian people are often fearful people who hide behind their role. Is this surprising? They appear to have neither support nor supervision, are accused of being clinically out of date, are often disrespected by their teams and don't support one another. When we examine the internal drivers that motivate the roles of persecutor, blamer and placator, we note that *'managers are only human after all – but do you really want us to feel sorry for them?'* Again, I challenge the group to own their contribution: for instance, do they ever give positive feedback to their managers? Do they support them when they get something right for the team? If team members only present problems and never celebrate successes is it any wonder management avoids them? I ask *'So why doesn't the Clinical Director supervise and develop his managers?'* A shortage of time seems to figure here, as he himself constantly struggles to maintain his patient workload and consultancy duties while simultaneously managing the hospital. In this regard, he is set up to fail as his workload is nigh unmanageable: *'We used to have two-hour sessions every week and a breakfast meeting to cover the post, but now I rarely see him, and his clients are piling up for his decisions'.* *'X is human, he is personable, and will say sorry later if he feels he was out of order'.* With a Director who role models good-quality relationships, it is sad that other managers seem unable to follow his example.

The Way Forward

(4th May) As this action-learning group draws to an end (we have one more session planned) we consider how, and to whom, we will present our findings. As the Clinical Director released the money to resource this exercise, it is decided a full report of our activities and findings should go to him, with two further full accounts for him to circulate to others as he sees fit. It is further suggested that we invite the Clinical Director to give feedback on our documentation and findings, and say that we would welcome any proposals he might have concerning our recommendations. It is further suggested that an Executive Summary of about two pages be circulated amongst each member of this action-learning group. It is observed that there are many others, such as the members of the teams we in this group represent, who would also welcome feedback, but that this should only be provided at the behest of the Clinical Director, the sponsor of the exercise.

We also evaluate the fruits of this group. Participants felt for the first time they were listened to, heard and attended to in a sympathetic (though sometimes tough-loving) way: *'It was good to let off steam so long held in check, while being encouraged to try new strategies and to communicate in fresh ways'; 'Even if nothing comes of our inquiry, systemically, we will have grown as people through this experience and developed friends in other disciplines'; 'I feel less isolated and more capable now; I don't think I'll allow myself to settle into a rut again now I'm aware of many more options'.*

The Report

In the weeks and months following our meetings there is much frenzied emailing between participants as our report of this inquiry is circulated. Two participants who had missed the latter sessions feel unsure about a formal report being submitted and are fearful of the back lash. This is debated amongst group members by email, and eventually resolves when specific comments, which two of our number are unhappy with, are removed. The following is the text of the report we eventually submitted to the Clinical Director and the commissioning committee in its entirety.

A Multidisciplinary Inquiry into Determinants of Work-based Stress

1) Context and Remit – Overview of the Action Group's Development

In May of last year the facilitator met with a working party of staff representatives empowered by the Clinical Director to consider a strategy for staff support and development. Following this meeting, an action-learning group of multidisciplinary participants was suggested and subsequently accepted, commencing with a three-hour appreciative inquiry followed by twelve ninety-minute meetings extending over a six-month period. It was further suggested that this group should generate recommendations as to the best way forward for maintaining staff support. Should this pilot be successful, it was further envisaged that skills in coaching and group facilitation might be offered to selected staff of St X's, so that they might be trained as facilitators to offer peer learning and input to the wider community beyond the pilot group. In this context, the above recommendations are suggested.

Although we started with very wide-ranging intentions, the following themes came especially to the fore of our inquiry:

- Qualitative inquiry into the current work situation and its opportunities
- An illumination of current organisational needs and work-based issues
- The generation of problem-solving strategies for the workplace
- Personal sharing and the transfer of relevant knowledge

…and less time was made available for:

- Opportunities for participants to construct their own individually tailored learning contracts
- Exposure to coaching and facilitation plus training to these approaches
- Opportunities for skills practice and peer coaching.

In practice, the action-learning sessions, especially in the earlier meetings, focused upon what participants presented. Indeed the earlier sessions appeared to provide a much-needed venue for letting off steam, verbalising what had previously been left unsaid, and orientating to the world-view of other disciplines. As it gradually emerged that similar problems existed across disciplines, a united voice seemed to emerge re the short-comings of management.

Later in the life of the group we explored strategies for change and examined the prospective usefulness of the action-learning group to foster change.

Individually, participants were willing to:

- Explore their individual and personal development needs
- Reflect on their interpersonal relationships and ability to manage themselves and others
- Give feedback and to receive the same from peers.

They were rather more resistive due to the managerial climate to:

- Keeping a record of their implementation of learning in the workplace
- Rehearsing skills with a view to applying the same in the workplace
- Developing coaching and facilitative skills.

118

As to outcomes, participants seem to have begun the process of:

- Appreciating their current situation and behaviours and how these impact upon others
- Illuminating a clearer picture of 'what is actually happening', 'what is perceived to be happening', and 'what needs to happen' to improve the quality of care provision and staff support within St X's.

2) Record Keeping and Facilitation

The facilitative approach was essentially client-centred, addressing emergent themes with hand-outs being provided to build upon earlier themes. As to the recording of themes, a verbatim record of discussion was kept, circulated, and amended at subsequent meetings. These themes are listed in the following section which offers a mixture of direct quotes, commentary and illustrative examples drawn from working practice.

3) Report of the Initial Appreciative Inquiry – A Multidisciplinary Investigation into Problems and Dilemmas of the Workplace

Within a three-hour appreciative inquiry held on the 4th November focusing upon our experience of the workplace and working conditions, the following themes arose:

'What is it like to work here?'

- 'Compared to how it was prior to Trust status – and even to merely three years ago – the pace is much faster and demands are much greater than they were previously'
- 'These days, chasing petty details such as paperwork and form filling tends to subtract from time spent delivering specialist treatments and quality patient care'
- 'Protocol seems directed to chasing "stars" or abstract performance targets rather than improving practice'
- 'There is no time to reflect or plan as we are constantly drawn into fire fighting'
- 'Managerial policy often conflicts with quality care and undermines clinical policy'
- 'Small things add up and leave us feeling increasingly undervalued – such as taking away our Christmas shopping day'
- 'As crisis management rules, I have to make a crisis to be heard – although I don't like myself for what I have become in my effort to be heard'
- 'Management seems to fault-find and criticise and constantly implies we should always give more but never says what we are doing well'
- 'I just wish that at times when I've stood in for senior staff or worked extra hours to cover clinical needs someone would just say thanks'.

Generally, the group recognises that if things go on as they are in the current climate of crisis management, with crises coming thicker and faster and ever more resources being withdrawn, that '...if something drastic doesn't happen soon care will deteriorate and the system will collapse'. In the meantime, it appears that more balanced feedback and an occasional thank you would go a long way to improving the working climate.

'What has been an especial low point at work over the last year?'

- Having twenty-five deaths over the two weeks of Christmas, 'receiving no recognition for what I was going through, plus being pressured and chased at this time to fulfil protocol by maintaining the flow of forms on time'
- 'Working one's heart out and receiving no thanks for going the extra mile to keep things afloat'
- 'Having a manager appointed who didn't know the current up-to-date ways of clinical practice although they acted as if they did'
- 'Having to fight for basic recognition of patient needs'
- 'Being instructed to answer the phone within three rings – and this being given priority over much more crucial care provision and clinical criteria'.

Working at full stretch and without thanks seems commonplace within the clinical culture. Without balanced feedback and recognition by seniors of what they are doing well, staff naturally enough feel unvalued. Add to this the reality of remote decision making, where the Chief Executive is never seen and would not be recognised even if he walked on site, and the sense of powerlessness grows even more acute. Interestingly, St X's appears to suffer by its proximity to the larger hospital complex, in that 'overspill from next-door' can fill up the reserved beds when St X's is identified as part of the whole, yet this same 'pool mentality' doesn't extend to porters from outside St X's crossing over to help. Indeed, '...the general lack of multidisciplinary communication at the operative level' appears to cause many problems. And as to why this remains unresolved, well, managers are suggested to be defensively territorial to the extent that they actively discourage cross-disciplinary communication.

'What in the workplace encourages you to stay and raises your spirits?'

- 'Receiving new equipment (even though such equipment was commonplace elsewhere) for this was at least a recognition from above that the working arena was supported and, indirectly, was in turn felt as supportive to staff'
- 'The intimate and warm relationships enjoyed through close contact with clients'
- 'The way staff pulled together during a crisis and helped across the disciplines'
- 'The peer support, banter and goodwill expressed by fellow staff even when under pressure'
- 'When, for one day at least, the system ran as it should rather than frustrated professional activity'
- 'Working nights or out-of-office hours when petty management issues were relaxed and staff could use their professional expertise and authority without having to fight to do so'
- 'Going part-time and feeling so much more space in my head, having more time with my family and a healthier life balance'.

Indeed, it's almost as if a Blitz mentality, a sort of 'we have to draw together and sort things out ourselves' prevails, as 'management can't be relied upon for support'.

'What would you like to happen if you had something akin to a magic wand?'

- 'To slow down the system so we can catch up with ourselves and reflect on where we are going'
- 'Clinical power to maintain a realistic bed policy'
- 'Managerial recognition of what I am doing well'.

Simply, the above wish-list seems supports the observation that '...we just want to be let get on with our jobs' without undue outside interference.

'So what do we appear to have learnt from this inquiry?'

- 'It is not just me who feels frustrated and caused to deliver a service where I can't give of my best; we all do, so I need not blame myself nor feel myself a failure'
- 'We now have a place where we can share our frustrations, be heard and witnessed, and experience the support of peers'
- 'As my professional problems appear to be shared by others and experienced by other disciplines, it appears the system may be at fault'
- 'If existing policies and managerial strategies are seen to be causing us similar difficulties, perhaps we can join together to make a multidisciplinary case for supporting positive change'.

Hopefully future groups will help us to express, identify and form strategies for better dealing with the frustrations of the workplace, while fostering the degree of empowerment necessary to add value to ourselves and our clinical functions.

4) A Summary of the Initial Findings

In sum, I formed the opinion of a dedicated and hard-working staff group, who felt under-resourced by the system in general and under-supported by specific managers in particular. Indeed, it seemed that management attention, in the main, was more keenly centred upon 'performance targets' and activities that merited 'stars' rather than the more fundamental issue of improving day-to-day care. This was felt to be even more frustrating, as centres with three stars were regularly rated by our patients as inferior in standard to this un-stared area. As things stood, it felt as if excellence of care could never be appreciated, no matter how hard we worked or how well we did. Consequently, the impression given was of a ghastly game being enacted, where management directed its attention on areas that had little impact on care, but had a great deal of impact on 'spin' and 'image'. For example we noted the following crazy events that made us doubt the sanity of 'the System' and its management:

- 'Being prevented from ordering more felt-nib pens or a new printer in the interests of saving money, whilst a new off-site storage system for patient records costs £25 per request to see the old notes; and because these were stored in boxes with bar codes denoting batches rather than names, we often need to request three or more boxes at a cost of £75 to find a case record'
- 'Having to waste time taking a disc with an urgent letter to a patient typed up on it to other departments and to beg for a printer, as cost cutting meant a

printer wasn't supplied to a busy clerical office'
- 'Having two booked beds filled with patients from other areas and having to make a stink to have them moved so that the two booked-in clients could have their chemotherapy on time (timing being essential to maintain maximum efficiency)'.

5) Illuminative Points

1) Symbolically, if St X's is compared to a person, though a great deal of activity and hard work is taking place in the organism as a whole and the arms and legs are going at a frantic rate, the thinking process seems to be functioning without sensory awareness and evidence-based feedback, with the consequence that policies and strategies are not anchored in practice and therefore fail to improve performance.

2) At the relational level, even if we account for the 'us and them' dynamic that so often materialises between 'managers' and those who are 'managed' in an organisation, it still appears that a person-sensitive and clinically-informed management style, one which celebrates good practice and acknowledges personal effort and attends to the effect of policy while soliciting feedback of those at the client interface, could do much to alleviate the current frustrations experienced by staff within St X's.

6) Recommendations – Action Points

1) In order to prevent a rift developing between 'managers' and 'those who are managed', we suggest that practice meetings are instigated where managers and clinicians may regularly review not only 'how to promote excellence in clinical practice' but their 'managerial relationships', 'team dynamics' and ongoing 'systems of personal and peer support'

2) In order to promote hygienic inter-staff relationships, we suggest practice meetings are initially attended by an external facilitator who might provide feedback on communication styles and team dynamics with a view to building a supportive person-centred culture

3) In order to improve clinical communication and involvement, we suggest that as a matter of routine practitioners are invited to contribute issues for discussion prior to senior management reviews, and that the wider team is de-briefed on the action points and outcome of such meeting

4) In order to develop and support managers we suggest they receive regular group supervision with a view to developing a supportive and developmental managerial peer culture, and that bottom-up appraisal is performed so that they might appreciate how they are perceived by those they manage.

Postscript

The outcome of the inquiry was that the group deemed our report to be a true record of what happened and an honest representation of our recommendations and the Clinical Director privately admitted the truth of our findings. However, in a meeting with his managers he distanced himself from the report and the researcher, even going so far as to call the report 'unprofessional' – seemingly due to its portrayal of emotion. Nevertheless, he was pressured by this multidisciplinary inquiry, partly seeded at his behest, to act on its findings (possibly to save face with participating staff) and to employ other more conventional trainers to address the problems it raised. From this reaction, it might be suggested that the research acted as a 'whistle-blowing' exercise, where true to form, symbolically, the messenger was shot and the researcher was cast out as a representation of the organisational shadow.

When researchers raise to awareness what an organisation would prefer to deny, they often find themselves hung by their own petard, martyrs of their own research inquiry.

In terms of my facilitative style, within this inquiry I was primarily attentive to the group and individual field; I sought to encourage and to provide the curiosity and permissiveness necessary to enable those involved to flower. Essentially, I followed the unfolding process rather than initiated or sought to extend the same. I guess the quality of my presence conveyed something of those qualities being withheld or denied elsewhere in the system, that is to say: an appreciation of those involved; interest in their plight; high-quality listening; personal and interpersonal support. In this way 'support for the person' was made available alongside inquiry into the circumstances that prevailed.

As for the decision to let the record of our inquiry and its emerging themes inform our report, this was felt by the group to be the best and most authentic way to inform the wider system and to honour the experiences of all involved. If the wider 'system' wanted to hear 'the truth', here it was in stark form. Possibly a little repressed anger informed this decision but, for the most part, the need to 'capture the reality of the working climate' and to 'foster a more positive attitude to care and people management' seemed to drive the group.

Some Post-reading Reflective Triggers:

- I'm aware of how diffuse relational phases of orientation, identification, exploration and resolution (see 3.6) appear to be in real time, both in the study as a whole and within the various meetings; and also how qualities of inquiry such as 'tasks', 'processes' and research methods all flow together in real life.

- I wonder as to the possible interplay of Menzies' systems of social defence (3.2) within the hospital culture of this study.

- Applying the insights of field theory (see 2.1 and 2.5) as a shaper of reality, I find myself reflecting upon how events and people appear to be organised; what influences of the field might serve to explain the group's behaviour; what is unique about the research field; what appears to be in the process of becoming; and what we might have been blind to or excluded from our vision.

123

- Considering the phenomenological reality and findings of the above learning group, I am caused to speculate upon how this might be further analysed in terms of: *the relationship of the Figure and Ground* – the degree to which findings belong to either 'the figure' (what momentarily peaks and holds attention) or 'the ground' (the background or long-term structure); *Differentiation and Confluence* – the degree to which findings are self contained or have a tendency to merge with other phenomenon; *Resilience and Reconfiguring* – the degree findings resist merger (resilience) or have ability 'to absorb change or disturbance' or to reconstitute themselves (reconfiguration); the *Laminated Field* – the degree findings interrelate between differing layers and levels of experience.

- I am left at the end of this study wondering about the interrelationship of tuition and inquiry – for instance, content was introduced within this study relating to leadership styles; facilitative interventions; conflict resolution; stress responses; burnout; group dynamics. Educative inquiry and personal and professional development combined with research in this way to facilitate change.

- I am also caused to wonder about the wisdom of letting verbatim comments remain in the final report when we were attempting to be heard by senior managers in such a politically defensive working culture. Perhaps we ought to have just circulated findings of the appreciative inquiry rather than the hard evidence of the ongoing group but, as an advocate as much as a researcher, I didn't want to bullshit the organisation or diminish the experiential reality of group members.

Exploring Experience and Illuminating Data

exploration

Begin with the possible;
begin with one step.
There is always a limit,
you cannot do more than you can.
If you try to do too much,
you will do nothing.

Ouspensky in Hayward 1990

Chapter four

Creating a Culture of Inquiry –
Setting the Scene for Group Exploration

4 Creating a Culture of Inquiry – Setting the Scene for Group Exploration

The people we are in relationship with are our best mirror, reflecting our beliefs, values and desires; simultaneously we act as their mirrors. But when they get too close to us and mirror back our shadow – we push them away. So if you wish to see your shadow – look at those you abhor or reject.

Preamble

This chapter explores how a practitioner-researcher might cultivate a climate of permission and experimentation within a group, community or organisation, so as to facilitate a culture conducive to group inquiry. The contribution of therapeutic community practice is surveyed to this end, to illuminate an approach to collaborative group inquiry that develops the person while educating the organisation. The researcher-subject relationship and facilitation are explored to this end and a review of leadership style is performed to enable a researcher to diagnose and to profile their own research facilitation style. The models shared in this chapter can also be applied to the analysis and shaping of information. Hopefully, by the close of this chapter, you will have a richer appreciation of how to permit the fullness of the human condition to enter and inform your inquiry.

4.1 The Inquiring Attitude – Values to Live and Research By

Excellence in research as much as in group facilitation, coaching or counselling, is abetted by the amount of personal development a practitioner has undertaken, the degree of democracy and facilitative transparency they permit, and their internal stock of self-awareness and relational skill. Simply, we are reminded here that 'the person' cannot be separated from the 'inquiry' they undertake:

> There is no rule of thumb that tells a researcher precisely how to focus a study. The extent to which a research question is broad or narrow depends on purpose, the resources available, the time available, and the interests of those involved
>
> *Patton 1995 p.166*

Inexperienced researchers are often reluctant to investigate or to receive feedback regarding their perceived motives, their role or their effect on others. Often hiding behind the mantle of 'the leader' or 'the researcher', novice researchers enact 'control' and strive to 'get things right' for fear of feeling exposed or shamed. It takes a substantial degree of emotional maturity for a person to own their confusion and vulnerability and to acknowledge this in the research field, especially when they are deemed responsible.

When researchers can raise to awareness and share their underlying motives, especially with those they facilitate or enrol as co-researchers, and are prepared to openly investigate their own biases and beliefs, they begin to convert 'naïve facilitative inquiry' into sound 'experiential research'. When practitioner-researchers share their interpretations and invite others to explore alongside themselves, they begin to enact collaborative inquiry, to facilitate cultural change and to seed the beginnings of a 'learning and researching community'. Personally, when setting out to build a research-minded culture where inquiry can flower, I have found it useful to first orientate my co-researchers, then raise working hypotheses we might proceed and experiment with, putting into practice the following principles:

- Work to flatten the prevailing authority pyramid of the group and to open up for examination authoritative and hierarchical responses when these occur.

- Risk sharing their thoughts, feelings, sensory awareness and fantasies with others, so as to raise awareness to the hidden agenda of social interaction.

- Engage in ongoing analysis of the social events that unfold and be prepared to explore the effect of these on themselves and others.

- Risk experimenting with the philosophy that problems are mostly in relation to others and capable of solution through face-to-face discussion.

- Persevere to constantly put to examination roles and behaviours with a view to increasing understanding and current awareness of a community's progress to date.

- Listen to the whole of themselves and endeavour to do the same with others.

- Open up to others and respect messages of stuckness and confusion when they arise.

- Accept emotions as energies rather than problems or symptoms to be resolved.

- Experiment with owning and exploring different ways of behaving and being.

- Engage with the here and with the now.

Approaching the above as *suggestions* and a *starting point for negotiation*, rather than as *rules*, I find helps to set a collaborative tone. As for the origin of the above principles, the first five are derived from therapeutic community practice (after Main 1980) – a group approach to psychiatry which will be discussed in the next section; the second five have been distilled from educational workshops of my own. Taken together, they set the scene for a facilitative culture conducive to group inquiry. Through this introductory process, a sense of tradition may be sensed, drawn upon, and opportunity afforded for people to decide on how they want to inquire – together. Negotiating and refining the above for more immediate consumption has distilled the following guidelines:

1) *Own*

Speak from the authority of your own experience, i.e. 'I think...'; 'I feel...'; 'I see or hear...'; 'I imagine...', rather than indirectly through the use of such phrases as 'one thinks...'; 'people tend to...' or by labelling others through such phrases as 'you are...'.

2) *Explore*

Engage in ongoing exploration and analysis of the social and interpersonal events that unfold, and remain curious to the effects of these upon the behaviour of yourself and others.

3) *Experiment*

Risk opening yourself to others and reducing your guard; honour your own stuckness or confusion and experiment with being tolerant of this in others; be prepared to explore new ways of expressing and being you.

4) *Respect*

Do not take beyond the group – nor share within it without the prior consent of those concerned – material of a confidential nature; take responsibility for sharing or holding onto your own secrets.

5) *Act*

Choose for yourself when to call a halt or to opt out of activities which appear wrong for you at the time; do not collude in situations that you feel are personally unhealthy.

Introducing the above guidelines, reflecting upon their prospective use and the shape they might take, I have found does much to shift a resistive culture to a growth-minded one. Indeed, these suggestions for ground rules as to how group inquiry might proceed are designed to enhance social contact and authentic communication while supporting other Gestalt notions facilitative of relational clarity – see **Figure 2.**

Orientating a group to the above ground rules while role-modelling the guiding principles that underpin them often constitutes a morning's work in itself! In culture-building terms, the rules themselves quickly become secondary to the negotiation process, which gives participants a chance to assess my facilitative bias, to find out about others, and to explore how they themselves might contribute to the emerging group. In short, it encourages group ownership and begins to create a culture and social container for future work (see the next case study). When this is in place, we may then set about exploring the nature of the community we are creating together. Time spent in building a research-minded culture, though slow at the beginning, facilitates faster movement and less hindrance at later stages of an inquiry.

The above discussion, and the principles suggested, are heavily influenced by humanism and its guiding principles of *holism, autonomy, experiential inquiry* and *democracy*. These affect me personally as a researcher and underpin the value-orientation of my own practitioner research in the following way:

Holism suggests that a person's mind, body, intellectual, emotional and spiritual qualities are integral to 'everything they do' and 'all they are'; consequently, an individual is best approached as a whole mind-body-spiritual being, rather than reduced to a role or one or more of their component parts. As every thing is multi-faceted and multi-influenced, there are no easy answers or simple solutions to human problems.

* As a researcher facilitating group inquiry, holism encourages me to approach groups as organic entities, which, though composed of conscious and unconscious elements of the individuals within them, nevertheless are seen primarily to take on a life of their own. Attending to the whole, I endeavour to foster a dialogue between the 'group' and the 'individuals within', which illuminates the interplay of all that emerges, inclusive of humankind's physical, social, emotional, imaginal and spiritual natures.

Autonomy supports the notion that, given the opportunity and resources, individuals are best placed to diagnose and resolve their own problems, as they know much more about themselves than I or anyone else can ever do.

* As a researcher alert to autonomy, I watch and listen very carefully to what the group and its participants present. Guided by the group's own wisdom and energetic currents I follow what emerges, sharing my observations. In this way I act as a flexible resource who works alongside others on an educational journey towards self-empowerment.

Experiential inquiry suggests it is important to meet life in an open and inquiring way, to attend to the unique nature of our present relationships, and to explore and experiment with becoming 'whole' in ourselves.

* As a researcher I am encouraged here and indeed encourage others – to take nothing for granted, but rather to inquire into everything. Through a focus upon 'what is unique' coupled with ongoing inquiry into our perceptions, beliefs and relationships with others, I seek to illuminate through experiential group inquiry, insight born from experience.

131

Figure 2 Some Gestalt Ground Rules for Direct Communication and Phenomenological Inquiry into What is Here and Now

Focus on What is Here and Now – don't waste time by ruminating on theory, the future or the past; practise paying attention to what is actually happening and to describing what you see and are aware of in the moment. I.e. *'I notice when you say we must plan for the future, we leap into fighting for our own territory, so I wonder if it might be useful to share our fears and to identify the support we need right now before we think ahead?'*

Accept Personal Responsibility – speak in the first person, say 'I' rather than 'we'; be clear if you are 'supporting', 'clarifying' or 'challenging'; speak for yourself and be clear about your 'needs'. I.e. *'Although we have agreed a way forward, I would feel more confident if we were to look at the alternatives and rattle-and-shake our plan so as to prepare ourselves for what might go wrong – do you feel the same way?'*

Question Rather than Defend – ask 'what' and 'how questions', which invite people to share their knowledge, rather than 'why questions' which cause them to justify themselves or to retreat; attempt to deepen your learning and contact and to expand your understanding. I.e. 'I'm curious as to how you see us moving this idea forward?'

Be Specific and Practical – practise being direct and owning your experience; say 'I feel cold towards this idea' rather than 'it feels cold'; avoid the use of 'it', as this distances us from the information available, our experiences and each other. I.e. *'I don't believe you have the resources or skills to achieve what you have set yourself to do, and I need to know the fall back position available if things go wrong?'*

Make Simple Statements – make short direct statements rather than take a position and defend it; simplify rather than construct elaborate statements which distort with explanation, or otherwise avoid the immediacy of direct experience. I.e. *'I feel supported by what you say and really admire the trouble you are taking to explain things to me'.*

Explore and Experiment – test ideas out; plan in the light of experience rather than freeze action until everything is tightly planned and understood; investigate rather than label: 'I guess that...' or 'I imagine that...', rather than 'you feel...' or 'you are...'; most interpretations and plans are based on projections and say more about the speaker than the issue. I.e. *'How might we test out this idea before committing ourselves more fully?'*

Clarify your Perceptions and Share your Evidence – be clear as to when you are seeing, hearing, thinking, feeling or imagining something. I.e. *'I felt relieved when you said we must make a decision soon, but felt scared when I remembered the last project we pushed through, which failed because we didn't spend time looking at the long-term costs'.*

Democracy supports the notion that we are interdependent rather than independent, and suggests that reason and negotiation should inform all we do. As we have more in common than 'out of common' with each other, to address the common good democratic process should underpin all decision making, and debate; sharing and transparency rather than authoritative imposition and covert agendas should therefore inform group norms.

* As a researcher alive to the democratic tradition I work to generate a negotiated and client-centred menu where everyone may be involved in forming the 'how' and the 'what' of what we explore, so that the inquiry is owned and of benefit to each of us. Democracy also keeps me alert to the need for healthy 'I-Thou' relationships, and to be watchful of communication that slides towards an egocentric 'I-I' and/or a reductionist 'I-It' stance in research.

Implicit within the above humanistic perspective is the notion that life and every path we travel represents a sacred journey, and every person and experience we meet presents us with a lesson worthy of respect. As to whether I'm walking my own talk or not, and living and practising within the Gestalt rules and humanistic principles suggested above, I find the following checklist a useful one to ground myself in the authentic facilitative presence I attempt to cultivate in group inquiry:

- Am I 'talking about' (using abstractions or generalisations) rather than 'dealing with' (asking for what I want and being intimate and personal)?
- Am I lecturing to the other person about 'what ought to be' rather than dealing with him or her on 'what is'?
- Am I saying 'I can't' when what I really mean is, 'I won't?'
- Am I asking a rhetorical question, pretending that I am looking for information when what I really want is to make a statement?
- Am I saying 'you, we, one...' etc., when I mean 'I'?
- Am I talking about the past when the real live issue is in the present?
- Am I saying where I stand on an issue and owning my true position?
- Am I saying 'No' when I mean 'No' – or am I avoiding real connection?
- Do I stop when I am finished talking or go on and on with examples or anecdotes?
- Am I broadcasting into the air, at the rug or to the group in general, rather than talking directly to the person(s) that I really want to reach?
- Do I send mixed messages (express anger with a smile on my face)?
- Am I really seeing and hearing what's going on or is my mind thinking about the future or past, or trying to imagine what someone else is thinking?

Because holistic research does not attempt to replace or remove other methods but rather seeks to include all, practitioner-researchers are able to retain their interactive authenticity and to invest a genuine depth of feeling and being into their work. This educational and facilitative stance, I am suggesting, is further enhanced by humanistic values which raise awareness of the human condition while encouraging the view that:

- People are a field of interrelated energies
- Empowerment is superior to control
- Individuals have ability to be authors of their own lives
- It is wholesome to allow the whole of oneself to meet with the whole of experience
- Progress is possible if we remain in dialogue with the self and others.

Movement in the above direction reduces the power-politics and hierarchical interference that stifles genuine inquiry. If a researcher is envisaged as too powerful by those they research they may rebel or, even more damagingly, feed a researcher with the information they believe they want to hear. The point I'm making is that hierarchy limits exploration, while peer-hood and democracy enhance it. Concentration on 'definition' and a tendency to 'expertism' can also rush facilitative inquiry too quickly towards answers, effectively foreclosing investigation. Humanistic principles guard against this, for they encourage us to acquire knowledge born from experience, rather than to impose knowledgeable solutions upon experience.

A forefather of humanistic psychology, Abraham Maslow (1965), who researched 'self-actualisers' – persons who were able to maintain peak performance throughout their lives – has something to say about the 'research attitude to life' I am advocating here. Indeed, it may be suggested that research-mindedness is itself a prerequisite for personal development and self-actualisation. For instance, Maslow found that self-actualisers, those who stayed curious and experimental, retained a childlike freshness alongside an ability to fully engage with the world, and in consequence were better able to:

- Perceive reality efficiently
- Tolerate uncertainty
- Accept themselves and others for what they are
- Be spontaneous in thought and behaviour
- Be problem-centred rather than self-centred
- Have a good sense of humour
- Be highly creative
- Be resistive to enculturalisation but not purposely unconventional

- Demonstrate concern for the welfare of mankind
- Be deeply appreciative of the basic experiences of life
- Establish deep satisfying relationships with a few, rather than many, people
- Look at life philosophically and objectively.

This ability to view things in the raw, to engage deeply and to stay open and receptive is, I suggest, fundamental to research excellence. Unless a practitioner-researcher can move towards a relational climate where empowerment rather than control predominates, and can capture a little of their earlier childlike enthusiasm and curiosity with the world, they will stifle their own and others' potential for living, inquiring and learning.

Reflections

Get a colleague/supervisor to use the criteria portrayed in **Figure 2**, and the Gestalt ground rules it describes which are intended to help focus a researcher upon 'what is here and now', to evaluate your own practice in communicating with your group.

4.2 Developing a Researching Community – Lessons from Therapeutic Community Practice

My understanding of what constitutes a 'learning and researching community' has been greatly influenced by contact with 'therapeutic community practice', a model for living, researching and learning that developed from a communal approach to psychiatric care.

Therapeutic communities, somewhat like action research, arose as a reaction to reductionist ways of approaching and treating behaviour. During the melting pot of the Second World War when it became apparent that psychological stress and disease were often symptomatic of wider dis-at-ease within the social system (Jansen 1980), and that large institutions often wrought a depersonalising effect upon those within them, the need became apparent for a more inclusive perspective, appreciative of the totality of organisational life, inclusive of its:

- Vital force or systemic energy
- Emotional climate
- Relational dynamic
- Quality of warmth and acceptance in general view

135

- Learning available through the engagement of institutional roles
- Morale building and therapeutic effect of communication
- Developing organisation culture. (After Rapoport 1960)

Exploring the therapeutic community as a model for humanising institutional life, Robert Rapoport (1960) in his classic study of the Henderson Hospital, identified four characteristics as central to its social-inquiring vein:

* **Permissiveness:** tolerance, acceptance of others and cultivation of the ability to witness a wide degree of behavioural response without undue distress or the acting out of punishment, victimisation or compulsive rescuing.

* **Communalism:** allowing intimate relations to flower, encouraging sharing, informality and free communication to knit the community together at a pace and time appropriate to those involved.

* **Democratisation:** encouraging all members to equally share in the exercise of power and decision making via regular community meetings and face-to-face discussion.

* **Reality-Confrontation:** presenting individuals with the consequences of their actions, while expressing that they are responsible to their peer community.

As a model of how to approach face-to-face collaborative communal inquiry, the therapeutic community offers up an example of a researching culture where subjects may become self-managing and responsible for inquiry into themselves.

In terms of their facilitation, a practitioner-researcher working in the therapeutic community mode, Gestalt-like, does not impose so much as illuminate, clarify and verify. By standing aside a little, they allow the community to develop of its own accord, while keeping the spirit of democracy and inquiry alive through regular planning meetings and debriefs. But do not suppose that a practitioner-researcher becomes invisible through this process or loses themselves within the group they study, for although working alongside and responsible to the community, they nevertheless represent a powerful and authentic presence in their own right.

In the account that follows, a practical example is provided of how a therapeutic community approach – informed by Gestalt – was developed and used to support collaborative inquiry within the frame of an experiential workshop. This account also illustrates the emotional demands that are made on a practitioner-researcher who works in an open and facilitative way, especially when they attempt to resolve a particularly resistive patch through reality-confrontation.

Case Study

A Facilitative Approach to Community Inquiry – Maintaining an Authentic Presence

An interesting second day. I state my intention to be a more challenging presence in the group, referring as I do so to a model of facilitation which includes dimensions where: 'achieving the objectives', 'attributing meaning', 'raising the hidden agendas', 'managing feelings', 'forming the boundaries' and 'expressing authenticity' are strategically mapped. I state my intention to address this model in more detail later in the day, and circulate a handout describing an exercise where in pairs, we will explore our thoughts, feelings, sensations and fantasies – while focusing upon the person before us... I am met by stony silence. I say aloud:

'Is this the way this group responds to change?'

I ask for a volunteer to help me to demonstrate the exercise. After a further silence – and a little more prompting, 'M', a female participant who has been more vocal than most, volunteers to work with me. I start by sharing my thoughts:

'What I am wondering is how best to illustrate this exercise'.

I go on to share my feelings:

'I feel a little embarrassed and excited as to where this exercise might lead'.

Regards my sensations:

'I am aware of the warmth in the room, the hardness of my chair, the smell of coffee and the eyes of the person before me'.

My fantasies are:

'I imagine there is just the two of us and that we are alone having a picnic'.

'M' then proceeds with her thoughts, feelings, sensations and fantasies, and is equally open and able to engage. After we have completed two cycles I invite the group to form pairs and to do the same. No movement and no passive silence this time, rather an active resistance to going further. A dialogue ensues around how unexpected and unwanted it is in Chinese culture to share such things:

'To share feelings is not the Chinese way' I am told.

An example is provided as one of the elders shares that he has never seen his parents share a warm embrace or kiss. It appears as if the exercise we demonstrated produced a profound fear of intimacy – and possibly sexuality – in some bystanders.

I reiterate:

'Thoughts, feelings, senses and fantasies are ways we construct our world; if we are not prepared to explore these connections, how can we research what is happening, or begin to appreciate the baseline we start from?'

▶

I gently challenge the group to: 'Enter the experience in order to collect evidence of how you relate'.

The atmosphere is one of trepidation. This threatened exposure generates much discussion about 'problems'; that this is 'meant to be education and not therapy', and leads to such statements as:

'To be charismatic is not the Chinese way'.

'Why don't you give us case studies of change?'

With emphasis I respond:

'We need to explore what is happening 'now' as a case study example of change, rather than fly into judgements'.

The group's stress crescendos. I raise to the group's attention that they are:

'...living and feeling the effects of facing up to possible change – right now. You are your own case study... Change is about breaking patterns! Do you want to talk about it or do it?'

I suggest they consider the supports they need at this moment to go beyond this, their habitual way of coping, and suggest:

'If we learn how to stay with uncertainty and to work this through, we may never need to fear change again.'

The impasse continues for some forty-five minutes with numerous challenges and counter-challenges. I again raise to the group's awareness that they are 'talking about' rather than 'exploring the change' they are currently experiencing. I make the observation that:

'To gain skills in managing change you have to live through it'.

I find myself quoting a Chinese saying and becoming more authoritative:

'To hear is to know, to see is to believe, to do is to understand. Change has to be experienced not planned out of experience.'

At this time I endeavour to be firm, yet gentle, so as to avoid bullying the group. My intention is to hold the group to the contract we earlier negotiated together.

'A', who is a senior and powerful organisational presence and reference for others, is openly critical; she can not make sense of what is happening or what she is meant to be learning; she has 'not learnt anything about strategies yet!' I remind the group that 'Emotions and attitudes may be educated as much as the intellect'.

I suggest that this is what they are doing right now! The group becomes split into those who see the benefit of experiential learning and those who do not. Some challenge 'A', and others try to help her understand the nature of experiential learning and what is being experienced. At this time it feels like three-quarters of the group are positive and a quarter are negative to the approach I am taking. As earlier experiences of experiential learning are shared by positive members of the group, heated debate ensues. This previously distant and polite group is now thoroughly aroused and openly debating in a highly charged emotional atmosphere. Some participants request more theory, others say they are learning much more like this. At this time I feel I am providing on-the-spot consultancy, processing the group dynamic and feeding back insights. This feels like the make-or-break point of the workshop.

After a time, breakthrough emerges as those who are positive towards the experience, seemingly, begin to educate and convert others to their view. Some who were earlier vocally rejecting of my approach, over coffee, now say they are beginning to appreciate what experiential learning and research are all about.

Barber 1995

In the case summary we see how the intermix of allowing space for community dynamics to work themselves through, attending to the group's pace, holding individuals to their pre-determined ground rules while maintaining an authentic presence – can surface data which would otherwise stay hidden. Indeed, unless you are facilitatively robust, you might easily conspire to keep data such as this well and truly hidden. I am reminded here of a Zen saying:

When not spurred, no awakening; when not cornered, no breaking through.

Suzuki 1974 p.157

In the aforementioned setting as the practitioner-researcher-consultant-facilitator roles began to merge, I felt paradoxically vulnerable yet strong. But if I had not been contracted to illustrate the nature of experiential learning and how I taught change management I would not have dared – nor felt permitted – to go as far as I did. In terms of verifying my own record of events, I circulated the above account to participants for their comments. In this way, opportunity was afforded for those involved to correct any misperceptions and to add interpretations of their own.

As we can see from the above case study, facilitative inquiry need not engender a cold and isolated 'researcher presence'. Akin to consultancy, collaborative group inquiry can solicit and indeed requires active engagement with the client group within their social-system. But a caution: remember, inquiry of this nature can stir up a hornets' nest, raise to awareness the 'group shadow' and through removal of the polite mask of the 'false social self' (Winnicott 1965) reveal uncomfortable feelings of the 'true self' so often hidden from view. Then again, if as a facilitator researching into the nature of a community or group, you want to encourage an authentic and deeper description of events, you will need to be authentic yourself. This in turn may demand that you remove your own social mask – along with any defensive or pseudo-professional distance you attach to your facilitative role.

Without our professional mask we may meet role insecurity, but if we are unable to tolerate openness and vulnerability, how dare we ask those we facilitate to do the same? Remember, practitioner-researchers are themselves the prime organ of inquiry, and personal and interpersonal sensitivity represent the cutting edge of 'the self' as an investigative tool.

In re-reading the above case study I am again reminded of Scott Peck's observation that:

> Confrontation, even angry communication is sometimes necessary to bring into focus the clear reality of the barriers that separate us before they can be knocked down.
>
> *Peck 1993 p.357*

Knocking down and removing barriers is part and parcel of building a robust researching community. This is done with the intention that we extend our vision and deepen our appreciation of reality. As humanistic researchers, we have an ethical duty to facilitate with respect and love.

Returning to our developmental model of the facilitator-client relationship discussed in Chapter 3 (3.6), various emotional seasons are suggested to unfold naturally in collaborative inquiry. Approach this description as a working hypothesis of *what can happen*, rather than a factual map of the territory.

Case Study

Influences of Community – Relational Dynamics within the Facilitator-Client Relationship

Tuckman (1965) has identified a five-stage model of developmental progression in work groups: forming (introducing), storming (testing the competition), norming (forming rules), performing (addressing the task) and mourning (ending the relationship). I find that these stages are less obvious in process-centred groups. A practitioner-researcher, facilitating inquiry in the less structured group or community, is more likely – in my experience – to meet the following dynamics as their collaborative inquiry develops and matures:

The Orientation Phase: As the facilitator and inquiry group meet and begin to acclimatise to each other, the following dynamics commonly emerge:

* *Dependency* – initially the facilitator as 'the leader' is depended on to set the scene, to initiate and to generally 'parent' the group.

* *Excitation* – as expectations of 'the unknown' and 'beginnings' surface and flight and fight dynamics are heightened, the researcher-cum-facilitator is watched very carefully for clues as to what he or she wants of the group.

The Identification Phase: As the facilitator-group relationship develops and members set about identifying and planning the focus of their inquiry, now, before trust truly develops, the group may test out the facilitator through the following behaviours:

* *Individual Resistance* – individuals, as the initial excitement wanes, feeling threatened by the size and energy of the group, may now: hide their reactions, retreat into silence, behave stereotypically or release their emotional tensions by dramatisation. Roles of victim, persecutor, rebel and rescuer can now occur, or over-intellectualisation arise in an attempt to reason away the mounting unease.

* *Group Resistance* – here the group may relate in a superficial, cocktail-party mode, become mildly cynical in a polite 'league of gentlemen' way, blame the facilitator in an effort to avoid responsibility, or scapegoat external agencies to draw attention away from anxieties within itself.

The Exploration Phase: If during the above kinds of resistance the facilitator is not thrown off-stride and is found to portray an authentic non-punishing presence, trust develops and participants are able to plan and put their pre-arranged methods of inquiry into action. At this stage, as contact and communication deepen, from out the earlier resistance the following positive behaviours may be seen to emerge:

* *Introspection* – individuals, as they begin to attune to themselves and to the here-and-now, may enter a phase of contactful and intimate sharing, where issues previously unfinished or unaddressed in earlier group relationships can be revisited.

* *Contactful Attentiveness* – participants may begin to relate in an empathic way, share intimacies, check out their perceptions and invite feedback from others.

The Resolution Phase: With the end of the group and the inquiry in sight, the facilitator and participants debrief, give meaning to events and prepare to complete their relationship. If the experience is seen as a positive one, the following occurs:

* *Personal Contracting* – here participants decide what insights and behaviours to take beyond the group, network with others, affirm their learning and take from the experience strategies for implementation in other areas of their lives.

Though the above dynamics sometimes arise in group inquiries of the short term, they flower more conspicuously in groups of seven or more members and of a day or more lifespan. They are also more readily discernible in settings where a researcher or a facilitator adopts a process-centred rather than task-centred approach, and where leadership is rather more democratic or laissez faire, rather than authoritative or prescriptive. In more authoritative task-led climates Tuckman's (1965) model is more discernible, for although having similar dynamics as above, in task groups they tend to go underground to fuel a hidden agenda.

What lessons do you take from the above case studies and how do they relate to your own practice as a practitioner-researcher?

(December) I find myself alerted again to the undercurrents of my research group, the developmental nature of a group and the unconscious or 'out of awareness' influences that may be driving us; I'm also aware of how useful it might be as a researcher to adopt a position which supports Permissiveness, Communalism, Democratisation and Reality-Confrontation, and see how I can use this to build a culture of inquiry. This said, I wonder about the ethics of facilitating inquiry at so deep a level.

As a trigger-point for reflection upon your own study, how well do you account for: the vital force or systemic energy of the institution you are working within; the emotional climate of your inquiry group; the quality of warmth and acceptance in view; the learning available through the engagement of institutional roles; the morale building and therapeutic effect of communication.

(December) I'm aware of how I've been so focused upon individual players that I've largely forgotten to step back and consider the cultural water people are swimming in, let alone the effects of my research as a morale-building exercise, yet this does appear to be taking place, albeit indirectly.

4.3 Facilitative Choices in Group Inquiry – Towards Mindful Intervention

Often whilst travelling back on the train following a day of investigative inquiry I review my performance by profiling my facilitation of inquiry and investigative stance on the six dimensions shown below (adapted from Heron 1989):

Directive   *(How we defined and achieved the task and objectives)*   Non-Directive

10   9   8   7   6   5   4   3   2   1   0

Interpretative   *(How we raised information and attributed meaning)*   Non-Interpretative

10   9   8   7   6   5   4   3   2   1   0

Confronting   *(How we raised awareness of hidden agendas and motives)*   Non-Confronting

10   9   8   7   6   5   4   3   2   1   0

Cathartic   *(How we addressed feelings and dealt with emotional energy)*   Non-Cathartic

10   9   8   7   6   5   4   3   2   1   0

Structuring	(How we formed our values, boundaries and rules)	Un-Structuring

10 9 8 7 6 5 4 3 2 1 0

Disclosing	(How we shared, met and expressed our true feelings)	Non-Disclosing

10 9 8 7 6 5 4 3 2 1 0

As to what exactly I am attempting to profile, the above categories are more fully explained and detailed below:

'**Directing**' is somewhat like prescribing or ordering, occurs when you state what you believe should happen, and is often concerned with how participants might fulfil the group task.

'**Interpreting**' links to the allocation of meaning, such as when a facilitator shares the reason they see behind a group's dynamic.

'**Confronting**' denotes the degree of challenge you use to get at the deeper issues, or when you try to raise awareness to the blind spots of a person or group.

'**Cathartic**' interventions seek to release emotional energy, as when you encourage laughter to break the ice or allow any angers or fears to surface.

'**Structuring**' focuses upon the ground rules a group negotiates and the cultural values and maps that are used to shape experience.

'**Disclosing**' relates to the level and degree of personal sharing you solicit, and how well a group relates at the authentic level.

The further to the left-hand side I rate myself, the more active and interventionist is my research facilitation and the more leadership-centred is the group. Here my inquiry stance supports an active style, best suited to a directing of purpose and the structuring of research tasks. The more towards the right-hand side the less interventionist, observational, field attentive and phenomenological my research style, and the more self-directed and self-illuminating the group tends to be. When centrally placed upon the above scale, the more democratic and dialogical becomes my research style.

As for my own investigative stance – and indeed my profile upon the above scale – I find that although it is constantly changing I can plot its movement on the above tool. With a measurement such as this to hand, I can identify what I contributed on days when my research inquiry went well and what I did at times when I felt it failed or fell short of expectations. Having to hand a means of mapping the interventions I make allows me to form a working hypothesis as to what I might do *'more of'* or *'less of'* to increase my effectiveness. By this means, my research style and inquiring role also becomes a subject for study.

143

Turn to your reflective journal, consider your facilitative role as a researcher within your inquiry group and profile yourself on the scale described below – then ask a colleague to rate your facilitative style.

+ 10   9   8   7   6   5   4   3   2   1   0 –

Directive   *(How we defined and achieved the task and objectives)*   Non-Directive

Interpretative *(How we raised information and attributed meaning)*   Non-Interpretative

Confronting *(How we raised awareness of hidden agendas and motives)* Non-Confronting

Cathartic   *(How we addressed feelings and dealt with emotional energy)*   Non-Cathartic

Structuring   (How we formed our values, boundaries and rules)   Un-Structuring

Disclosing   (How we shared, met and expressed our true feelings)   Non-Disclosing

(10 August 2006) When self-profiling my own style I revealed the following result: directive – 2; interpretative – 9; confronting 2; cathartic – 1; structuring – 8; disclosing – 2; yet when I gave it to a colleague to profile on my behalf he rated me much more directive (8) and much less interpretative (5). Possibly my inner thoughts are much more interpretative than my outer communication; I also wonder if I'm more directive than I realise? I note how although I rate myself to be non-directive, that I am nevertheless highly structuring. Do I therefore covertly shape the group rather than make my intentions clear and up-front? I'm also aware that although I'm very feeling-centred, personally, I am cagey about addressing emotions or disclosing the same in my research group. I wonder about the effects of all this on my research.

4.4 Researching from within the Group – The Researcher as Data in a Research Field

It has been argued in this work that carers, counsellors, consultants and other practitioner-researchers who work intimately alongside others, who must facilitate a group or client-systems movement and account for tacit and emotional ways of knowing, plus everyone else who shapes social behaviour, need to be intimately involved. We can't learn to drive just from watching others drive, and we can't understand a group or organisation's dynamics just by observing behaviour. But, because group workers share in the same 'intimate "family-like" group field' as their clients, feelings such as rejection, competitiveness, impulses to control and to retaliate – common currency to group life – constantly threaten their facilitative effectiveness. Facilitators wear many hats in a collaborative inquiry. For although *leaders* and/or *researchers*, they are also *a person* with feelings and sensitivities, *a group member* and *peer*, a *holder of professional authority*, a *consultant* and a *subject*, someone who *educates and illuminates while facilitating change.*

If I were studying the quantity, regularity and financial cost of training events in an organisation I would not need to consider my degree of social involvement. But, if I were interested in how clients assessed value for money during training – and wanted to go deeper than a series of interviews or a questionnaire – participation would have to be considered. This would especially be the case if I thought emotional factors and relationships played a part in the phenomenon being studied. In this case, I might decide to sample a series of training events as a participant, and decide to explore my own responses in the heuristic mode. In this way, I would not so much *get data from 'the horse's mouth'* – as *become a horse* myself. So, is the researcher here using introspection and participation as a means to uncover information, or are they *the data itself on a journey of discovery*? Phenomenologically, whatever we think we are, we are already in danger of becoming.

For me, the roles of social researcher, counsellor, consultant and group facilitator have an interchangeable quality, in that each performs collaborative inquiry in order to raise personal sensitivity and individual awareness. Letting go of what you have been taught and releasing a little of your certainty so that you meet afresh with the unknown are for me prerequisites of good quality performance in all these areas. If you know 'where you are' and 'what you want', why bother to inquire? If you enter research with 'the answers' why not write a letter instead! *Research is about cultivating doubt, being prepared to question everything and making confusion a friend.*

In order to cultivate a sense of objective subjectivity, researchers who explore experientially from within an experience, besides facilitative skills, need emotional and intellectual support. The role of the research supervisor, a shadow consultant who draws attention to your facilitative blind spots and who supplies these needs is explored in the next chapter.

> The only thing that makes life possible is permanent intolerable uncertainty; the joy of not knowing what comes next.
> *Ursula Le Guin in Haywood & Cohen 1990 un-numbered*

4.5 Raising the Unaware to Awareness – The Shadow Side of Facilitative Inquiry

A researcher, especially a researcher in a collaborative or group setting, does well to remember that most communication is non-verbal and that attitude, identification with others, energetic level, emotional tone and receptivity play a large part in how social reality is construed. Some aspects of non-verbal communication are easy to spot, such as the effects of gender and age within relationships. Other aspects are less readily discernible – the way a subject's memory may associate you with figures of their past or the symbolic role you are accorded by a group. In order to appreciate the unconscious message and emotional undertone you evoke, it becomes necessary to look at the shadow – or covert – side of behaviour and what this communicates. This is especially important in first meetings when people thrust out interpretations of their own in order to fill their information gaps. Stereotypic 'projective responses' such as this do much to unconsciously shape what later unfolds and need to be constantly brought into awareness for closer examination. Indeed, when we examine ourselves closely we find a rich mix of rationality and fantasy, cultural and personal bias, idiosyncratic meaning interwoven into common sense, conscious and unconscious processes.

The unconscious, or 'shadow' as it is termed in Jungian literature, contains undeveloped and unexpressed potential of all kinds, all that is hidden from view behind the social mask of our ego: 'The shadow acts like a psychic immune system, defining what is self and not self' (Zweig & Abrams 1991: p.xviii). The best as well as the worst of us is seen to reside in the shadow, such as our store of love, compassion and joy, as well as our angers, envies and fears. Everything we fear is too much for others to handle. Some authors suggest it also includes lost depths of the soul (Assagioli 1976). Just as people have personas and shadows, so do groups and organisations (Hinshelwood 1987).

As a Gestaltist, my view of the so called 'unconscious' – what the analysts see as the store of repressed behaviour and a powerful primordial driver of human action – includes the Jungian notion of the shadow, but extends to everything that is beyond a person or group's current awareness:

> ...talking of the unconscious, we prefer to talk about the at-this-moment-unaware. This term is much broader and wider than the term 'unconscious'. This unawareness contains not only repressed material, but material which never came to awareness, and material which has faded or has been assimilated or has been built into larger gestalts.
>
> *Perls 1976 p.54*

Bly (1988) compares the shadow to an invisible bag into which we put everything our parents and teachers don't like and have taken trouble to police out of us. When children are told to 'stop that' or 'don't do that again', they assign that part of themselves to the black bag of the shadow. By the age of twelve, Bly – speaking metaphorically – suggests our shadow is a mile long! When we eventually look within the bag to view the collection of disowned material we have acquired, say in a therapeutic or personal development setting, its contents appear alien and a threat to all we have become. The shadow in this light holds everything we have exiled in order to become the person/self we portray. But what is denied in ourselves has a tendency to return in a disguised form, and often ends up displaced upon others:

> When an individual makes an attempt to see his shadow, he becomes aware of (and often ashamed of) those qualities and impulses he denies in himself but can plainly see in other people – such as egotism, mental laziness, and sloppiness; unreal fantasies, schemes and plots.
>
> *Marie-Lousie Van Franz in Zweig & Abrams 1991 pp.34–5*

Practitioner-researchers, facilitating at deeper levels of human experience, need to provide sufficient support for individuals to remove their social masks, and so must remove their own professional mask – while remaining professional in behaviour – if they are to fully engage with experience and to access their potential. In this regard, as researchers, we must facilitate within ourselves – as much as others – insight to the undertone or subtext of behaviour.

People are emotional and imaginative beings who engage in many more symbolic interactions (Blumer 1969) than rational ones. If a practitioner-researcher ignores the more abstract, symbolic or 'shadowy' aspects of their role, they will not only be confused and helpless when their store of logic runs out, but will tend to record stereotypic rather than sound information. Authenticity is a requisite of quality inquiry and the uncovering of reliable data.

Case Study

The Role of Unconscious Co-Creation within Inquiry

Joan Wilmot (2005) records how her partner and herself were suddenly overcome in an inquiry they were co-facilitating by a potent sense of utter powerlessness. They had used all their tried and tested facilitative tools to no avail and nothing they seemed to do appeared to either impact the group or shift their feelings of powerlessness. During the coffee break they conferred together. As powerlessness was not common to their own facilitative experience, they speculated as to whether this might be emanating from the group. Following coffee they shared their experience with the group – while holding back the hypothesis that they might be picking up some of the group's own distress. When they shared with the group their own sense of powerlessness and then asked them how they themselves felt at work, individuals shared that they often felt useless and incompetent within the workplace, indeed they did so right now, and until the facilitators had shared their own sense of powerlessness they had seen the facilitators as pretty incompetent also!

Recognising, seeing through and over and beyond your own projections, as well as holding and reflecting back the projections of others, attempting to resolve the same while all the time exploring what is projected upon them, is an essential practitioner-researcher skill, especially if we are to illuminate the undertone of our inquiry.

There is also another caution: as researchers, we should always remember that we are in danger of getting from a group what we give as well as what we withhold; perception, especially when informed by an all too firmly held hypothesis, runs the risk of us feeding a projective reality.

Goffman's (1978) recognition of the tendency for people to 'assume' rather than 'check out', and to project out 'untested stereotypes' to fill their information gaps, does much to explain how individuals may be subverted from a consciously agreed task, especially within groups:

> Group members set about their conscious task, but constantly interfering with efficient execution of that task are unconscious emotional drives and feelings of members. As these feelings intrude upon the mind of one individual they are sensed by another, who may act in sympathy... to a greater or lesser degree, according to his 'valency' for a popular basic assumption.
>
> *Whiteley & Gordon 1979 pp.16–7*

Many families and management teams, educational and indeed research communities I find often run on similar untested lines as these.

As a holistic facilitator and researcher, though primarily Gestalt and phenomenological, I do not turn my back on behavioural or analytic notions but rather allow these to serve as facets of and working hypotheses within the whole field. In this way 'what is not Gestalt' is allowed to inform my vision in this way as much as 'what is Gestalt'.

Knowing the basic assumptions and developmental dynamics that groups may cast upon them, prepares a facilitator for the shadow side of group life and permits them to experiment with the same. For example, Zeisel (1981) suggests a facilitator or researcher can test out group assumptions through subtly changing their role or presentation, and then observing the social ripples which result. For instance, when I sense that a group is becoming overly dependent upon me, I tend to take a less active facilitative role. As a participant-researcher rather than a leader, I can then begin to glean from this newly acquired position knowledge of those who are able to take the inquiry further when I start to wilt. Sometimes facilitative abstinence in research is an excellent catalyst of learning.

If a leader – symbolic or actual – is not prepared to be led, how will others begin to own the research process as their own or yet again begin to empower themselves?

Reflections

In relation to unconscious processes, what 'basic' or untested assumptions might be proliferating in your own research group, and how might you counterbalance the emergence of further untested assumptions?

(December) I am aware of the tendency of my research group to depend upon my leadership and initiative. If this were to continue, I suspect people may give me what they want me to hear rather than what they really think. To safeguard against this, I will endeavour to be more person- and process-centred in my style, more non-directive in my facilitation, check out how confident others feel with the process we are engaged in and take more of a backseat in the decision-making processes we engage.

4.6 Unconscious Bias – Actively Interfering with the Interference

Unlike quantitative research where 'the person' of the researcher relates minimally with those studied, qualitative researchers who work intimately alongside others need to be familiar with the ways semi-conscious and unconscious psychological mechanisms skew information.

Collaborative researchers akin to group facilitators, cannot afford to take 'the obvious' for granted or to content themselves with appearances. In the passages now cited, I define common defensive reactions – distorters of information – provide examples of their effect within groups and highlight suggestions for their redress.

Repression:- *Definition:* This involves the exclusion of a painful or stress-inducing thought, feeling, memory or impulse from awareness. The more emotional energy you push out of conscious awareness, so the theory goes, the more fuel you provide for unconscious, emotionalised and distorted thoughts and behaviour. All unconscious behaviour stems from this root of repression.

Example: When repression is habitual and fully fledged, any amount of direct questioning fails, as there is a deeply rooted refusal to face the facts or address the issues. Conversely, if you continue to confront what is avoided, your persistence will only increase a subject's or group's entrenchment and anxiety.

Strategy: A researcher's job here might be to free up the underlying threat that fuels repression, which is perhaps best performed by building in cultural supports rather than focusing in upon individuals themselves. Sometimes a researcher's role-modelling of 'relaxed attentiveness' can take

149

the urgency out of events, defusing the feelings of 'getting it wrong' or 'shame' that originally led to repression. Resolve the sense of 'anxious excitation' that often prevails in repressive climates, and what was earlier denied may now flow back into view. Asking a group what rules they would like to operate by, imparting humour or fostering acceptance, all dilute the need for repression.

Denial:- *Definition:* When an individual or group discards or distorts reality in such a way that the original event becomes unrecognisable, they are within the throes of denial.

Example: Denial is commonly found in times of culture shock, such as when a practitioner-researcher in the early phase of a relationship moves too quickly towards a sensitive agenda. Sometimes jocular behaviour may cloak denial. Mild, good-humoured cynicism can also give rise to a 'league of gentlemen' dynamic, such as when people attempt to avoid or dampen proceedings, or stall for time to dilute or move away from uncomfortable zones of inquiry.

Strategy: A practitioner-researcher might raise awareness to denial and gently draw attention to the purpose it is serving in a group. They might also negotiate rules where people are encouraged to be more direct, by speaking in the first person: 'I think...'; 'I feel...'.

Identification:- *Definition:* This mechanism relates to the wish to be like and/or assume the characteristics of another; often to the degree the subject becomes estranged from their own authentic self. Unconscious imitation of this nature is an integral part of socialisation and sexual programming; it is therefore well established within each of us.

Example: Identification may happen in groups where passive reciprocity has taken the place of problem resolution. Individuals so affected tend to become over confirming, supporting and identified with an external object, be this an organisation, a boss or a researcher. An individual responding in this way feels by turns, seductive and dependent, and may cause us to be less questioning or exploratory than we would otherwise be. Group confluence, where everything the facilitator suggests is readily agreed with, is a classic feature of over-identification.

Strategy: When identification occurs in a group it is useful to raise to awareness the socialising influences of the setting, its norms, plus what happens when these norms are breached. Alternative strategies to the more usual ones may also be explored. Another way is to interrupt collusion by highlighting individual difference and drawing attention to what is unique. Investing more challenge and gently raising to awareness hidden agendas can also help here.

150

Projection:- *Definition:* Projection describes an unconscious means of dealing with unacceptable and uncomfortable feelings in oneself, by splitting them off and projecting them outwards. What has origin in oneself is, through this process, attributed to others.

Example: Subjects may project their own suspicions and discomfort upon a researcher/facilitator and criticise everything they say and do. Scapegoating and blaming of others outside the group is another feature of projective behaviour.

Strategy: A practitioner-researcher might offer counter information or encourage individuals to check out and to consider the evidence behind their assumptions. Asking a person to supply external evidence to support their viewpoint or to stipulate what observations, values or beliefs have informed them, can also lead towards greater discrimination and objective evaluation.

Rationalisation:- *Definition:* Here reasoning is employed to deflect from or hide the emotional impact and/or significance of an event.

Example: An uncomfortable question or uncomfortable incident might be re-interpreted and reasoned away intellectually, without exploration of the core issue. When a theoretical presentation is held onto at all costs and no space is allowed for other views or self-critique, it is likely a person or group is suffering the hubris of rationalisation.

Strategy: Inquiry may be made into the emotional significance of an argument or debate and attention drawn to the purpose 'reason' is serving. Counter-positions and critiques may also be invited. Surfacing the underlying discomfort that motivates rationalisation and encouraging a discussion of this can also prove useful.

Displacement:- *Definition:* The discharge of pent-up emotions onto events/persons who are less threatening than those who initiated the original emotional reactions.

Example: Sometimes, anger which originated with a manager in the workplace may be carried over to safer targets in the inquiry group, or displaced upon the researcher.

Strategy: It is sometimes useful to ask people to check in with what sort of day they've had, to share the preoccupations they carry with them or to ask them to voice what they are thinking right now.

Regression:- *Definition:* A reversion to earlier – age inappropriate – behaviour in order to avoid responsibility or current environmental demands may occur when an individual's emotional and intellectual resources are overwhelmed by a crisis situation.

151

Example: A person's regression may be compounded by their perception of subordinate status, feelings of passivity and inadequacy, or by a sense of being at the mercy of a strange environment or caught in the throes of a childlike past.

Strategy: Practitioner-researchers need to be on the lookout for any hierarchical, authoritarian or parental responses that creep into their presentation, and should work towards peer-hood in their relationships. Role-modelling and supporting humanistic values I find do much to undo this dynamic.

The above mechanisms skew research inquiry. Their continued presence denotes a considerable degree of psychological stress which might well lead us to hypothesise about the psychological health of the relationship, a group or community under study.

No review of unconscious influence would be complete without recognition of transference, counter-transference and resistance, three major ingredients of untested assumptions that surface in groups. Phenomena that do much to skew the information and data a practitioner-researcher receives are as follows:

Transference:

The re-enactment or repetition of past conflicts with significant others – parents, teachers, lovers etc. – to the extent that feelings, behaviours, and attitudes that spring from these earlier relationships are transferred into the current setting (Brammer et al. 1989). Transferential reactions take many forms, for instance an individual or organisation, race or species may be loved, hated, or otherwise idealised and/or greeted in a habitual un-checked-out way. An individual in the throes of transference may be suggested to be avoiding current or anticipated emotional discomfort by sticking to 'the tried and the tested'.

Counter-transference:

This concept represents the reciprocal way a receiver of transference (cum-researcher in the context of this text) may be seduced or seduce themselves into responding as if they are indeed in reality the idealised figure projected upon them – father, guide, lover etc. You are more susceptible to counter-transference when you, albeit unconsciously, carry unresolved feelings relating to the transference you receive; i.e. if you try to feel special in compensation for a deeply held sense of inadequacy you will be more likely let yourself be placed on an idealised pedestal.

Resistance:

Describes an oppositional pattern of relating that impedes contact, change and movement, by interfering with the ability of a group or person to take responsibility for the part they play in current events of their life (Brammer et al. 1989):

> All movement engenders resistance. Since experience is in constant flux, it takes place against an inner resistance. This inner resistance of mine I experience as a reluctance to change my own ways of doing things, of behaving as I typically do in daily life.
>
> *Zinker 1978 p.34*

Resistance, transference and counter-transference originate at the level of an idealised or imagined relationship, and can catapult an individual from an authentic 'here and now' position to one haunted by emotions of the past. Attuned to earlier emotional instincts and assumptions a practitioner-researcher's counter-transference may then show itself in their:

- Not listening or paying attention to a specific message
- Finding it difficult to shift positions and tightening up
- Becoming sympathetic rather than empathetic or overtly emotional when faced by certain people or events
- Constantly reflecting or interpreting too soon what is happening
- Consistently missing or underestimating another's depth of feeling
- Being unable to identify with and feeling emotionally remote from a client or colleague
- Discovering a tendency to argue with a certain person or being defensive or otherwise vulnerable in their company
- Being driven to control in a parental way
- Feeling that this is a best or worst person or group to work for or with
- Being preoccupied with a client or colleague between meetings
- Being consistently late to meetings
- Attempting to solicit strong emotions from someone by making dramatic statements
- Compulsively giving advice
- Feeling a compulsion to be active and to deliver at all costs
- Dreaming about a person or event
- Being too busy to make time for something or someone
- Working excessively hard then complaining of overwork.

Adapted from Brammer et al. 1989 by Barber 1999a

When you catch yourself acting as you did in your family of origin, you are well within the grip of transference. So, given that we can recognise transferential influences within ourselves and others, how might we work with and through them? Some guidance in this regard is suggested below:

1 Start by recognising a person's feelings for what they are, transference, and not taking what comes your way personally. This can also help others unhook themselves from you.

2 Look within yourself for the possible source of your feelings and reactions. Ask yourself: 'Who does this person remind me of?' 'What impels me to behave in the way I do?' 'What emotional needs of myself am I seeking to meet in this relationship?'

3 Talk over your responses with a colleague or supervisor.

4 Raise awareness to your motives e.g. 'I'm feeling very involved with this issue as I have just left a similar situation recently'; apologise when your responses run away from you: 'Sorry to have interrupted you just then, I guess I'm a little over-eager'.

5 Increase your own personal awareness by appointing a shadow consultant or supervisor, by joining a personal growth group or by seeing a counsellor.

Barber 1999a

Monitoring the shadow side of facilitation is especially important in collaborative inquiry, where a practitioner-researcher facilitates inquiry from within the fabric of a group. Below, a collaborative inquiry into a learning community's relational dynamics is described in psychodynamic terms, to illuminate the energetic undercurrents a researcher might meet when in group inquiry – whether they are interested in group dynamics or not! A static approach to group inquiry tends to miss the essence of the thing, for dynamic phenomena require similarly dynamic research tools. The simultaneous management of research and social involvement is far from easy, for the risk of a practitioner-researcher losing him- or herself within the field, falling prey to 'transference' and surrendering their research stance remains ever present. To prevent this from happening, supervision is a necessity. A shadow consultant or research supervisor's job is a research-minded one designed to 'inquire into the researcher and their facilitative vision', inclusive of:

- *The contextual frame of yourself and your method of inquiry* – your skills, experience, beliefs and values; knowledge; methodological position; the literary and research tradition your facilitation hails from

- *The characteristics of those your facilitation/research involves* – who they are, what they do, what roles they engage, what they expect from you and the effects of this inquiry

- *The nature of the problem or theme for investigation* – perceptions of problems, needs, the interests that drew the various players together

- *The nature of the wider field the inquiry affects* – private or public sector effects; present macroscopic and microscopic influences upon

154

the study; what it sets out to change, improve or add value to

- *The current situation and its possible problems* – the need to pilot, review, select various investigative and/or diagnostic tools, or to devise new avenues of investigation

- *The study's relationship to its host environment* – the subject and study's relationship to the environment; its world view and reality orientation; what it seeks to support or emphasise; what it challenges and understates

- *The nature of the facilitator-client relationship* – how the inquiry relationship formed; the leadership style you adopted and how this changed through time; transferential and shadow dynamics that influenced the whole; what you thought and felt about the relational dynamic you co-created

- *The types of intervention you employed* – the actions taken to inquire into the issues identified; whether these were facilitative or authoritative; whether they emanated at the contractual, idealised or authentic level of relationship

- *The nature of the inquiry itself* – its biases and character; politics and the 'isms' it consciously and unconsciously supports

- *The results* – the effect and outcome of your inquiry; its relevance to others in the field, to other professionals and professions; the necessity for further study and/or investigation

- *The overall critical analysis of the inquiry* – with hindsight the strengths and weaknesses you perceive in your research design; what needs to be improved if and when there is a next time; what you would do differently if starting out fresh again.

The supervisor-supervisee relationship is explored in more detail in the next section.

Reflections

In terms of the above unconscious processes, do they appear to proliferate in your workplace and the groups you are researching?

(December) I'm more than ever aware of the resistance in my workplace and within the research group to contemplate 'change' in real terms; in the academic climate I function within there appears to be a tendency to 'rationalise' and ruminate 'until the cows come home' rather than to take new action. I guess we are over-fixated on planning and ironing out all the problems before we risk involvement. Maybe I should write up this as 'contextual framing' in my study?

4.7 Perceptive and Methodological Bias – Illuminating your own Research Shadow

A surprising number of supervisees, facilitators, researchers and indeed counsellors, find it difficult to differentiate between 'interpretation' and 'observation', primarily because they have not developed sufficient sensitivity to separate out when they are seeing, hearing or feeling something. Taken to extremes, an individual may end up projecting out ideas and imaginative concepts upon the world, so that they don't perceive, so much as transmit, 'meaning'.

To explore the difference between describing and interpreting, and to illuminate perception style I have found it useful to refer the work of Mitroff and Kilmann (1978). Exploring how researchers approach and refine knowledge, Mitroff and Kilmann identified four styles of inquiry, which broadly correspond to Carl Jung's psychological types. In **Figure 3,** four styles are shown: structuring; interpreting; experiencing; relating. A researcher who combines thinking with intuition is deemed to be an *analytical scientist*; one who combines thinking and sensing a *conceptual theorist*; another interlinking feelings and intuition is suggested to be a *particular humanist*; a researcher who functions primarily via feelings and senses is taken to be a *conceptual humanist*. In essence, these positions are indicative of an individual's personal and unconscious bias, their perceptive style. To understand the rationale behind Mitroff and Kilmann's thesis we need to be privy to Jung's thinking. A Jungian perspective would suggest that people take information from the *external* or *internal* world via their senses or intuitions. *As sensory or intuitive engagement cannot occur simultaneously,* so the theory goes, *they have to tune into one or the other.* Those who take information in by the senses are seen as interested in details and specifics, to prefer 'realistic facts' and to pay attention to 'the present' and 'the practical' (Reason 1981). Those who take in intuitive data via their imagination are seen as more concerned with 'the whole' or the gestalt, and are suggested to be idealists, interested in hypotheses and 'what might be', which in turn tends to create 'novel, innovative viewpoints' (Reason 1981).

With regard to the decisions people make about the information they receive, that is to say how they attribute meaning to what they perceive, Jung suggests they either do this by accessing their thinking or their feeling. Individuals who prefer thinking are said to use reason to make sense of their information which is at core impersonal, formal and theoretical. Thinking, in one sense, is independent of human needs and concerns; it seeks 'the truth' and/or abstract generalisations (Reason 1981). Feelings, conversely, are intimate and integral. In research terms, the positions described lead to the following classifications:

Researchers who fall within the intuitive-feeling **(particular humanist)** domain seek to create a new artistic/expressive synthesis which expresses the human condition; story telling and expressive techniques such as psychodrama or art may be used here, to generate imaginative case studies.

Researchers who fall within the intuitive-thinking **(analytic scientist)** domain aim towards imaginative theory building through conceptual exploration; these are the theory builders who seek to integrate clarity with precision.

Researchers who fall within the sensing-thinking **(conceptual theorist)** domain tend towards analysis, the pursuit of new hypotheses, and see meaningful knowledge and action as synonymous with accuracy and reliability.

Researchers who fall within the sensing-feeling **(conceptual humanist)** domain tend to focus upon what is unique rather than general laws; in-depth study of a group or team through participant observation, facilitation or collaborative inquiry in order to create new social models may be employed here.

In the above schema we begin to appreciate some very different ways of *'doing'* and *'thinking about'* research. What may be of interest to you is not so much the stylistic category into which you fall, as the categories you fail to address. That is to say, your research blind spots and the part of the whole you inadvertently miss. As holistic researchers we need to access all of these perceptive and conceptual domains.

Reflections

As triggers to discussion with your research supervisor, you might wish to consider the question 'How might I begin to appreciate and recognise the prior learning-cum-personal bias that colours my vision?'

(December) I guess before asking others I could consider my past conditioning and personality. For instance, I think my family of origin, which was working class and very practical in orientation, has given me an impatience with 'theory for theory's sake' and a bias for direct practical action. Because I'm shy in nature (though many don't seem to recognise this) I tend to duck away from confronting issues directly. If I let these influence me as a researcher, I guess there is a danger my research will 'do a lot' but fail to anchor itself in the literature or compare itself with other studies. This seems like something else I need to alert my supervisor to.

In terms of **Figure 3** and its categorisation of:

Conceptual Humanist (sensing-feeling)

Analytical Scientist (intuitive-thinking)

Particular Humanist (intuitive-feeling)

Conceptual Theorist (sensing-thinking)

...consider in discussion with your supervisor or a co-researcher or knowing colleague the question 'Which style is furthest from your own researching stance?'

(December) I think I am primarily a sensing-feeling person and least comfortable in the intuitive-thinking domain; because of this, as a holistically inclined practitioner-researcher I may skim over analysis, become sloppy in my production of hypotheses and fail to test the same through more rigorous experimentation. I know from this I will need encouragement to be more precise and rigorous in clarifying my research design and its specific purposes.

Figure 3 **Relating Perception to Knowledge and Inquiry**

THINKING

Structuring:

(Relating thinking and intuition) Performing the role of an **analytic scientist** who searches for certainty and precision in order to clarify aims, purpose, and to test working hypotheses via controlled experimentation.

Interpreting:

(Relating thinking and sensing) Performing the role of a **conceptual theorist** who uses imaginative thinking to critique existing theory, refine hypotheses, create and build new models of reality.

INTUITION   SENSING

Experiencing:

(Relating feelings and intuition) Performing the role of a **particular humanist** who seeks knowledge through feelings, via focusing upon experience and in-depth case study and fieldwork.

Relating:

(Relating feelings and senses) Performing the role of a **conceptual humanist** who seeks to create new maps of experience from conceptual maps based on social engagement and dialogical inquiry.

FEELINGS

Paul Barber 1999a after Mitroff & Kilmann 1978

158

4.8 An Exercise in Self-Supervision – Monitoring the Efficiency of your Inquiry

Having now hopefully become more familiar with the rationale behind research supervision, I invite you to awaken your own internal supervisor through consideration of the following themes and questions, so you might enact regular quality research control and so refine and test the rigour of your research design.

Setting the contextual frame of inquiry:

(Your skills, experience, beliefs and values)

- What models or theories and values or beliefs inform your practice?
- Do you tend to collect more information from your senses (what you hear and see) or what you intuitively pick up from the environment?
- Do you listen more carefully to your reasoning or feelings for guidance and meaning?

Illuminating those your inquiry involves:

(Who they are, what they do, what purposes they serve, what they expect)

- Who does the inquiry involve and why were they selected?
- How do they evaluate themselves and how does your view differ to theirs?
- What did you possibly symbolise to the subjects involved (expert; consultant; counsellor; an agent of the management etc.)?

Identifying the nature of the problem:

(Perceptions of problems, needs, interests that drew the various players together)

- How did clients of the inquiry see the initial problem?
- How did you see the initial problem?
- How did others perceive the initial problem?

Locating your inquiry within the wider field:

(Private or public sector; present macroscopic and microscopic issues affecting the study)

- What wider influences or conditions currently affect events within the field?
- What local conditions or influences currently influence the field?
- Where does this study fit in relation to earlier studies and the wider literature?

159

Evaluating the current situation and its possible problems:

(The need to pilot, review, select various investigative and/or diagnostic tools)

- What further investigations are necessary to substantiate current working hypotheses?
- What did you expect to find, what did you really find and what were you most surprised to find?
- How might present influences degenerate into possible future problems?

Assessing the research field's relationship to its environment:

(The subject field's relationship to the environment, world view and reality orientation)

- What was the nature of the field's contact with its physical/sensory and social/cultural environment?
- What was the nature of the field's relationship to its emotional and symbolic environment?
- What was the nature of the field's relationship to and contact with its spiritual or higher purpose?

Exploring the nature of the facilitator/researcher-client relationship:

(How relationships formed, how the leadership style involved and how this changed through time)

- How did the way you were perceived on entry to the field, change over time?
- To which levels of relationship do you tend to attend: the contractual relationship (the stated purpose and task); the symbolic relationship (emotions and symbols); the authentic relationship (what is really and honestly happening)?
- Was your facilitative/relational style primarily authoritative (controlling), collaborative (democratic and peer based), laissez faire (autonomous)?

Illuminating the nature of your interventions:

(The actions taken to inquire into the issues identified)

- How did you plan your interventions and did they achieve what you set out to do?
- How did you record and evaluate the effect of your interventions?
- How many cycles of planning, acting, observing and reflecting were performed?

Reviewing the expressive nature of your inquiry:

(The effect and outcome of your work)

- In what way did you and your inquiry add value or make a difference to the field and the people involved, and how was this difference measured and accounted for?
- How focused were you upon raising and expressing emotions (your position on the cathartic and non-cathartic continuum)?
- How focused were you upon expressing authenticity and deeper aspects of your humanity (your position on the disclosing and non-disclosing continuum)?

Critiquing the study's developmental whole:

(With hindsight your research design's strengths and weaknesses and what needs to improve)

- What did you do well and not so well, and did you prove what you set out to prove?
- What social/political/professional values were supported by your work and did you say all you wanted to say?
- Were you sufficiently aware of the social stereotyping, deceptions, and lines of inquiry that were actively discouraged?

John Rowen (1981), a leading humanist whose work stimulated my thinking through the above categories, suggests that you periodically return to the questions below in order to spring clean the ethical base and relational health of the researcher-research relationship and to keep it facilitatively on track:

Efficiency *(my professional effectiveness):*

- How familiar am I with the field?
- What are my working hypotheses?

Authenticity *(knowledge of my true self):*

- Am I aware of my motives and bias?
- Am I open to my feelings and experience?

Alienation *(what it is I dismiss or miss):*

- Do those involved truly listen to me and each other?
- How trusting are we?

Politics *(how I handle power):*

- What social and relational pressures affect me?
- What political assumptions do I work to and support?

Patriarchy *(what I patronise in my work):*

- Do my conclusions/analysis make sexist or other limiting assumptions?
- What patterns of domination are played out in my work?

Dialectical *(how I keep everything in dialogue):*

- Am I aware of contradictions in my work?
- Is conflict encouraged and worked through?

Legitimacy *(what I deem appropriate and right):*

- What power do others have in my work?
- What problems are deemed inappropriate for address?

Relevancy *(the usefulness and added value I bring):*

- Is my work really of use to those it involves?
- What will this consultancy change?

Return to this chapter and its associated questions regularly to ensure the depth and validity of your facilitation and its investigative approach. Keep the above notions ever present when you are designing an inquiry or beginning to analyse your data. Awaken and listen to your own internal supervisor, and little will go amiss.

Having segmented and deconstructed the research field through an attention to supervision, in the following chapter we return to an appreciation of the whole, via an appraisal of field theory.

> Compared to what we ought to be, we are half awake.
>
> *William James quoted in Boldt 1993*

Reflections

In relationship to the headings below:

- The contextual frame of your inquiry (your skills, experience, beliefs and values)
- The nature of those your inquiry involves (who they are, what they do)
- The nature of the problem (perceptions of problems, needs and interests)
- The nature of the wider field (private or public sector; macroscopic/microscopic issues)

- The current situation and its possible problems (the need to pilot, review inquiry tools)
- The inquiry's relationship to its environment (the inquiry's relationship to the field)
- The nature of the facilitator/researcher-client relationship (how relationships formed and evolved)
- The nature of your interventions (whether facilitative or authoritative)
- The nature of the inquiry (its bias and character)
- The review of the inquiry (the effect and outcome of your work)
- A critical analysis of the inquiry (your research design's strengths and weaknesses)

…use the above categories of self-supervision to assess yourself and to open discussion with your supervisor as to how they might impact upon your research.

Rate your involvement with the qualities below in your study by ticking the headings provided:

	Actively Address	Very Aware	Aware	Unaware
Efficiency				
Authenticity				
Alienation				
Politics				
Patriarchy				
Dialectic				
Legitimacy				
Relevancy				

(December) I'm aware of how much more aware of the politics and relevancy of my research I have become since reading this text, and how I have begun to address authenticity, alienation and dialectical aspects of my research. I still though, tend to forget about the influence of patriarchy and legitimacy in my study. Still, no one's perfect.

EXTENDED CASE STUDY B

Community Inquiry as an Intervention for Organisational Change

Preparatory Trigger Points. While reading this case study you might pause to consider:

- How a culture of inquiry (see 4.1) was co-created and participants were encouraged to own and speak from the authority of their experience, to explore and engage in analysis of social events, to experiment and risk opening themselves to others, to respect confidentiality and take responsibility for their own actions;

- How values (1.4) of *holism, autonomy, experiential inquiry* and *democracy* were cultivated to foster the humanistic value-orientation of this study;

- How Robert Rapoport's Therapeutic Community principles of *permissiveness* (supporting tolerance and acceptance of others), *communalism* (furthering intimacy and communal sharing), *democratisation* (encouraging all members to share in the exercise of power and decision via face-to-face discussion), and *reality-confrontation* (presenting individuals with the consequences of their actions upon the community) were facilitatively seeded at the communal level (see 4.2);

- How resistance appeared to arise in the *orientation, identification, exploration* and *resolution* phases of the study (see 4.2), and how unconscious influences of *transference, counter-transference* and *resistance* (see 4.6) are seen to surface periodically throughout this study.

Preamble: This study illuminates the co-creation of a learning and inquiring community within a commercial setting. Field theory and collaborative inquiry flavour the approach described, and a general case study frames the whole. As to how this venture began, following a well received two day external workshop on group facilitation – during which I am told by a senior consultant that if I had been no good this group would have walked out in the first five minutes – held within a consultancy in central England, the company founder – its current Chairman – approaches me with a view to developing his organisation. He wants me because his most difficult, as well as his most efficient, managers found my workshop useful, and because he believes he has become too embedded in the organisation to be an effective developer of his staff. As I say I am interested in opening negotiations the following story unfolds.

Phase 1) *Orientation:* Into the Dragon's Lair – Organisational Resistance to Change

As most staff, including the major power holders, of the organisation in question had been recruited personally by the Chairman himself in the 1980s through so-called 'seminaries' (personal encounter workshops) which incorporated a potent mixture of group encounter and charismatic spirituality, my 'contractor' cum sponsor exercises enormous political power and charismatic control within company life. Because of this events progress rapidly.

As discussions progress a commercially cited MSc in Change (the flagship course of my unit) is suggested, but negotiations are far from plain sailing. Initially, the University sees the company's eagerness to get things under way as pushy and

164

naïve, and the company interprets the University's slow, over-careful response as faint-hearted and unenthusiastic. Due to the University's caution, the company (largely in retaliation) becomes nit-picking and legalistic with regard to contractual arrangements and guarantees. But this resistance is possibly symptomatic of another dynamic explored below.

Gestalt-informed consultants (Critchley and Casey 1989) see organisations as living fields which sometimes become stuck within a 'sensation-withdrawal cycle'. They suggest that all living things, organisations included, meet their needs by organically moving through the following developmental stages:

Sensation (sensory feedback from the self and environment); Awareness (alertness to feelings and needs); Mobilisation of energy (raising motivation for need fulfilment); Excitement (engagement of physiological energy); Action (behavioural enactment); Contact (meeting with an experience of satisfaction); Withdrawal (natural completion and rest).

Taking this model as our guide, the University's culture in general and the unit, to which the researcher was attached, in particular may be suggested to have become stuck between 'awareness' and the 'mobilisation of energy'. For example, some way into the negotiation process, though fully informed and aware, the University still appeared to lack the confidence to act. When teams/organisations are stuck at this point, there is much intellectual rumination but little action, for fear of unleashing powerful emotions which threaten intellectual controls. Projecting blame and holding onto hurts and angers is said to be the norm in these so called 'knowing-and-angry organisations' (Critchley & Casey 1989). Organisations representative of minority groups commonly exhibit these symptoms, and the author's unit, promoting such 'fringe activities' as experiential learning and humanism on a predominantly engineering and technological campus, fits neatly into this category.

Phase 2) *Identification:* Forming a Strategic Way Forward

From the outset, I was clear that I did not want to rush headlong into a new working environment at the cost of my employment by the University or my ongoing private practice. The venture was also too big for one person and necessitated multiple resources and focuses. Eventually, I suggest running a Masters in Change Agent Skills and Strategies in the said company's commercial setting. The benefits of this to the company are seen as multifaceted:

- Disruption to the working life of the organisation would be minimal
- The workplace could be used as a practice area
- Assignments around change facilitation would provide in-house consultancy
- Travel costs would be reduced
- Spin-offs to others in the company could be generated on site
- Academic status could be given to the company's work
- Professional and personal development would proceed side by side
- Reflection on current practice and future developments would be fostered.

From the University side the following gains were recognised:

- A ready-made cohort of fee-paying students has been identified
- A new academic-commercial partnership can be seeded
- The venture could be re-framed as a research exercise.

After a prolonged period of floating in limbo and mounting frustration with my senior managers, realising it is impossible to supply the securities being demanded, I force the pace by reframing the proposed off-site master's course as an experiment that would tackle problems as they arose. To the University culture the notion of experimentation is kosher and serves to sanctify the fledgling partnership. Within six months interviews are completed and a commercially based MSc is under way with a cross-section of twenty-four participants from the company's management and the shop floor.

Eventually, incentive payments come through, staff within the company are identified to administrate, and a doctorate student is employed to liaise between the two institutions. This reduces tutorial fears of over-commitment but brings another dynamic into play, a split between tutors who deal directly with organisation and those who do not. Interesting how the solution to one problem may create new levels and kinds of problems as a field's ecology is impacted. As for my contribution to unhygienic team relations, I am rather too keen to take the risk of proceeding and dealing with problems as they arise rather than employ the academic norm of waiting until certainty is assured. 'Holding the dream' and keeping this alive is my prime intention at this time when information is still fluid and a practical container is as yet to form. In hindsight, I believe I transferred in a sense of urgency from the company's exuberant culture and was acting from a mind-set informed by a commercial rather than academic timescale. Still, I keep the pressure up and within six months of the original contact the first commercially based MSc in Change is under way with twenty-four participants.

Phase 3) *Exploration:* Awakening Dragons – Fostering a Dialogical Approach to Learning

In the introductory three-day block, within a palatial commercial building where our cognitive agenda is to raise awareness to the nature of learning and our affective task is to bond as a peer-learning community, participants and tutors began to evolve a way of being together. At the start of each day we spend from thirty to ninety minutes – depending upon the nature of the emerging issues – seated in a community circle raising attention to current individual and community learning needs, while reflecting upon the dynamics we are co-creating together. This process surfaces emerging conflicts and frustrations, while providing opportunity for tutors to resolve the same through timely facilitation. Following our checking-in process we plan how we will address the academic content of the day, inclusive of mini-lectures, experiential experiments, self-directed activity and assignment preparation. At the close of the day participants reform the community group to debrief, share evaluations, celebrate their gains and to say their goodbyes; also within this first meeting a good deal of old scores and resentments surface. My notes of the time, recorded in field theory terms from questions surfaced by Parlett (1991) and grouped under subheadings of 'external impressions', 'my internal reactions' and 'possible future action', record:

a) How are people and events organised here?

External Impressions:

- Historically, a core group of people appear to have lived, loved, fallen in and out of love and been friends for what seems like forever in this community

- Some of the longer serving members of the community appear to take it on themselves – and be looked to by others – to police the community rules

- Community members, being familiar with 'other people's stuff', tend to ridicule or laugh at those who act characteristically and/or true to the company stereotype

- To be female in this organisation seems to confer consent to emotionally bully others

- Some seem to need to overstate their difference to avoid being swamped by the group.

My Internal Reactions:

- Shock at how punitive some women of this community are permitted to be, almost as if they have divine protection or a permit to abuse

- Surprise at the carefulness of the men.

Possible Future Action:

- Facilitate all-male and all-female groups in a fishbowl setting?

- Investigate further the male and female stereotypes this culture produces?

- Look at the role 'sex' plays as a competitive and/or controlling tool?

- Examine how male and female roles in the community keep each other trapped?

b) What influences of the present field explain current behaviour?

External Impressions:

- A highly competitive group with strong players for power and dominance

- Powerful members make long speeches rather than enter into dialogue with others

- Tendency to 'tell people how it is' rather than inquire

- Competition for attention and airtime.

My Internal Reactions:

- With so much being said it is not easy to be heard or to enter gently into the group.

Possible Future Action:

- Encourage attention and more sensitive listening and role model same?

- Facilitate exercise in deeper levels of listening with the heart as well as the ear?

c) What is unique about the present field?

External Impressions:

- A gifted group of individuals who are potential stars in their own right
- The organisation seems to genuinely value people and appears to offer opportunities for individuals to maximise their potential
- Senior management appears person-centred and caring
- People appear to want a 'quick fix' and actionable skills, rather than to mindfully and carefully acquire the same
- This is a 'people pleasing culture' (quote)
- Individuals openly share their personal and transpersonal beliefs
- Individuals can be very loving and caring of each other
- Some individuals are very committed to the organisation and some appear trapped within it.

My Internal Reactions:

- I find this group very easy to like.

Possible Future Action:

- Monitor and draw attention to the community's development?

d) What is in the process of becoming?

External Impressions:

- If the quieter members are permitted to stay quiet and the noisier ones noisy, the community will split into activators and those who hold hidden resentments and hurts?
- If things go on as they are, a 1960s encounter group could become the norm?

My Internal Reactions:

- I was aware of letting this run this time round to get at the emerging pattern, so as to see the organic form this group co-creates
- I was fascinated by how sophisticated and yet naïve the community could be.

Possible Future Action:

- Gently encourage the quieter ones to speak and noisier ones to hold back?
- Challenge each individual to break their usual group pattern?
- Let the pattern run until the community sorts itself out?
- Facilitate an event that illuminates the emerging pattern?
- Combine the above approaches?
- Go with the trend and run an encounter group?

e) What am I blind to or excluding at this time?

External Impressions:

- I sometimes came out more strongly than I intended when policing the ground rules of striving to be authentic, respecting others, or in focusing the group upon what was happening 'now'

- Conflict seemed to be held onto until near the end, when all manner of grievances arose as time was conveniently running out

- A tendency for senior community members to swing a little between depending on and rebelling against authoritative facilitation.

My Inner Reactions:

- Having an acute sense of impatience when – in a personal biased way – I felt that 'time', or 'my time' was being squandered

- I believe the undertone of my communication was 'life is too short for us to waste playing out the usual rescuer-victim-persecutory dramas you play out to get attention here'

- Held back my power to let others develop their life dramas.

Possible Future Action:

- When the group is stronger state the ground rules clearly that I am prepared to live or die for and invite challenge?

- Be less patient with repetitive deflective behaviour that appears to be getting nowhere?

- Challenge the resistances?

This record, in the interests of openness is circulated and discussed within the community. Its external impressions are subsequently verified as recognisable to others. Hopefully, from my description you can begin to appreciate the emotionally expressive nature of this company, with its 'tell it like it is' character and competitive 'I want to be a star' culture.

Interestingly, the above description, in terms of Critchley and Casey's (1989) organisational categorisation, fits that of the 'hysterical organisation' interrupted between sensation and awareness:

> Organisations stuck here are in sharp contrast to the suppressed organisation – instead of denying feelings, these organisations go overboard with their feelings and much of their time is taken up with experiencing and expressing sensation. Where they fail is in extracting any sort of sense from this welter of sensation – they have plenty of excitement but they do not know what it means for the organisation's health Many such organisations get stuck because by and large they enjoy the experience of sensation.
>
> *Critchley & Casey 1989*

Another feature essential for an understanding of the company is the emotional dependence individuals feel upon the Chairman who, having originally drawn the working community together, retains an immense personal following because of this earlier facilitative role. Indeed, Heelas (1987) in the1980s had compared the company in question to a cult, and even now, the Chairman takes very seriously indeed his obligation to provide individuals with unsolicited developmental experiences. But, as with all intimate relationships, a large degree of transference proliferates. Sometimes he becomes so trapped within his facilitative/parental role that he enacts with gusto a 'beneficent parent' one minute and a 'punitive parent' the next. So personally felt are the dynamics that neutrality is rarely in the equation. He is either loved or rejected – or loving and rejecting – by turns. No doubt this is as exhausting for him as it is for others, yet, on the plus side, this intense emotional climate is felt to be generative of a good deal of heightened contact and emotional learning.

In regard to the company's earlier history and cult-like nature, a participant describing a usual working day in his subsequent master's dissertation observes how every morning the workforce came together. To start the working day a Zilgeon gong, the large sort found in orchestras, is sounded by each person prior to their daily 'cleaning ritual':

> Some people just hit it, others make it reverberate and the sound just grows and grows like rolling thunder. We now begin the ritual of cleaning. For the next ten minutes we will silently clean our work area and any other part of the building we are allocated. Everyone has their own spray can of Pledge and a J cloth... The idea here is that we experience creating our own space... This cleaning is like all the showy effort you see in a theatre to prepare for the performance, which is not a bad analogy because during the day it is a show.
>
> *Pollecoffe 1998*

Following the cessation of cleaning, again sounded by the gong, a countdown to the working day is enacted:

> Over the years the countdowns have grown more elaborate. And the movements you make whilst singing grow more complex, as a step or facial expression is added. Although there are favourites and stalwarts like 'Match of the Day' or 'Hawaii Five O' (Book him Danno) they change by the day. Today is the 'Flintstones Countdown':
>
>> Phoners meet the phoners
>> They're a modern working family
>> When you're with the phoners
>> You'll go down in history.
>> Do Da Dada Da Dada Da
>> Da Da Da Da Dada Do
>> (Everyone does a twist, during this bit)
>> (...) Ten Nine, Eight, Seven, Six, Five, Four, Three, Two, One...
>
> *Pollecoffe 1998*

The above gives further support to the notion that this is a dramatic histrionic company. In this light, systemically, what the University offers in terms of emotional containment and reflectivity the company obviously needs, and what the company displays in terms of emotional expression and creativity – possibly the University needs even more? *But then what organisations 'need' and what they 'want' are rarely the same thing.*

What is missing to my mind in this exciting, often quoted as being 'sexy', climate is objective witnessing and critical reflection upon the processes involved – in short, supervision or shadow consultancy. The research-mindedness encouraged by the peer-learning community and the academic demands of the master's course can offer a very useful cultural counterbalance here.

Phase 3) *Exploration (continued):* Policing the Community Boundaries

After about two months, the course pattern becomes established and tutors and participants and academia and commerce become more accustomed to each other. Though the educational process for the most part ran smoothly, there were some interesting challenges over the following months. For example, the Chairman and founder who invited me into the organisation decides to sell the company and to leave. With the pending retirement of the Chairman-cum-founder imminent, an era is seen to be rapidly coming to an end. Having drawn the community together through developmental seminars, virtually fathering the current community in the process, the Chairman's leaving evokes a response within the company's community that is not unlike that of a trusted parent deserting his family. So many past and future dreams seemed to be woven around him.

The ensuing emotional distress on all sides is deep and long-lived. Individuals swing between adoring and rejecting, feeling grateful for the past and fearing the future – a feature which continues for a considerable period long after the patriarch has left.

The Chairman is a man of charisma and charm, amazing candour and a great inspirer of visions. After he leaves the organisation it feels – even for me – as if my patron and the MSc's learning community's champion has gone.

With the departure of the Chairman and the company's sale a phase of destabilisation now ensues. Intense effort and energy are now invested in a life-or-death drama as the company seeks to prove itself. Organisational pressures begin to threaten the timely return of course assignments to the degree that I feel compelled to circulate the following letter to participants:

> While I am accepting – and sympathetic to the fact – that commercial pressures and overseas postings make part-time study difficult, I interpret my role as Director of the external MSc as one where I am employed by you (my clients) and the conjoint partnership of the University and the commercial funding body to bring the MSc to a successful conclusion. ...I am holding you to your contract with yourself, your company and myself, to meet the requirements of the MSc programme. ...You may choose to feel alerted; supported; told off; patronised or cared for. Whatever reaction and whatever you feel is fine, just as long as we open further dialogue.

The above missive is received positively – bar one – and says masses about: anxieties myself and the tutor team entertain re commercial pressures swamping academic boundaries; our attempt to re-interpret and relate academic concerns commercially; the fine balance between policing deadlines and maintaining personal support; plus the demands of a course off-campus that feels at a great psychic as well as geographical distance from our academic campus.

Phase 4) *Resolution 1:* **A Collaborative Inquiry into the Effectiveness of the Consultancy**

At the end of the taught modules (April 1998) a weekend is organised for a collaborative inquiry where the programme might be evaluated; this inquiry is framed in the manner of action research (Lewin 1946) and is attentive to progression through several recurring cycles of:

- Clarifying and planning – raising awareness to the purposes and structuring of inquiry

- Engaging and observing – experientially engaging and observing the process of inquiry

- Integrating and debriefing – reflecting upon the information raised through inquiry.

In the following account, working largely to Therapeutic Community principles, participants themselves report on their course experience and how this influences their organisational and working life:

Participants note that the peer learning community has:

'Been challenging of working practices'; 'exerted a collective effect upon the organisation, by way of setting people free from their history'; 'There have also been many major life changes such as marriage; babies being born; changes of employment; movement out of the organisation – events that were less common previously'; 'Aware of my personal foibles and blind spots, of deepening my experience and ability to learn, and re-learning lessons I thought I had learnt – but hadn't'; 'For me a healing process; I have become softer, and questioning of what I'll do with the rest of my life'; 'Clearer as to what is mine and what are others' processes that affect me'; 'I've been energised by questioning unconscious assumptions I have woken to... Feel much more compassionate, wise and able to contribute and add to the commercial environment'; 'I don't need to be angry and bullying which I did to others as they did to me to avoid being controlled'; 'The experience of being me is quite different than two years ago... A lot of the froth has gone away'; 'Several lifetimes of learning have been crammed into what felt like half an hour; reawakening of the cosmic law that what you give is what you get – ten-fold... Presence and love, or pissed-off-ness!'

It is recognised that the course has acted as **a healing force/organisational family therapy:**

'Before I didn't feel qualified as a human being. So many years of negative feedback. I now value my humbleness and skill in working with people here.' 'People have aged ten years in terms of their mindfulness and gravitas; largely brought about by the humanism the tutors have injected. (...) Feel more whole as a human being'. 'I am now able to make change intentionally; learning to be responsible for the situation I've put myself in. (...) I'm more confident with my clients'. 'I've reinvented myself and my career on this course'. (...) 'The portrayal of appropriate boundaries by the tutors I found especially valuable'.

Regarding the **difference in boundaries between business and education it is noted that:**

'Boundaries in a business context are usually positive and non-negotiable. Educational ones were more humanistic and person-centred, and this may have given some people permission to break them.' 'There is also the difference between business being action-driven and academia being reflective. Developing an attitude to work and life that is inquiry-based was not easy with commercial pressures in your face'(...)'Trying to get away with it – fake it until you make it.' 'After all, we are good sales people who market things. Be, do, have – are all part of our culture.' 'Front, was a lot of our survival, and the articulation of needs was not strong here. The greater cause of work always came before people. We did not share needs for fear of looking stupid'.

Examining the **effects of the educational community upon the organisation, we observe:**

'Working with my clients is very different now, I'm drawing out their ability rather than imposing upon them; more empowering in nature. Also my models to gain clients and maintain my market are more collaborative in style. My doing and acting is now balanced by encouragement to reflect.' 'Gains re transferring inquiry with people to the workplace and enjoying people more'. 'Greater sensitivity in the organisation towards people and their needs'. 'Changes to the company have been in our completing and working through the old culture, which enabled us to put a full stop to our previous conflicts' (...) 'The amount of time spent dealing with difficult issues is now much shorter'. 'The initial impact of the MSc centred around the exclusiveness of those chosen for the course, and splits between the haves and have-nots... This group acted out a rebellion, pulling away from the organisational cocoon to form its own identity – which did not help. This said, the MSc kept us sane through a very organisationally traumatising time. The course helped to build up our new culture.' 'This group processed something for the organisation, and took this back again resolved in part. The old way had reached the end of the road and the MSc gave the company a new direction. Look how the company has doubled in size since the MSc began!' (...) 'Increased skills means increased charge-out rates to clients' (...) 'Greater holding and containment'. 'More emotional intelligence, re being informed by feelings rather than being taken by them and acting impulsively'. (...) 'Put us in front of clients and you will see your style from here coming through; the care as well as the expertise.'

Phase 4) *Resolution 2:* In Terms of Change – Was this Inquiry a Phoenix or a Death-Knell?

From the foregoing study it would appear substantial gains were made in developing individuals in areas of self and interpersonal awareness, in fostering motivation and an appreciation of team and organisational dynamics. The person-valuing culture of the community appears to have also supported individuals through the hiatus of a change of company ownership and done much to heal trauma of the past, while building individual resilience.

Reflecting upon the ability of the peer-learning community to facilitate organisational change, it is suggested there was transfer of learning from the course community to the organisation.

Regarding the feasibility of a learning community – within the framework of a master's – serving to promote personal and professional development, team building, quality supervision and organisational renewal, participant feedback attests some success in this regard.

As I write this paper some four years after the above events, all who participated in the programme have left the company. All bar one – who left in the first block – completed the taught component of the course to achieve a postgraduate diploma. Over four-fifths have gained the MSc, three have opted for the diploma and two have gone on forward to doctorate study – and this from a cohort who were primarily without a first degree and entered via a non-traditional and non-academic path.

After the chairman's departure the company doubled – then trebled in size. Over-expansion and a drive to replace 'the old' with 'the new' led to redundancies and most of our earlier course participants at this time chose to work freelance.

So, in company terms, was this experiment representative of a phoenix or a death knell? Evidence from ongoing conversations and an informal appreciative inquiry (Cooperrider & Srivasta 1987) conducted largely in a conference setting, suggests it challenged those personal and institutional patterns – remnants of the earlier cult culture – that kept people and the organisation stuck, and in so doing increased the options all round.

So what did I learn from the above experience?

First, I have come to realise the paradoxical nature of change, that it is better to raise awareness and to build in community support than to aim to change something or somebody directly.

Second, I appreciate the truth of Stapley's (1996) observation that change agents have responsibility for 'relating to the emotional and cognitive state' of a client system, and should see themselves as parent-like, temporarily sustaining a holding environment wherein clients can be facilitated beyond unhelpful methods of thinking and behaving, and supported while they deal with the anxiety and uncertainty that accompanies change. *As a supportive container, the peer-learning community performed its function excellently.*

Third, I have come to recognise that organisations make collective demands of the individual that infiltrate and subjugate them to a 'collective consciousness' which 'sucks them into the personality structure or dynamic field of the group', with a consequence that when the organisation is threatened, the individual becomes threatened. *From this perspective, a change agent romantically represents a Saint George figure, a slayer of dragons, who struggles to release the organisation's grip on the individual and his 'still small voice reflective wisdom'.* The peer-learning community was an asset here.

Finally, I now realise the importance of continually clarifying 'contractual' and 'idealised' levels of communication within the community, while maintaining and fostering a dialogue with the 'authentic level' and the core truths of all who were involved.

Boud and Walker (1998) have drawn attention to the need for reflection to be supported by the cultural, social and political context. The learning community described in this paper represents a vehicle well suited to this purpose. As to the form reflection takes within the peer community described in this paper, earlier inquiry into the same (Barber 1990b; 1996b) suggests that Gestalt influence stimulates holistic reflection, inclusive of phenomena associated with physical-sensory, social-cultural, emotional-transferential, imaginal-projective and intuitive-transpersonal levels of experience (see **Figure B1**).

Looking wider afield, alienation and depersonalisation have long been recognised to attend work (Merton 1968), organisational life (Herrick & Maccaby 1975) and modern living (Josephson & Josephson 1972). If we are to leave these behind as we enter the twenty-first century, we will need to educate people and organisations in a different way to how we do at present. The Gestalt-informed peer-learning community described here points to one such alternative, and a tried and tested 'different' way at that. Indeed, the research-minded culture of a Gestalt-informed community, in the author's experience, also provides a fitting medium for the study and facilitation of those emergent creative influences complexity and chaos theorists (Reason & Goodwin 1999) have sought to address, but all too often failed to contain and shape within organisational life.

> Contemporary society worships at the altar of functionalism. Concepts such as process, method, model and project have come to infiltrate our language and determine how we describe our relation to the world. The recovery of soul means the rediscovery of Otherness; this would awaken again the sense of mystery, possibility and compassion. Stated philosophically, being could find expression in doing.
>
> *O'Donohue 1997 p.179*

> To many people the workplace is unsatisfactory and permits neither growth nor creativity. More often than not, it is an anonymous place where function and image have control. Since work demands such labour and effort, it has always made the worker vulnerable.
>
> *O'Donohue 1997 p.171*

Some Post-reading Reflective Triggers:

- I wonder how effective this study was in supporting such underlying Gestalt principles as: a focus on what is here and now and cultivating personal responsibility (see **Figure 2**).

- I'm curious as to how the profile of my practitioner-researcher cum facilitative style would pan out if I were to analyse it in terms of my direction-non/direction etc. (see 4.3).

- I am caused to consider how the interplay of *repression, denial, identification, projection, rationalisation, displacement, regression* (see 4.6) might explain group behaviour within the study.

- In relation to Mitroff and Kilmann's (1978) four styles of research inquiry (see **Figure 3** – 4.7) I wonder which best represents the style suggested in this study.

- In terms of this study's ethical and relational health (Rowen 1981 – see 4.8) I wonder how it rates in terms of *efficiency, authenticity, alienation, politics, patriarchy, dialectical legitimacy and relevancy* etc.

Figure B1   Experiential Levels of Reflection

i) Reflecting upon Physical-Sensory Phenomena:

[Gathering and attending to sensory information – developing sensory intelligence]

Learning to observe and listen:- attending to the environment; focusing upon what is presented; identifying physical support systems; differentiating between thoughts and feelings and observations; developing awareness and sensitivity to our physiological needs.

ii) Reflecting upon Social-Cultural Phenomena:

[Relating and understanding the cultural context – developing social intelligence]

Learning about how we socially and intellectually structure and relate:- forming rules and roles; informing others; prescribing; reflecting in a critical way; defining the purpose and task; building a learning community; creating a safe environment; meeting relational needs.

iii) Reflecting upon Emotional-Transferential Phenomena:

[Expressing and directing emotional energy – developing emotional intelligence]

Learning about our emotional responses and patterns:- understanding and expressing feelings; releasing blockages of emotional energy; reviewing how our present relates to our past; raising awareness to family scripts; releasing ourselves from the presenting past.

iv) Reflecting upon Imaginal-Projective Phenomena:

[Exploring and integrating imagination with the self – developing self intelligence]

Learning about the hidden self:- identifying our sub-personalities; illuminating inner motives and ego defences; unpacking how imagination informs us; exploring our persona and ego needs; undoing projective identifications and control dramas; raising the shadow.

v) Reflecting upon Intuitive-Transpersonal Phenomena:

[Becoming and speculating upon potential beyond the self – developing intuitive intelligence]

Learning about how and where we belong:- valuing ourselves and others; becoming authentic and identifying core values; developing holistic vision; illuminating your life's purpose; awakening to wisdom above and beyond the self; relating ourselves to the cosmos.

Towards an
Integrated Whole

resolution

*Experience is determined by yourself -
not the circumstances of your life...*

Bellin in Hayward 1990

Chapter five

Towards a Holistic Model of Facilitative
Inquiry – Mapping a Multiple Reality

5 Towards a Holistic Model of Facilitative Inquiry – Mapping a Multiple Reality

We must surrender ourselves to chaos and experience its lessons if we are to harvest its fruits; without letting go of the known, throwing away our intellectual maps and by engagement with the unknown, chaos cannot be transformed into a new order.

Preamble

In this chapter earlier material of the text is integrated into a developmental model of facilitative inquiry. Inquiry cycles are further refined and 'research as learning' is considered. The role of 'action' and 'reflection' is also made explicit, along with the need to anchor a research study to its contextual frame of past, present and future influence. Developing field theory's concept of a laminated reality a little further, our phenomenological map is refined to illuminate physical/sensory, social/cultural, emotional/transferential, imaginal/projective and transpersonal/symbolic levels of influence. These levels are then examined with reference to the unique qualities each represents, plus the inquiry methods best suited to their exploration and representation. By the close of this chapter you will have to hand a series of models to enable you to design a holistic study and to shape and analyse the information you acquire. With research cycles, developmental relational phrases and experiential levels dovetailed together a model is provided for mapping and analysing multi-dimensions of reality.

5.1 Progressing in a Cyclic Way – Researching as Experiential Learning

Researching and learning cycles are not new. Every mindful act we make requires elements of intention and motivation, planning and strategic enactment, plus a spell of reflective integration or debrief, which when taken together describe a natural cyclic movement. Cycles of inquiry underpin action research, experiential learning and group facilitation. Indeed, counsellors and consultants, teachers and social workers, all progress through a developmental orientation-to-resolution relationship (see iv and 2.3) in which bio-energetic elements of the Gestalt contact-withdrawal cycle (described in Extended Case Study B) may be suggested to combine with psycho-social influences to effect 'social inquiry'.

Orientation:

Sensation – awakening to an emerging focus for investigation within the sensate world;

Identification:

Awareness – planning and raising awareness to possible strategies/directions of inquiry;

Mobilisation – drawing resources together and focusing energy for action;

Exploration:

Excitement – directing emotional energies/motivation towards an actual act of inquiry;

Action – focusing behaviour/awareness in order to engage practically within the field;

Contact – entering fully and robustly into the social field to engage with experience;

Resolution:

Withdrawal – moving beyond an experience to map and reflect upon what has been learnt.

The model in emergence here is refined, developed and put into action later in this text.

Multi-layered inquiry cycles such as this, enacted at microscopic and macroscopic levels, coexist simultaneously. Cycles exist within cycles; when one ends – another begins. The life of an inquiry cycle may be over in minutes or extend over an hour or a day. The inquiry cycles of a study may last months or years, while that of ourselves takes a lifetime to complete.

Inquiring cycles with phases of 'reflection', 'experience' and 'critical evaluation', though the bedrock of action research have long been recognised to permeate experiential learning (Kolb & Fry 1975; Fry & Kolb 1979; Reinhertz 1981). Indeed, Heron's (1981 and 1989) models of qualitative researching and learning, when combined, illustrate the marriage of *learning* to *inquiring* cycles very well.

In the collaborative inquiry cycle suggested below, created from a synthesis of two of John Heron's works (Heron 1981 and 1989), a learning cycle is seen to progress from *conceptual learning* through to experiential learning alongside a research cycle that travels from *propositional belief* through to *propositional knowledge* which, when combined, harness education and research together:

Stage 1 – **Conceptual learning**: a phase where group participants learn about and gradually gain familiarity with the concept of collaborative inquiry while they build up intellectual knowledge around a research theme. *(This is a time in inquiry when **propositional beliefs** are reviewed, participants share some initial working hypotheses, consider their respective roles, agree a focus, identify what to investigate or change, define their general and specific lines of inquiry and decide upon the assessment procedures and the research records they will keep.)*

Stage 2 – **Imaginal learning**: a phase where participants start to intuitively grasp the whole picture – the gestalt, begin to perceive the underlying rationale and to appreciate the prevailing pattern that holds the whole

181

together. *(Here **practical knowledge** is developed as participants – as co-researchers – map and record the processes that unfold, apply the methods they illuminated in Stage 1, test the hypotheses they have proposed and examine the results, before modifying their original hypotheses in light of the practical evidence they have acquired.)*

Stage 3 – **Practical learning**: participants learn the 'how' of research through active practical application. *(At this phase of an inquiry **experiential knowledge** is developed as participants become immersed in mutual encounter and experience. Here group participants put on hold their earlier judgements, bias and rigid perceptions, so as to learn from what is new and emerging; values and beliefs that stem from ideas and notions generated within the earlier stages are now reappraised in the light of more recent engagement and experience.)*

Stage 4 – **Experiential learning**: participants generate insight through encounter, and acquire deeper knowledge and resonance with what unfolds through the integration of their developing experiential skill. *(At this time propositional belief transforms into **propositional knowledge** as participants, after an appropriate time when Stages 2 and 3 have produced sufficient data, set about reviewing their findings. Here hypotheses are rejected, methods of inquiry evaluated and further themes for investigation considered. The research status of this stage is derived from the thoroughness of earlier stages, plus the number of times the above inquiry cycle has been applied.)*

Personally, in the role of organisational consultant, I have used the above cycle to advantage when performing collaborative inquiry with a view to improving a group's team performance or to improve its productivity, especially when the host culture is uncomfortable with a more fluid, unstructured phenomenological approach. I have also found this model a viable vehicle for conflict resolution.

So here we have a prime example of research – in the form of a facilitative inquiry – doubling as education and consultancy; a natural enough process for holistic inquiry which often demands multi-skills and multi-tasking in service of the multiple dimensions it seeks to account for and serve. In this context, being alert to the position of a group or team within their own naturally evolving learning and researching cycles, helps me as a practitioner-researcher to speculate and hypothesise where they might most productively journey to next. In this context, inquiry cycles provide structure and opportunity, while helping to map routes from confusion to clarity and from *problem identification* to *corporate resolution*. But beware: your cycles need to travel at sufficient depth to do justice to the complexity of what is experienced. With depth especially in mind, we will next consider the roles that *'action'* and *'reflection'* play in social inquiry.

182

Reflections

In terms of the Gestalt sensation-to-withdrawal cycle, where do you feel most comfortable working and where do you feel most challenged? Try to focus on which part of the cycle you are working in as you engage with others in your research and use the cycle to reflect on your practice.

(January) Re Gestalt's sensation-withdrawal cycle I am most comfortable with sensation, excitement, action, contact, withdrawal – less with mobilisation! I think I get blocked here quite a bit, as I find it hard to identify what I really want or to focus my energies towards a singular theme. It's as if my wheels spin at a great rate but I don't always move very far! I think I need help from my supervisor to prioritise my research aims.

In terms of Heron's model of collaborative inquiry, what is your preferred learning style? Again, use the different styles to help you reflect on your practice.

(January) In Heron's terms my preferred learning style is an 'imaginal' one, I enjoy reflection and considering the options – it's choosing I have a problem with! Conversely, the form of knowledge I most like to elicit, this is 'experiential'; especially when there are others involved. I suspect there is a link somewhere here with why I find it hard to mobilise myself.

5.2 Balancing Mindful Action with Critical Reflection – Integrating the Heart and Mind

Inquiry cycles, when put to best use, raise to mind the fine balance between 'action' – *doing and discriminating* – and 'contemplation' – *discriminating and critically reflecting*. They also maintain a dialogue between 'tasks' and 'processes' of research, the art and science of inquiry.

As a practitioner-researcher in the *'doing and experiencing phase'* I am often divergent and expressive, going with the flow and on the alert for new patterns and experiences. In the *'discriminating and critical reflection phase'* I tend towards convergent thinking, focus upon specific events and meanings and am altogether tighter as I seek to map the social territory we have earlier engaged and explored.

In **Figure 4** the relative positions of 'action' and 'contemplation' – the 'art' and 'science' of inquiry – are further illuminated; though action and contemplation may at first view appear separate and distinct, bear in mind that as with Yin and Yang, they represent differing phases of a singular evolutionary cycle flowing into itself.

Reflection upon my own practice as a practitioner-researcher suggests to me that the *'doing and experiencing'* phase, which I associate with artistic and expressive elements of the research process, is where I experience the whole field in a way reminiscent of the Gestalt process. In this state I allow and accept confusion, using this in a purposeful fashion to facilitate a loosening of the preconceptions I bring with me. Through this process I open my vision, renew my curiosity and awaken my creativity. This experiential phase of inquiry enacts a *'staying with what is'* and helps to prevent a flight into intellectualisation and/or premature conceptualisation. Simply, it keeps the pattern of my perception open.

In the *'discriminating and reflecting'*, a more scientific and critical phase, I reverse the above dynamic, stand back from immediacy of the field and personal experience to allow intellectual rigour to come into its own. Here I separate out parts of the field for critical analysis, speculate upon interconnections and contemplate the ways I might map or model what has been experienced. This reflective stage also includes the communication and publication of findings and the opening of a dialogue beyond the research field.

In relation to **Figure 4** and our earlier discussion of research styles (4.7), in the *doing and experiencing* phase when I ponder 'where to focus', I act as a ***particular humanist*** who works in a sensing and feeling way, and when I 'immerse myself experientially' I engage as ***conceptual humanist*** attuned to intuition and feeling. Conversely, in the *discriminating and reflecting phase* as I attempt to 'make sense' of my findings, this necessitates my becoming an ***analytical scientist*** who integrates sensation and thinking. When I consider the next step, the practicalities and 'the how of inquiry' I adopt the role of a ***conceptual theorist*** who works in a sensing-thinking mode. In this way, not only the research method but the researchers themselves enact an inquiry cycle. In the research field this cycle is externalised, while in the researcher, it is internal.

In terms of the practitioner-researcher relationship and collaborative inquiry, this pans out as follows:

*In the **orientation** and **identification** phases, energy is directed to building rapport, developing a workable relationship and culture of inquiry. In this phase, questions of: 'How are we going to work together?' and 'Where do we focus and how do we proceed?' come to the fore. The key tasks in this phase are ones of identifying resources, promoting research-mindedness and developing research skills, surfacing bias and motivation, gaining familiarity with the field, drawing ethical and political boundaries, raising to awareness initial hypotheses, agreeing roles, defining an initial focus, identifying upon what to focus and where to investigate, defining the line of inquiry and deciding upon the records that will be kept.*

Figure 4 Phases of Action and Contemplation in Education and Inquiry

ACTION *(Yang > Yin)*

CONTEMPLATION *(Yin > Yang)*

DOING and EXPERIENCING
(Attending to the field;
engaging with experience;
Yang flowing into Yin – art)

DISCRIMINATING and REFLECTING
(Attending to specifics; meditating
upon experience; Yin flowing into
Yang – science)

Behaviours Associated with each Stance:-

Participating and observing

Following the field's rhythmic flow

Experiencing the social dynamic

Expressing the self through action

Relating to the here and now

Viewing things as a whole

Objectively evaluating experience

Creating models from out of
experience

Rattle and shaking experiential
learning

Reflecting on the self as witness

Relating to past experience

Perceiving the segments and parts

Questions I Ask of Myself and Others:-

What is our experience now?

What emotions arise within us?

What influences us?

What relationships are we forming?

What interests us?

What are we doing now?

What sense do we make of events?

What theories support our
experience?

What insights remain?

What effect does our relationship
have?

What have we learnt?

What might we have done differently?

Qualities of Reality Addressed in each Position:-

Experiential

Feelings and senses

External and objective

Active and expressive

Meditative

Thoughts and intuitions

Internal and subjective

Reflective and contemplative

Paul Barber 2001b

185

In the **exploration phase**, energy is directed towards engaging practically with people and the cultural field. Participants now become increasingly immersed in the life of the inquiry and in mapping the processes that unfold. Main questions in this phase are ones of: 'What is happening and how does it feel?' and 'How might we best record our current reality?' The major tasks in this phase are ones of applying the strategies and methods illuminated in the previous phases, examining what results, recording feedback, modifying earlier working hypotheses and the research design in light of current experience and evidence, and evaluating current needs and demands. Here many mini orientation-identification-exploration-resolution cycles are enacted, as various interrelated themes and developmental patterns are followed, experimented with and recorded. Inquiry in this phase spirals ever outwards and demands focused facilitation.

In the **resolution phase**, energy is directed towards pulling together the mini-explorations of the previous phase so as to pool and to interpret data, to unpack the total experience and to illuminate learning. The main question in this phase is: 'So what have we learnt and how are we going to communicate it?' Socially and conceptually, participants work together to map and to critique their experiences, and to complete and debrief upon the inquiry as a whole.

The main tasks now are ones of review, reflecting upon the gains and costs, noting areas for improvement, forming new models and recommendations, feeding impressions outwards and publishing these beyond the study. Hopefully, with new knowledge in hand, earlier hypotheses can be rejected and further themes for investigation considered.

Reflections

How well do you balance action and contemplation? Consider how the questions in **Figure 4** and Heron's learning styles impact on your own practitioner research.

(January) I personally work best at an 'imaginal' and 'experiential' level, but am less experienced in facilitating imaginative reflection in others. Out of this process we (the research group) need to come up with integrating theories and propositions to help us move forward. To achieve this I need to find a way of building in regular periods for 'group contemplation' and discrimination, an activity to help us analyse or realise with greater clarity 'where we are now' and 'where we might journey to next'. But how do I do this?

Case Study

An Integrated Holistic Inquiry Cycle in Action

The account below is taken from a collaborative inquiry into community dynamics, two-thirds of the way through a six-month consultation. As the study was ongoing, the phases of orientation are seen to overlap. Only one mini-cycle is described:

1) The Orientation and Identification Phases:-

(Energetic stages: Sensation – awakening to an emerging focus within the sensate world; Awareness – raising awareness to the possible strategies/ directions of inquiry; Mobilisation – drawing resources together and focusing energy for action)

When I first met the group the interceding days seemed to fall away, but very soon, after an initial welcome, an emotional wall seemed to develop and I feel afresh the resistive feelings of old, and intuitively go into a highly watchful and alert facilitative mode. This group of some twenty people does not feel a safe place to be.

As is the agreed pattern, we spend from 10.30–13.00 within the community group, constructing an agenda for the remainder of the day. As is my style, I participate in negotiation and add to the sense-making that emerges, all the while raising the group's awareness to its earlier agreements, but leaving the direction to be decided by the group itself.

As this consultancy seeks to facilitate community decision making, it makes sense to leave this to them. After thirty minutes I comment upon what I have seen. I observe that we are three-quarters way through the programme, and that today we appear to be revisiting old behaviours and themes, such as confronting others re their commitment. I wonder aloud 'if those doing the confronting were asking the same question of themselves?' And, as nothing happens by accident, in so far as individual behaviour takes place within the context of the community field, suggest 'this might be a roundabout way of the group, reaffirming its emotional investment in the inquiry?'

C, a member who appears especially quiet this morning, suddenly launches into a presentation of how much she has gained from this group... 'it is excellent', she is 'learning a lot', but 'didn't speak unless she had something useful to say'. Her earlier quietness does not go unchallenged, and jibes focusing upon her earlier defensiveness now begin to come her way. Although she usually withdrew into shyness, today she argues, shares her feelings, and proceeds to interpret the group and to analyse her own behaviour for some thirty minutes. In earlier sessions her contributions had come in ten to fifteen second bursts. Other group members speak of their pleasure at hearing her voice; they laugh and joke and warmly welcome this, her 'new verbal self' to the group. It feels today, as if she has created her own rite-of-passage into the group.

A little later, C raises the idea of videoing the community at work. As the group seems energetically stirred by this suggestion, I offer to bring a video

187

camera in after the coffee break. 'But are there other agendas around to explore?' I inquire. As these do not materialise, I ask the group 'why do you want to video our sessions? What might we gain?' One member says that as quality feedback has helped him more than anything in this programme, he firmly believes video will enhance this process. Eventually we focus upon exploring non-verbal behaviours, perhaps 'by videoing a session, playing this back, freezing a frame and interpreting what is on the screen, prior to checking this out with those who were actually portrayed?' As we exit for coffee there appears to be an excited buzz in the air.

2) The Exploration Phase:-

(Energetic stages: Excitement – directing emotional energies/motivation towards action; Action – focusing behaviour/awareness upon practical engagement; Contact – entering fully and robustly into the social experience)

Following coffee I wheel the video and a TV monitor into the room. 'How do you feel about this new group member?' I ask. 'Bit scared now, don't know what it might pick up' one member replies. 'So it might be useful to consider how different we are when being videoed on camera, to when we are off it' I suggest. 'With a new member, even a mechanical one, the group changes'.

I raise to awareness the effect of the video upon ourselves and the group's emotional field. 'Will we be so busy performing and spectatoring ourselves, that we will become stilted actors rather than spontaneous interactors?' A member notes that she would like to explore how others perceive her, another adds 'I'd like to explore my ability to read non-verbal signals. I haven't seen myself on video before – and I'm curious to how I come across.'

The theme that arose prior to coffee returns, as a member states he would like to try his hand at interpreting non-verbal behaviour, prior to checking out, with others, what they are really thinking and feeling. Eventually decide to video an open community group, where an agenda will be allowed to emerge of its own accord. 'Maybe then we will be better able to see our blind spots and more subtle influences to the group dynamic?'. O opts to man the camera. 'So you're formally opting for the observer role' someone notes. O laughs, and admits to feeling most comfortable in the witnessing role, the role he often occupies within the group; besides doing this openly, rather than covertly, feels very new for him.

We begin the community meeting with a few minutes of anxious silence, as people wait for something to happen. Someone notes that B has been unusually withdrawn from the community today. He has reaped a good deal of confrontation in earlier sessions, re his quietness. The group appears to want to goad him into action.

Initially, B is superficial and light, hard to engage, and is challenged by one of the community as being 'gamey' and 'avoidant' in his responses. All questions and approaches he is now actively avoiding, twisting them back as the inquirer's, rather than his, issue. I state my discomfort at what appears to me to be scapegoating. I ask B how he feels. 'Fine' he says.

188

One of the group says that he 'feels played with and discounted' by B. I open the issue out a little more by asking 'So what are we doing now in our relationship with B? And what do we really want from him?' 'I feel rejected' says one. 'I don't trust him' says another.

The group appears to sense an angry core beneath B's passive exterior. 'But is the group projecting its own fear and lack of trust on B, rather than owning this itself?' I ask.

B is further challenged about his 'true feelings'.

At first he refuses to acknowledge there is an issue. He 'doesn't understand why the group is giving him such a hard time', and 'why can't he stay as he is?' I share an observation, namely, that there 'seems to be a mismatch between his smiling cool exterior, and what I am experiencing as a charged emotional field around him', which I 'rightly or wrongly' can easily interpret as hostility. 'Could this be why the group is pursuing him so much?' He says he doesn't know. He now becomes argumentative. I raise my own energy in return. He now begins to jump from one intellectual point to another, all the time blocking, twisting and turning issues back as before. I ask if he would mind if I replay his responses to me, back to him. 'OK' he consents.

I tease, taunt, twist things back on him in the manner he demonstrated with me. I challenge him to really say what is going on. Fierce eye contact comes my way. I ask B what he wants? He says he doesn't want to please me. I soften my approach, and ask if he is really pleasing himself? He looks sad. I report gently, what I perceive as having happened so far, namely resistance, a mismatch between what was said and his bodily response. I observe what I emotionally experience as a swing in his attitude, between what feels to be 'a persecutor and victim stance'. I wonder aloud if others have a similar perception? Other members confirm similar responses to my own.

B admits shyly that, since our last session, he has felt angry with me, and the group in general. Consciously, he is at a loss to explain this. He just feels like withdrawing for a while, but he doesn't know how to ask for this. I say it's fine for him to withdraw, 'as long as the community knows what's going on'. He laughs, 'it all seems so easy when I ask for what I need'.

A friend of B who accompanies him on the train joins in the laughter, and asks him if its OK to share their morning conversation? B says yes. It transpires B 'promised he wouldn't say anything in the group today'. 'Well, you've really blown that one' I say. We laugh and agree to break for lunch. Before we adjourn, participants raise a desire to analyse my facilitation, via video – post lunch.

3) The Resolution Phase:-

(Energetic stage: Withdrawal – moving beyond experience to map and reflect on what has been learnt)

Following lunch we review the video. Analysis of my facilitation is still to the fore. As the video is screened participants freeze certain frames and question me accordingly. I am asked why I mirrored back B's communication to me. I

189

note that I didn't feel seen or heard by him, and felt as if wrapped in an imagined world not of my own making. As it didn't feel appropriate at the time to say this, I chose a more contactful method. I was also hopeful, that in giving more information to B, in the shape of my mirroring his responses, his 'don't know' response might change. Though I had chosen to go with the field and its energies, I share – in hindsight – that subconsciously I might have acted into being set up by the group to sort B out, on their behalf. A sort of counter transference reaction? Though I was unaware of the camera at the time, I concede that an unconscious degree of 'performance' may have crept into my facilitation.

Symbolically, I am aware of another important variable that might also be at play in the above dynamic, namely, B is black and I am white. I verbalise this awareness. This theme, though uncomfortable, is further examined. Other black members of the group admit to having felt uncomfortable when I was challenging B. They felt split between supporting me intellectually and B emotionally. B notes that his annoyance with me could well have been fuelled by his negative earlier experience of 'white teachers back home'. My moving from challenge to gentle attentiveness, symbolised for him, my de-role from a persecutory figure to a more nurturing one. My tone of voice was seen by B as especially helpful here. Up until this stage, racial difference had not been openly addressed in this group, perhaps this inadvertently created tension and generated a need for this to burst forth in the disguised form it did? Some thirty minutes are taken in discussion of the community's blindness to racial difference. With regard to our next cycle of inquiry, we decide this will be focused upon racial difference and experience.

As the session draws to a close, we debrief from the day, by each sharing 'what we have most liked' and 'least liked' about today, and how we 'might change the quality of our contribution next time.'

Barber 1986

Inquiry cycles, when shared and made known to a researching community, provide an investigative focus. When focus is lost, even if this focus is merely one of attending to what is arising now, loss of research integration and purpose is not far behind.

A practitioner-researcher who is facilitating collaborative inquiry needs to differentiate between what is obvious and what a group keeps tacit, unknown, disowned and unrecognised, with a view to integrating these into conscious awareness. The facilitative inquiry performed by a holistic practitioner-researcher, in this regard, not only enacts inquiry but is directed towards re-educating and developing people through the mending of splits in awareness and function. We are also reminded that if emotive and shadowy themes are let run and infuse the undertone of a group, they eventually break out – as seen in the disguised form of the above study where racial tensions had remained latent and covert. From this perspective, a group's relational hygiene, plus the relational health of a holistic researcher's role necessitates that we attend to conflict wherever and in whatever form it arises. But as we are blind to so many of our motives, this is far easier said than done. Again, a case emerges for quality supervision and shadow consultancy of all professionals and practitioner-researchers who conduct qualitative inquiry. Counsellors have long had quality supervision which addresses emotions and the unconscious, but few non-therapeutic facilitators receive such shadow consultancy. This needs to change.

Reflections

What are your reflections on reading the above case study? Consider the usefulness of the above four stages to orient yourself in your own practitioner research work, and the feasibility of writing up your reflections in the ways suggested above.

(January) I'm aware of my need for a structure to begin, develop and end individual group inquiry sessions, and this model represents a useful device. I'm also beginning to appreciate the energetic patterns of engagement symbolised by the Gestalt cycle which is suggested to permeate and underpin the inquiring relationship, but don't know how to use it yet.

I'm now acutely aware of how a lack of attention at the beginning may slow down movement later. For instance, I suspect I leapt into the identification phase and 'the task' of inquiry far too quickly, before allowing a sufficient period of orientation and 'team-building', which I paid for later when trust and confidentiality became live issues and we had to put inquiry on hold while we paused to renegotiate ground rules and group procedures. If I'd have paid more attention to group development within the orientation phase and to 'contracting' in the identification phase I believe I'd be further along in my research by now.

5.3 Positioning a Researcher in the Middle Ground – Embodying a Holistic Mind-set

This work has argued that social inquiry while alert to external forces and conditions, needs to also account for the inner experience of life, where intuition and symbolic meanings are given form; for it is suggested that *fantasy and feelings* are as strong – if not stronger – determinants of behaviour than what is *seen, heard, and intellectually planned*. Simply, it is proposed that to capture the complexity of individuals and groups, facilitators and researchers should, like Gestaltists: be aware of the whole *(holistic)* field; appreciate what happens when it happens *(quantity)* and how it happens *(quality)*; incorporate perceptions *(sensory data)* and visions *(imaginative data)*; engage with the social field they work within in a vibrant authentic *(humanistic)* way; switch between scales of person and personal detail *(what is specifically in focus)* and the community and its context *(the field)*.

To do justice to the human condition and social interaction, it is has been further proposed in this work that facilitative inquiry is best served by an approach to research which appreciates and keeps in dialogue: *culture and relationship building; collaborative inquiry; intellectual, sensory, emotional and imaginal data collection; phenomenological exploration; personal development and learning; experience and theorisation; field and group dynamics; inner and outer world experience; cycles of inquiry; the known and the unknown.*

Engaging experientially and reporting holistically at first hand the raw experiences of life, eventually leads a practitioner-facilitator into territory where continua of:

- Past and Future
- Feelings and Thoughts
- Abstracts and Particularities
- Senses and Intuitions
- Action and Observation

…must all be considered.

Conversely, remaining in one or other of the polar positions illuminated above, such as concentrating to the exclusion of other dimensions solely on *'the past'* (historical records) or *'the future'* (missions and strategies), is not productive of good research practice. Polarisation does not generate sound vision. It is rather upon the growing edge between known extremes – in what Gestalt refers to as 'the middle ground' – that a true creative synthesis occurs. In **Figure 5**, the 'fertile middle ground' of inquiry is suggested to exist at a point of balance where synthesis and integration can occur of the past-future; feelings-thoughts; acting-observing; abstractions-particulars; sensing-intuition. From this perspective, 'attuning to the present'; 'acknowledging confusion'; 'witnessing self'; 'being at one with experience' and 'creating new vision' are seen to create a balanced integration of influence. This, the *'at balance'* position of the middle ground, somewhat like a tennis player in mid-court, represents the point of readiness a

192

Figure 5 Dimensions of Holistic/Gestalt Inquiry

Qualitative concerns   *<The Fertile Middle Ground>*   *Quantitative concerns*

THE FUTURE

(Speculating upon what is becoming and an inquiry's as yet unrealised and latent effects and results)

ATTUNING TO THE PRESENT

(Noticing how the field is currently unfolding, maintaining the ethics and agreed rules of inquiry)

THE PAST

(Charting a theme or the study's ancestry and earlier chronological development, its roots and historical origins)

FEELINGS

(Being impacted and moved by the energy of emotional drives and meanings that arise from intimate engagement)

ACKNOWLEDGING CONFUSION

(Accepting confusion while remaining alert to the unknown, being led by influences here and now)

THOUGHTS

(Reflecting on experience, making sense of what has occurred, forming models and maps to communicate and to represent past events)

ACTING

(Playing the role of group leader in order to guide members/co-researchers through their inquiry cycles and research tasks)

WITNESSING SELF

(Acknowledging and counterbalancing influences of your self, your bias and perception style, theoretical and structural needs upon and within inquiry)

OBSERVING

(Watching the drama of a study unfold and recording events in the manner of a participating non-involved observer)

ABSTRACTIONS

(Looking beyond the concrete to catch tacit and symbolic/imaginal meanings and effects)

BEING AT ONE WITH EXPERIENCE

(Engaging wholeheartedly with events and dynamics within the research field)

PARTICULARS

(Focusing upon details and attending to what is actually happening, when it happens and how often)

INTUITION

(Attuning to the hunches, imaginative and symbolic meanings that arise)

CREATING NEW VISION

(Synthesising sensory data and evidence with intuition so as to generate new connections)

SENSING

(Attending to the external world and what is seen and heard)

Adapted from Barber 2000

practitioner-researcher must retain if they are to preserve maximum movement and facilitative flexibility. The middle ground portrayed in **Figure 5,** a vantage point from whence to view and work holistically, is brought about through mindful balance, not merely through the research process but within the practitioner themselves.

Consider for a moment the more detailed terrain and territory of the above continua, and what balance such as this really implies in research terms:

(Past – Future)

Glancing forward and back orientates us to our potentialities and history; when our attention is stuck in the past or future we are powerless; our only real power is now, in the unfolding moment; we cannot step into the same community field or moment twice, for river-like they are always in flow.

(Feelings – Thoughts)

Trying to get your thoughts clear of feelings or your feelings free of thoughts is a wasteful occupation; we are holistic beings with fantasies, a physical body, wishes and desires; better as a practitioner-researcher you learn to live with complexity and let confusion and paradox be your guides rather than let them become your enemies.

(Acting – Observing)

Being an actor or observer puts you either at centre stage or in the audience; far better to stay mobile and able to engage with varying degrees of participation, whenever situations or events demand it.

(Abstractions – Particulars)

Having one's head in the clouds and full of abstractions or being detail-fixated are traps, better to ground yourself in experience and float in and out and rest between these positions.

(Senses – Intuition)

By synthesising sensory and intuitive information we generate new vision; when inquiry is imaginatively inspired the creative potential released is immense.

The above continua alert me afresh to the multiplicity of holistic research; they also serve as an appraisal of my facilitative position and so act as a self-referencing aid. They warn me that if I concentrate on one dimension and exclude others then the holistic quality of my inquiry will suffer and become unbalanced. For example, if I focus on abstractions while blinding myself to specifics, I may illuminate the wider-ranging field conditions but remain blind to individual experience and effects. Remember, holism attempts to include everything that percolates into awareness at any one time. In terms of facilitation, this means:

194

- Keeping the Past-Future dimension in mind – this reminds me to pay attention to the context and timeline of an inquiry's projected trajectory

- Reviewing the Feeling-Thought dimension – this alerts me to the need to allow and to facilitate expression, and to attend to the emotional and intellectual meaning participants ascribe to events

- Being aware of the Acting-Observing dimension – this alerts me to the need to lead and to provide structure, and when necessary to vacate the leadership role so that I may observe the leadership patterns of others

- Journeying along the Abstractions-Particulars dimension – this keeps me alert to macro and micro influences, and helps sustain a dialogue between the wider context plus the individuals involved

- Attending to the Senses-Intuition dimension – this raises awareness to how our inner and outer worlds interrelate, impact, inform and stimulate one another to generate knowledge and meaning.

When we place the aforementioned influences into a chronological frame, an interesting multi-layered orientation to reality results – see **Figure 6**. Note how *'reality as felt'* and *'reality as sensed'* stand nearest to the immediacy of what is currently happening *'now'*, and how *'reality as intellectually constructed'*, schooled via socialisation and tradition, stands closest to the *'past'*. By contrast, 'reality as imagined and intuited' looks to the *'future'*, imaginatively feeling the way ahead – for what we dream today informs our reality tomorrow. Hopefully this discussion will prevent you from repeating such classic errors in your facilitation and in your analysis and writing up as:

- Excluding the relationship of the Past-Future, causing your facilitation or account of the same to lose its contextual, chronological and developmental frame, so that in consequence it appears static, abstract, and without a sense of dynamic progression or over-guiding aim.

- Denying the interrelationship of Thoughts-Feelings, so that you isolate conceptual mapping from field experience, causing what results to feel unsupported and removed from what actually happened. If you shield the participants of your facilitation or the readers of your account from the emotional impact of an inquiry, they will fail to recognise or appreciate how your own experiential store of prior learning and knowledge tacitly informs your facilitation.

- Dismissing the Acting-Observing dimension causes you to lose sense of how you as a facilitator impacted the field. All that you inadvertently or intentionally did to influence the group tends to be missed, as well as those choices you made to pursue certain lines of inquiry or to drop others.

- Failing to perceive and account for the Abstractions-Particulars continuum causes you to fail to discriminate and describe macro and micro influences and effects. In consequence, participants upon the day – or readers of a written account later – will be unable to tell when you are standing back to interpret or attribute meaning, or immersed and attending to actual events.

- Paying little heed to the Sensing-Intuition dimension, causes practical evidence to merge with imaginative speculation; consequently, your facilitative rationale will appear confluent and ungrounded, and your creativity and imaginative leaps will be unrelated to their points of origin. This will give your practice and write up the appearance of being impractical and un-evidenced.

Figure 6 The Phenomenological Wave Within Holistic/Gestalt Inquiry

THE PAST
(Historical and remembered influences)

Reality as Intellectually and Socially Constructed
(What I think is happening now in the light of
earlier knowledge, experience and learning acquired
from the research field)

Reality as Felt
(My experience of emotional energies and
meanings that arise from within me)

NOW
(Unfolding influences of the moment)

Reality as Sensed
(What I see, hear and touch in the sensate and
physical world I exist and function within)

Reality as Imagined and Intuited
(Metaphors and intuitive imagery that
provide symbolic/spiritual meaning)

THE FUTURE
(Influences forming or yet to form)

Adapted from Barber 2000

Ideally, standing within the balanced position of the middle ground, a practitioner-researcher retains their 'sense of being' while relaxing into a state of alerted flexibility. So placed, they are better able to acknowledge everything within and before them. In this connected and balanced state a researcher contacts and contemplates their experience while the phenomenological wave – of **Figure 6** – washes over and through them as they stand firmly in the present. Here we glimpse the poetry of holistic Gestalt inquiry, the muse from whence its art flows.

> The experience of transition, a simple movement through time, easily eludes people as they cope with complex daily requirements. Yet since nothing stays still, except as we imagine it, we all live at the transition point between now and next. It is through this movement that people stay fresh and through it that the stories of our lives grow.
>
> *Polster 1987 p.67*

Reflections

Consider the middle ground of **Figure 5**:

- Attuning to the present (Staying in the here and now to maintain potential)
- Acknowledging confusion (Staying with confusion and being alert to its message)
- Witnessing self (Acknowledging the influences of self within and upon the field)
- Being at one with experience (Entering fully into experience of the field)
- Creating new vision (Synthesising senses and intuition to make new connections).

Where do your strengths and weaknesses as a practitioner-researcher seem to lie? Of which categories are you most forgetful or least attentive? And what needs to happen to enrich or to further develop your facilitative and researching style?

(February) 'Staying with confusion' still challenges me – but with a model to hand I'm getting much better at focusing upon what is unfolding and can hold back a little more on having to make sense and plan everything. I know now that 'confusion' is a process I have to journey through towards clarity, not something I must avoid at all costs, as was the case; consequently I am able to experiment more. I'm also becoming more aware of immediate influences and can 'witness myself' in action, but I'm still finding it difficult to 'create new visions' and connections and fall back too often on old and

trusted models, into which I try to force-fit my experiences. This said I'm more able to respond without having to rationalise everything I'm doing, so I think I'm beginning to portray a more natural sense of 'presence' and authenticity. I started out wanting to change my department but have ended up changed myself! I'll have to re-entitle my study 'research as a form of personal therapy' if things go on like this!

In the context of **Figure 6**:

1) Past (Historical influences)
2) Objective external influences (Reality as intellectually constructed and sensed)
3) Now (Unfolding influences of the moment)
4) Subjective internal Influences (Reality as felt and intuited)
5) Future (Influences yet to form).

Appraise yourself in terms of which of the above most influences your research vision and those involved in your research.

(February) I must admit the group inquiry is throwing up a lot of historical influences and little speculation upon the future. We seem to be stuck with 'reality as felt and intuited' and hurts and resentments of the past. I guess I need to encourage people to co-create new visions of what might be achieved in the future, or better still get them to verbalise what they most need right now to help them move forward.

5.4 Towards a Phenomenological Map of Reality – Opening to All and Everything

Although everything is constantly flowing in and out of awareness and is by nature transient, sometimes we must freeze our perceptions if we are to assimilate more deeply or to communicate them to others. With this in mind, I offer in **Figure 7** an experiential map of reality that first evolved through doctoral study (Barber 1990b), which was later refined through collaborative inquiry as a guide for group facilitation and organisational consulting (Barber 1992; 1994; 1999b). The levels outlined in **Figure 7** have been mentioned a number of times in previous chapters. Now, towards the close of this book I am returning to this model as a framework for mapping and embracing all that has gone before.

Treat this model as a container in which to pour your own awareness, or relate to it as you would a mirror – to help you check out areas otherwise hidden from a casual view. Remember, both structure and non-structure are impermanent, and like Yin and Yang transform one into the other.

198

Paradoxically, with a map before me, I notice that my busy intellect and its restless need for structure abate and, paradoxically, I am released through a conceptual framework to 'go with the flow'. Too much freedom can be alienating, too little stifling, but with the boundaries mapped I have safety and freedom within a form that contains me.

The model encapsulated in **Figure 7** illustrates insights I have gleaned from practice as a practitioner-researcher/facilitator in psychotherapy, consultancy and education. Each level is phenomenological, which is to say it represents *'what we perceive'* rather than *'what is'*. In regard to the realities presented, it is suggested that:

*'**sensory/physical reality'*** is located within the realms of the 'conscious'; that our attunement to *'**social/cultural reality'*** bridges 'conscious' and 'semi-conscious' realms of experience, and that *'**emotional/transferential reality'*** starts in the 'semi-conscious' but leads to the 'unconscious' realm. Conversely, *'**imaginative/projected reality'*** is positioned in the 'unconscious' alongside *'**intuitive/transpersonal** reality'*. This model may be used as a facilitative map, an orientator for data collection, or as a guide for phenomenological analysis.

Certain practitioner-researchers often concentrate their work in one or more of the above levels; they are not holistic. Impressionistically, I would suggest that *scientists* are often preoccupied with physical/sensory reality, *sociologists* with social/cultural reality, *therapists* with the emotional/transferential level, *artists* with imaginal-projective reality and *mystics* with transpersonal-intuitive reality. Paradoxically, when you limit your focus to one level in order to feel more in control, with the greater part of reality out of focus you are least in control and least aware. It is sobering to realise, that at any one time there is always more 'unknown' than 'known' in the cosmos around you.

Covert agendas often remain that way because they represent areas of personal or social discomfort. In holistic inquiry we recognise that interruptions to awareness need to be drawn to attention and explored, especially when a raising of personal awareness or systemic change is desired, as when facilitating inquiry in educational, team-building, and consulting for change and action research settings.

Emotionalised conflicts always run the risk of being cut off and denied, especially in formal settings where they threaten the status quo. But what is avoided at the beginning of a practitioner-researcher relationship, say within the orientation phase, can often become fair game later on in the exploration phase when trust has been established and greater risk may be tolerated. Get your timing right, handle covert or fearful events gently and respectfully, and they will eventually lose their steam.

Figure 7 Levels of Experiential Reality

CONSCIOUS

Sensory/Physical Reality as evidenced through our senses

Here we explore our experience through the route of our senses, what we see, hear and touch, as we engage with our own physiological being and meet our various biological needs. Here we need to differentiate between observations and interpretation.

(Research Activity: gathering data and attending to the sensory and physical environment)

Social/Cultural Reality as conventionally taught and intellectually constructed

Here we view experience as representative of the conventional social world and the norms culture enshrines, seek out leadership and purpose, structure time in task-driven ways, and recreate our more usual roles and cultural engagements.

(Research Activity: engaging and analysing the cultural context, values and norms)

SEMICONSCIOUS

Emotional/Transferential Reality as felt in reference to earlier experience

Here we recreate and enact earlier relational patterns, transfer prior learning and memories of the past to the present, and are thus re-stimulated into earlier emotional reactions and/or dramas as we act out victim, persecutor and/or rescuer behaviour scripts.

(Research Activity: charting motivational patterns and releasing emotional blocks)

UNCONSCIOUS

Imagined/Projective Reality as conjured up via projected images from the self

Here we experience with reference to the fantasies and the imagined reality we project out and see reflected back in the world, including the imaginary figures and archetypes we have internalised and unconsciously compare ourselves to and mould ourselves upon.

(Research Activity; exploring metaphor and the effects of unconscious bias and meaning)

Intuitive/Transpersonal Reality as intuitively and symbolically created

Here our experience is informed by the collective unconscious and a meeting with the unknown and unknowable, as glimpsed through our tacit connection with the divine, mystical, symbolic and other transpersonal phenomena over and beyond the self.

(Research Activity: exploring unknown potentialities and surfacing spiritual values)

Adapted from Barber 2001b

200

Groups and institutions, like the individuals who bring them to life, have conscious and unconscious components. *Again we are alerted: shun the group shadow, and at a later date it will seriously damage your inquiry and a group's developmental potential and health.*

Below, an illustration of some of the covert factors and influences which commonly attend group participation is provided, along with strategies a practitioner-researcher might employ to remedy, re-balance themselves and their groups, and so reorientate to the more productive balance of the middle ground.

Case Study

An Exploration of Covert Fears and the Steps we Might Take Towards Their Resolution

A few years back I conducted a study into the origin of 'fears' within group settings, plus the strategies available to resolve them (Barber 1994). Even with experienced practitioner-researchers and group facilitators, I found:

At the **physical-sensory level** fears were apt to arise of misperceiving evidence; being overwhelmed by stimuli and sensory data; drifting out of touch with environmental engagement. * As to the remedy, I found that attuning to intellect; forming conceptual maps; allowing intuition to inform and to give meaning to experience all helped counterbalance fears at the physical level.

At the **social-cultural level** fears were related to: offending others; being seen as different; receiving ridicule or rejection; being criticised or rejected. * As to a remedy, the following helped support people through these fears: attuning to sensory data; surfacing one's personal value; defining the ethical base; developing a more solid inner sense of being.

At the **emotional-transferential level** fears rooted in the past emerged concerning: becoming powerless and childlike; being punished; being unloved or overwhelmed by demands of intimacy. * As to a remedy for these fears: attuning to the here and now and to sensory experience, and exploring and experimenting in the present all appeared to help.

At the **imaginal-projective level** fears manifested of being made worse by exposure to others' emotional distress; of losing control; of hurting others. * As to a remedy for these reactions: attuning to sensory and environmental data; checking out your perceptions of others who were seen helped to build support.

At the **intuitive-transpersonal level** fears were seen to arise of being extinguished; going mad; meeting with a fearful unknown or the unknowable. * As to a remedy for these fears, people gained support from attuning to their theories and thoughts, developing relational supports and attending to their bodily sensations.

Simply, by extending vision and appreciation of the whole, fears were able to

> be counterbalanced by the generation of a wider platform of support. So in this light, what exactly are fears? Something we put in the gap between where we are now, and the future? In this context, focusing on a part rather than the whole, we haunt ourselves in the present by memories of the past and fantasies of the future.

So how might a practitioner-researcher/facilitator set about inquiring, gathering and making sense of information within the various levels outlined in **Figure 7**?

* *My awareness of* **'sensory reality'** *is best served by precise scientific observation of what I am seeing and hearing, by an event diary or video or tape recording, by case study and non-participant observation.*

* *My understanding of* **'taught and intellectually constructed reality'** *I find is enhanced through role and cultural analysis, history-taking, ethnographic study, participant observation or group interview, questionnaire, appreciative inquiry, action research and collaborative inquiry, in which individuals are encouraged to explore their beliefs and value systems.*

* *At the level of* **'reality as felt'** *I find behavioural analysis of emotional messages and taboos – as solicited from interview and questionnaire – useful; likewise structural analysis of the various egos at play (in transactional analysis fashion) and thematic analysis. Collaborative and heuristic inquiry which reviews a group's historical patterns and emotive memories of the past can also serve us well here.*

* *My appreciation of* **'projective reality'** *is enhanced by group interview and/or collaborative inquiry which focuses upon how individuals construct their reality, or which encourages them to share metaphors and stories relating to the arising theme. The sharing of myths, enacting of plays and reviews, or 'sculpting' – where several individuals, each in turn, arrange participants in clusters and positions they see as meaningful to them, prior to analysing the same – plus expressive art work where each member draws a badge or symbol for themselves and others who are present, can also capture this imaginative undertone.*

* *At the level of* **'reality as intuitively created'** *I find the sharing of free associations, dream analysis, guided visualisation and meditative approaches, plus the approach of heuristic and appreciative inquiry are my favoured tools for illuminating the inherent symbolism.*

Again, I need to emphasise a caution: for although in the above map specific qualities are allocated to specific levels, in practice they are far less clear than they appear on paper. In real life these influences overlap and flow together in a far more fluid way than is diagramatically suggested. Imagine these levels as over-lapping and inter-communicating hues of colour, consciousness as light and the unconscious as darkening shade and a more realistic metaphor arises.

Reflections

Which of the categories presented in **Figure 7** (reality as evidenced by our senses; reality as taught and intellectually constructed; reality as felt with reference to earlier experiences; reality as imagined via projections of the self; reality as intuitively created) do you consider most important for your own study and at which levels do you tend to concentrate your own facilitative attention and research vision?

(February) I'm aware of how I'm generally good at contacting my feelings and that I'm getting better at communicating them; I'm also proficient in recording sensory experience and appreciating 'reality as taught', but that my research vision is still blurred as to how to illuminate fantasy and 'reality as imagined'. I guess I need to speculate more, to encourage others to speculate and to possibly ask my co-researchers such questions as: 'If this group were a family – what would its children be like?' (in order to illuminate our culture) or 'What do you imagine the best and worst outcomes of this inquiry might be?' (to illuminate their fears). I'm beginning to realise how much a research study depends upon the awareness and 'presence' of the researcher and how much I have grown through this study.

5.5 Holistic Research in Action – Surfacing Tacit Knowledge and Covert Data

When you enter a group or community to collect information, you may at first find a world that is strangely familiar, especially if this is a field you often work within. On subsequent reflection, when you begin to revise your initial impression and enter more deeply into the inquiry process, you are likely to find it full of relationships and meanings that are alien to you. First impressions are often false impressions, especially when you are trying to calm your initial nervousness within a new setting. As noted earlier, at times such as this, when you are seeking to orientate and to establish yourself, a map becomes a valued and useful guide. Personally, as a practitioner-researcher, I find that the aforementioned experiential levels impact me in the following ways:

*The **'physical/sensory level'** is where I perceive myself as contacting and physiologically engaging the present – here I attend to what I see and hear and to what actually happens while listening and giving information, being present and engaging with subjects and the wider organisational field within which inquiry occurs, as I look out and explore:

- How the physical environment, space and organisational territory is organised
- The degree of energy and synergy individuals co-create and receive from one another
- How aware of sensory evidence, what they see and hear, people appear to be.

The **'social/cultural level'** is where I clarify tasks and build relationships – here I socially engage, strive to understand the research field's various rules and roles, form a research contract, define the research purpose and negotiate relevant strategies and interventions to achieve formally stated objectives, as I engage with the research field to inquire:

- How are people and events organised and managed here?
- What is the nature of the fluid cement that holds them together?
- Who are the formal and informal power holders and who maintains the rules?

* The **'emotional/transferential level'** is where I acknowledge feelings and manage emotional expression – here I raise energy, generate awareness to the historical and emotional patterns that drive both individuals and a group's inquiry, while endeavouring to unpack emotional and familial/organisational scripts present through a consideration of the:

- Established family patterns and power struggles people strive to re-enact
- Emotional dramas and roles individuals and the group have a tendency to act out
- Emotional re-stimulation that colours the current group dynamic.

* The **'projective/imaginal level'** is where I work to raise awareness to the hidden agenda and group unconscious – here resides the heart of a group's relational shadow, the heroic and mythical archetypes that drive us, personal bias and unconscious beliefs that fuel our individual, community and organisational blind spots. At this level I also perform my own shadow consultancy and supervision, asking such questions of myself and others as:

- What are we possibly blind to or excluding at this time?
- What fantasies or ego defences colour our vision and performance in this situation?
- Which part of ourselves is being expressed and who do we imagine our audience to be?

* The **'transpersonal/symbolic level'** is where valuing of the human condition and spiritual aspirations reside – here I invite people to reflect on their core values and meanings, encouraging them to creatively envision their own and their community's higher purpose. At this level my questioning has a tendency to become abstract and poetic:

- What is in the process of becoming?
- What might your soul have come here to learn from this situation?
- What images or visions arise for you at this time?

At the transpersonal level, mirroring, a process akin to active witnessing, provides an example of a non-invasive means of raising awareness and gathering data:

> When we mirror someone, we don't DO anything. We listen, we hear, but we don't DO. Mirroring that way creates a feedback loop that can facilitate awareness... Developing the capacity to mirror as not doing is extremely demanding. You must learn to forego all intention, including the intention to help. You have to trust a larger process.
>
> *Beaumont 1998 p.82*

Mirroring, like meditation, requires the cessation of sensory, social, emotional and imaginal activity. It requires a surrendering of the ego-driven self and an awakening to intuitive guidance and grace. *Meditating upon the person or group before you, suspending judgement while entering fully into experience, can sometimes catch the unexpected to evoke exploration of things transpersonal.*

Below, I offer an account of how the above model unfolded during a two-hour collaborative inquiry into 'stress in group settings' in a conference setting (Barber 1994). Hopefully, this more practical example will illuminate the effects of the aforementioned levels upon the researcher and within the research field.

Case Study

Accounting for the Influence of Experiential Levels in Group Inquiry

The following case study explores the propensity of a group to mirror personal and interpersonal processes at the physical-sensory, social-cultural, emotional-transferential, imaginal-projective and transpersonal-symbolic levels. Firstly I describe each level of influence, before sharing an example of this within the setting of a workshop within a conference setting.

The Group as a Mirror of the Senses

At this level of group territory I attend to the sensory data I am met with within a group. This includes: the number of participants; environmental features; the temperature of the room; the postures of participants; the level of verbal exchange; the dress code. Here I attend to the way I am physically supporting myself, reflect on my own breathing and posture, and position myself where I can view the whole community. I especially attend to this level when engaging with others and when assessing their ability: to be self-supporting; to handle environmental stimuli; to see and be seen; plus the quality of their person-to-person contact.

Engagement of this level in the workshop: Before the workshop began I acclimatised myself to the room, choosing a comfortable position from which to view the group. I noted the closeness of the room, the heat of midday, opened windows, and as the room filled and participants gathered, became aware of their physical discomfort and the resistance of some individuals to engage with their senses and to truly see and hear others.

Fleetingly, as the group formed, I thought I saw on people's faces expressions suggesting they were a little fearful of being overwhelmed by what might await them. I was also aware of the physical sensations I felt – bodily, I was alert without being over-stimulated and energised without undue physical discomfort or anxiety. When we experimented with forming small groups I was struck by the increased energy and verbal exchange, while in the large group we seemed to slow down and to find it difficult to speak and communicate. Some participants noted they felt more relaxed in the smaller group, others in the larger group. Some also observed that they felt more in tune with themselves in the large group, and more competitive for airtime in the smaller group.

By the close of the group communication seemed freer, attention and listening high, bodily energy and physical movement more free-flowing. I reasoned from this that contact with sensory reality was gradually enhanced during the group's lifespan.

The Group as a Mirror of Society

The social level I perceive as attached to – and stimulated by – the objective 'task' or social purpose of the group. Interestingly, it appears that at this level people re-enact the psychodynamics of socialisation – and the infant's commitment to the social world – all over again. At this level the facilitator is seen as a conventional social entity, that is to say, as representative of leadership and social authority.

Engagement of this level in the workshop: As the group formed there appeared to be a good deal of dependence on formal leadership, as I was seemingly expected to 'start things off' and to 'make things happen'. It was largely left to me, as 'leader', to 'form a conventional contract', and members expected that I would 'take responsibility for everything that happened or was about to happen'. They also seemed to anticipate that I would 'stay remote' and separate from themselves. Although a flip-chart and blackboard proclaimed the workshop aim, namely: 'To experientially inquire into stressors in groups and to open a dialogue between outer reality (sensory/intellectual constructs) and inner reality (emotional/imaginative perception)', this was generally ignored in favour of checking things out directly with me. At one stage I drew participants' attention to 'What was it like to wait for the workshop to begin?' And 'What

206

expectations do people have of this workshop?' Some said that they 'hoped for something different', some were '...irritated and hot with rushing from place to place in this conference', and 'wanted a time to relax and reflect'. Some participants also attempted to get into their more usual roles and to ignore all else.

As late members turned up there was concern about including them, especially as we were becoming short of chairs. At one point we decided to suspend the group to allow a search for chairs in nearby rooms. Inclusion and exclusion seemed to the fore at this stage, and I felt I was being checked out as to whether I was prepared to be as collaborative as I said I would be. There also appeared to be a search at this time for 'the rules'.

Periodically, following light-hearted comment a burst of what I took to be embarrassed laughter rippled around the room. One participant saw this as 'hysterical', another as a 'nervous release of energy'. As the group progressed there was more challenge and checking out of what was really happening, as we started to inquire into 'how it felt to be confronted by a large and loosely constructed group'. It seemed to help people settle when I gave permission 'to stay with uncertainty', or shared rationale such as 'if non-structure and uncertainty are what cause us stress, maybe staying with this might be productive?' Comfort was also afforded by my giving hand outs which brought a recognisable 'social' structure and purpose to our inquiry. By the end of the workshop dependence on this level seemed much reduced, with participants taking the initiative.

The Group as a Mirror of the Past

This level of the group is present for me whenever a participant's past is rekindled by current group events, or when earlier life scripts are re-stimulated. Participants at this level often view me in the stance of an earlier leader or authority from their past, sometimes assigning to me a parent-like role.

Where the level of the 'group as a mirror of society' solicits role play, the 'group as a mirror of the past' strikes a deeper layer more akin to psychodrama. The leadership style a facilitator adopts does much to influence a group's transferential quality. An empathic and nurturing facilitator is, I suggest, more likely to effect positive transference and to solicit a creative group. Conversely, a remote, critical facilitator invites negative parental transference and reaps destructive group processes.

Engagement of this level in the workshop: *This level was hard for me to verify in the short two-hour time span of the workshop. But one exercise, where we brought back a memory of childhood, gave this memory a title and examined how this related to where we are now, brought up for myself and my partner memories of infant school. This memory, we realised, represented the first large group of our lives, plus feelings of expectancy and uncertainty which related directly to where we were, now. The title I gave to this memory was 'how to be in a community'. Material of this level also intruded when I found myself thinking of an earlier conference where I had facilitated another open undirected group. As to the past patterns of others – I can only speculate, but I was intrigued by one participant who towards the end of the workshop told* *me: 'I came to scoff, yet find myself bowing my head before the altar'. I wondered about the negative experiences he had endured in earlier experiential groups before that day?*

I received feedback, post-workshop, from a participant who had some years previously worked with a former director of the Human Potential Research Group, the post I now held, and wondered if I was being compared or inviting memories of those times for her? By the close of the workshop this level seemed to exert less active an influence.

The Group as a Mirror of the Self

Because phenomena of this level lie at a deeper strata of group life than those of the previous levels, they are less affected by – or amenable to – intellectual rationalisation. A facilitator cannot hurry along insight here, but must wait for a group's readiness. At this level a consultant or facilitator functions as a screen upon which clients project imagined and fantasised meaning. In this way, a group leader may come to incarnate 'projective meanings' for the group, a fantasy figure given reality who in the 'projective eye' of a group is sometimes seen to represent a powerful figure released from imagination. How I as a facilitator tolerate and feedback projected idealisations such as this, I suggest, determines how well an individual or group can accept and work through their projections. I believe it is a truism that we perceive that which we can conceive.

Engagement of this level in the workshop: *I believe there were several incidents where participants projected qualities of their own, onto and into me. This was noticeable in language, especially where statements started with: 'You want us to...'; 'One always does...'; 'You are saying that because...'; 'People tend to...', where people spoke from a rich vein of assumption. Some astute members challenged others to check out their beliefs rather than thrust these out upon them. For example, after a participant described another as uncomfortable, yet seemed to more readily display this quality herself, she was challenged to own her own discomfort.*

At the beginning, when there appeared to be a good deal of emotional discomfort, the group seemed to projectively ascribe this to the physical environment; the lack of air in the room; the sun's heat. In terms of acting out projected energies, the drive at various times to open windows, to do something active and to make latecomers comfortable, all seemed to emanate from a store of internal and personalised dis-at-ease. It was also noted, by one participant, that the reticence of himself and others was understandable, for in this peer group of fellow professionals – researchers and therapists addressing the subject of stress – the sense of vulnerability was acute. I guessed from this that competence was being projected onto others, with the consequence that a residual trace of inadequacy remained within the self. By the end of the workshop imaginative projections appeared to have been checked out to the degree that factual and/or sensory data now balanced out projective reality.

The Group as a Mirror of the Universe

This level relates to what is largely subconscious and held within the 'collective unconscious' of the group. At this level thinking and feeling are secondary to spontaneous insight. When working at this level I have found intuitive, subtle,

208

non-directed interventions most fitting. The use of metaphor here reaches where cold reason and logic fail. When memories of the past and concerns of the ego begin to fade, a peaceful stillness can come upon us, wherein we meet with a deeper level of being where the unspoken is better perceived. Where at the ego generated imaginal-projective level the individual asks 'What's in it for me?' At the transpersonal-symbolic level an individual asks 'How can I add value and give of myself here?'

Engagement of this level in the workshop: *This level was lightly addressed when we shared fantasies relating to the symbolic animal the group brought to mind. Here symbols arose of 'a large slow lumbering animal like an elephant'; 'a large woolly fluffy sheep'; 'a turtle in a round hard shell'. A participant who drew attention to an imagined 'large hole' in the centre of the group – drew from me the image of water, which was in turn seen by some as 'still and clear', and others as 'choppy', but noticeably without sharks or other dangerous creatures in its depths. Reflections upon earlier groups, also illuminated, for some members, intuitive insights into what might be their life's purpose. There were also two periods of silence when participants seemed particularly attentive and self absorbed in a meditative fashion upon the quality of our being together. By the close of the workshop participants appeared more open to the unknown and unknowable, and more able to work at the level of metaphor.*

Barber 1994

In reviewing the above study, I feel that evidence generated from the transpersonal level of the group was heavily contaminated by the imaginal level, and that 'The Group as a Mirror of the Universe' was the least attended or pursued. Then again, this was an academic setting in a centre of learning, with psychologists and professional others – so what more could we really expect?

Practitioner-researchers in the guise of organisational consultants, change agents, counsellors and group facilitators upon various higher degree programmes have for many years tested and refined the above multi-layered model through their own facilitative and research practice. Many reported using it as an aid to enable them to stay open and receptive. As a support system it offers sufficient structure for a facilitator to stand in the experiential vortex, to endure chaos and to maintain a healthy boundary between self and others. In short, it prevents them from becoming overwhelmed by the vast array of data that bombards them and clamours for attention within group and organisational settings.

Over the years, I have observed how differing levels of reality tend to kick in and come to the forefront of awareness within various phases of a research study or consultancy. For instance, before I enter a new facilitative or research venture, in the pre-contact phase, I often notice that emotions and memories associated with similar events of my past crowd in. During this time I find that *'emotional/transferential'* and *'projective/imaginal'* energies well up within me. It is as if I am using my past as a reference, purging the

209

emotions and anxieties associated with a new challenge and creating imaginative scenarios to facilitate my entry into new territory. These projections, fuelled by an imagination that is working overtime, are thrown out to fill gaps of knowledge and experience. When I actually meet with the research field and the people concerned, I am aware of becoming more attuned to my senses and to *'sensory/physical'* influences; my pre-contact anxiety now recedes. When I actually engage with the job at hand and begin to facilitate inquiry, the *'socio-cultural'* world comes alive. In the resolution phase, when I begin to withdraw my emotional involvement and am more able to dis-identify with the field, I am more likely to witness events in an *'intuitive/transpersonal'* way. When I finally walk away to reflect upon and/or write up what has happened, creativity and insights flower, as imaginative and intuitive influences combine to stimulate a glimpse of a greater, more integrated whole.

In **Figure 8,** research perspectives *(methods)* and inquiry tools *(applications)* appropriate to exploration of the aforementioned experiential levels are described. Some methods are found at one level only while others reach through many. This is not to say all research methods are limited to where they are placed; they are merely cited where I personally find them preferable. You might well find otherwise and produce a very different picture.

In terms of the skill-mix holistic inquiry demands, at the physical-sensory level a practitioner-researcher cum facilitator of inquiry needs to gather information and to use *'focusing and interpretative skills'*. At the socio-cultural level they need to form a research contract and to use *'boundary and culture-setting skills'*. At the emotional-transferential level a facilitator needs to develop *'motivating and counselling skills'*. At the projective-imaginal level they need to work with shadow dynamics of the field and to hone their *'challenging and processing skills'*. And at the intuitive-transpersonal level, if he or she is to expand awareness, a practitioner-researcher will need to employ *'envisioning and valuing skills'*. Finally, most of all, they will need to cultivate curiosity and interest in people and to establish robust communication and an energetic contact with life.

> *How much longer will you go on letting your energy sleep?*
> *How much longer are you going to stay oblivious of the immensity of yourself?*
> *Don't lose time in conflict;*
> *lose no time in doubt – time can never be recovered*
> *and if you miss an opportunity*
> *it may take many lives before another comes your way again.*
> *Bhagwan Shree Rajneesh in Hayward 1990*

Figure 8 Experiential Levels of Learning and Researching

Researching and Learning at the Sensory/Physical Level [Gathering sensory data and attending to physical phenomenon] Learning to observe as a natural scientist:- attending to the environment; focusing on stimuli; identifying physical supports; differentiating between thoughts and feelings and observations; developing awareness/sensitivity to physiological needs and physical evidence.

Methods: Naturalistic inquiry; Grounded theory; Field theory; Holistic inquiry; Action research; Collaborative/Co-operative Inquiry. **Applications:** Participant and non-participant observation; field notes and journals; video and tape recording; sociograms.

Researching and Learning at the Social/Cultural Level [Relating and exploring the social and cultural frame] Learning about how we think and relate:- forming rules and roles; reflecting in a critical way; raising awareness to the purpose and task; building a learning community; creating a safe environment and fostering research-mindedness; exploring and meeting relational needs.

Methods: Ethnography; Case study; Action research; Collaborative/Co-operative inquiry; Postmodern approaches; Grounded theory; Field theory; Holistic inquiry. **Applications:** Participant observation; individual/group interviews; group inquiry; cultural analysis.

Researching and Learning at the Emotional/Transferential Level [Reflecting on past influences and exploring energy and motivation] Learning about our emotional responses and patterns:- understanding and expressing feelings; releasing blockages of emotional energy; raising awareness to behavioural patterns and family scripts; releasing ourselves from the presenting past.

Methods: Heuristic research; Phenomenological inquiry; Appreciative inquiry; Field theory; Holistic inquiry; Case study; Complexity theory. **Applications:** Participant observation; individual and group interviews; group inquiry; biographical review and history taking; re-enactment; psychodrama.

Researching and Learning at the Imaginal/Projective Level [Unpacking the shadow and exploring the effects of projection] Learning about personal bias and imagined meanings:- examining self; identifying our sub-personalities; illuminating inner motives and ego defences; unpacking how imagination informs facts; getting to know our persona and ego needs; undoing projective identifications and control dramas; raising the shadow and illuminating influences of the unconscious.

Methods: Heuristic research; Phenomenological inquiry; Appreciative inquiry; Field theory; Holistic and Collaborative inquiry; Chaos theory. **Applications:** Group inquiry; in-depth interview; guided fantasy; role-play; drawing or painting; reflective diary and journal recording; identifying with archetypes; dream analysis and dream sharing.

Researching and Learning at the Transpersonal/Symbolic Level [Attending to symbols and expressions of the soul] Learning about how and where we belong:- surfacing unrealised potential; valuing ourselves and others; becoming authentic; developing holistic vision; coming to know the real self; exploring your core self and values; illuminating your life's purpose; looking to the fertile void above and beyond the self.

Methods: Appreciative inquiry; Heuristic inquiry; Phenomenological inquiry; Field theory; Holistic and Collaborative inquiry; Chaos theory; and Complexity theory. **Applications:** Guided fantasy; meditation; therapeutic exploration; artistic expression and poetic description.

Paul Barber 2001b

211

Figure 8 provides us with a summary of which particular research methods might be used at the various levels of inquiring into experiential reality in a holistic way. Having now taken you through all of the previous phases, researcher qualities and mind-sets of inquiry we come back to the questions we asked right at the beginning: 'What is the purpose of your inquiry?' and 'What is the field/context your study will encompass?' as these dictate your methods.

Now look forward to how you might go about tightening up the design and framework for your inquiry, and map out in your reflective journal the possible methods you might employ or have already employed in each of the four developmental phases of your inquiry (orientation; identification; exploration; resolution).

(March) So I'm wondering how clearly I can delineate the orientation, identification, exploration and resolution phases of my inquiry to date, with a view to my future writing up of the inquiry's life. Certainly, all but the resolution phase – yet to come – are chronologically illuminated in my journal, plus cycles from orientation to resolution in each of my individual sessions, so I have the raw material if not an actual organising frame.

Looking back I'm aware of how during the orientation phase I spent much time building up a relationship with the department, locating possible sponsors and getting permission to approach students. I never expected that getting consent would take so long. I remember how informal interest groups also formed at this time. I have begun to apply a case study approach to build up further data here.

In the identification phase I recall sponsors were located, participants were identified for the inquiry group and trust in the inquiring community was deepened as the co-researchers and I surfaced our interests and commitment to working together, but that we failed to build in cultural ground rules or to firm up the social contract we would work to.

The exploration phase commenced as soon as we began to actively inquire together. This of course will be ongoing until we think sufficient data has been illuminated and our cycles of inquiry have happened often enough and delved at sufficient depth to give us confidence in our results. I guess I will have to pay greater attention to the thoroughness of my record, the depth and breadth of my inquiry cycles, and how earlier cycles inform later cycles and test out emerging hypotheses if I am to approach the write up of this research with confidence.

While encompassing an awareness of the five levels of inquiry (sensory/physical; socio/cultural; emotional/transferential; projective/imaginal; intuitive/transpersonal), contemplate how you might best address – or have to date addressed – these levels to get at the research data you need for your study. Good luck on your continuing journey.

(March) As for the various levels of sensory/physical, socio/cultural, emotional/transferential, imaginative/projective and intuitive/transpersonal, I've a good stock of sensory/physical and socio/cultural data readily to hand; have more recently inquired into the emotional/transferential patterns that shape our reality and have sufficient data to narrate the chronology of inquiry. So I can easily add within the above developmental phases an account of the methods and research tools I employed to surface our data to date.

Maybe I need to revisit my research journal and the influence of these levels then and now to glean their relative influence over time, and to identify what aspects of the field I have left out or over-attended to. Thank goodness I kept notes throughout the whole process!

I've recently started to raise imagined/projective influences within my inquiry group, which fielded such images as 'slaying dragons', 'deep sea fishing', 'working in a Victorian mill'; I wonder what these imply for the culture of work-based learning I'm trying to change!

I'm aware of how I haven't as yet considered the transpersonal/spiritual level, but I feel encouraged by **Figure 8** to go further into intuitive level and to facilitate a guided fantasy or an appreciative inquiry around 'what students expected to find before they came to work-based learning', 'what they found and the critical incidents that have informed them', 'what they would wish to change', 'what will become of them should things go on as they are', 'how they imagine their experience would have been without this inquiry group'.

I'm also aware of how rich and deep my own experience of work-based learning is, and have started to consider engaging a heuristic approach in order to liberate my own store of intuition and deeper experiential wisdom.

I guess I'm conscious data on my own voyage of self discovery!

EXTENDED CASE STUDY C

A Dialogical Approach to Organisational Consultancy – A Study of What Goes Wrong in Experiential Learning Climates when Cultural Supports are Diminished

Paul Barber, Jan Etienne, Paul Pivcevic and Brian Watts

Preparatory Triggers Points:

- While reading through this study contemplate again the feasibility of harnessing research to consultation and how awareness spirals outwards from propositional belief towards propositional knowledge through its ever expanding experiential engagement (see 5.1);

- Note that by staying with what was unfolding while retaining a robust dialogue with others the study accumulates an ever-richer description of the organisational field;

- Observe how the researchers gradually began to embody field energies and to 'feel' the organisational culture while retaining an objective stance;

- Consider the balance between 'action' and 'contemplation' and how a dialogical relationship with attuning to the present, acknowledging confusion, witnessing self, being at one with experience and creating new vision (5.3) was attempted throughout the study.

> *To save life it must be destroyed.*
> *When utterly destroyed,*
> *One dwells for the first time in peace.*
>
> *Zen poem*

Preamble: This account describes a research study contracted to perform critical incident analysis of an event that caused the suspension of a training programme in a public service organisation. It illuminates, via the voices of those involved, a clash between organisational and tutorial culture, and begins by reviewing an incident upon a personal development programme which occasioned the withdrawal of several participants, a battery of complaints and the placing of diversity training on hold pending an investigation by the consultation process described here. In its address this paper presents a multi-layered perspective, inclusive of the views of participants and trainers fielded from interview, empirical observations of the organisational field and analysis of the original incident that triggered concern. In this case study the researchers-cum-consultants were chosen because they were experienced facilitators, two of whom had direct and extensive experience of diversity training, and one because he was versed in Health and Safety. All were humanistic in their orientation and, except for one, had worked together before. In Gestalt fashion we were partial rather than impartial and owned our biases, namely a belief that individuals 'win' or they 'learn' – which means we were not into the business of allocating individual blame so much as illuminating the field conditions that influenced events; we also supported the notion – as humanistic facilitators – of the necessity of offering challenging educational experiences which take us beyond our comfort zone in the interests of personal growth, and believed that personal development of the individual, their attitudes social and relational sensitivity, cannot be separated from their professional skills. Within this paper the reports of interviewees are allowed to speak for themselves in

214

the manner of a case study. Because communication is seventy-five per cent non-verbal, and 'who we are' is as important as 'what we do', we suggest in this paper a way forward where personal development might proceed in a way which supports the person while honouring the continual learning culture of the organisation, and honouring the need for in-house work-based training to respect psychological health and emotional safety.

(Pre-contact)

Consultation as Ghost Busting – This Consultancy's Ancestry

This evaluation was initiated by an approach from the client organisation for the authors of this paper to risk-assess the provision of personal development within a programme of professional training, over which a spectre of fear and failure had recently begun to hover as the organisational shadow was drawn into light. Indeed, by the time we entered the organisation, diversity training was placed on hold following a training incident when several learners walked out amid a battery of formal complaints, and its continuation was dependent upon our findings.

From a Health and Safety and professional duty of care perspective the client organisation is to be commended for its rapid response, although at the individual human level this self-same action placed immense pressure upon the team of experiential facilitators who delivered the programme, who no doubt felt unsupported and singled out.

The organisation in question, which has a national remit, prides itself in delivering the very best of services and is at pains to enhance its public image. In this context, diversity training merits a very high profile, and contention and complaint in this area is felt most acutely.

When first asked to risk-assess diversity training by the client organisation, the Director of the consultancy employing our services envisaged the need for a wide-ranging team, with hands-on experience of designing and facilitating personal development and diversity, as well as evaluating diversity programmes. In this way, with the Director acting as midwife, our consulting family was born.

(Orientation)

Illuminating the Present – The Evolution and Expectations of Diversity Training in the Host Organisation

Though we had not worked together before this consultancy, we shared in a common professional stable informed by humanism and experiential learning as proffered by the Institute for the Development of Humanistic Psychology (IDHP). Upon our first meeting in a hotel close by Victoria Station, we found ourselves sufficiently comfortable within ourselves and our respective expertise so as not to compete for airtime or recognition, to the degree we bonded further by teasing and good humour. In this initial meeting we decided to collect data primarily by interview, in an emergent way guided by field conditions. Being humanists and working to humanistic principles (see **Figure C1**), in Gestalt fashion we favoured a dialogical approach to consultancy where we could work alongside the consulted, educate through dialogue and share our evidence and recommendations in a take it or leave it way. We also surfaced several fantasies as to what had happened within the organisation in question.

Figure C1 Humanism and Gestalt – Some Common Facilitative Principles

Holism suggests that a person's mental, physical, intellectual, emotional and spiritual qualities are integral to *'everything they do'* and *'all they are'*. Consequently, an individual is best approached as a whole mind-body-spiritual being rather than reduced to one or more of their parts. As every thing is multi-faceted and multi-influenced, we are cautioned that there are no easy answers or simple solutions to human problems.

* As a facilitator, holism encourages me to approach groups as organic entities, which, though composed of conscious and unconscious elements of the individuals within them, nevertheless express a life of their own. Attending to the whole I endeavour to foster a dialogue which illuminates the interplay of all that emerges, soma and soul.

Autonomy supports the notion that given the opportunity and resources, individuals are best placed to diagnose and resolve their own problems, for they know more about themselves than I or anyone else will ever do.

* As a facilitator alert to autonomy I watch and listen very carefully to what the group and its participants present. Guided by the group's own wisdom and energetic currents I follow what emerges, sharing my observations while inquiring into its dynamics.

Experiential inquiry, in service of personal development, suggests it is important to meet life in an open and inquiring way, to attend to the unique nature of our present relationships and to experiment with becoming the whole of ourselves.

* As a facilitator I encourage people to take nothing for granted, but rather to question everything. Through a focus upon 'what is unique' coupled with ongoing inquiry into our perceptions, beliefs and relationships with others, I seek to illuminate, through experiential group inquiry, insight born from experience.

Democracy supports the notion that we are interdependent rather than independent, and suggests that reason and negotiation should inform all we do. As we are social beings who share much in common, to further the common good democratic process should underpin all decision making and debate. Sharing and transparency rather than authoritative imposition and covert agendas, should therefore inform a group or a community's norms.

* As a facilitator I work to negotiate a client-centred menu where everyone may be involved in forming the 'how' and 'what' of what is on offer. Democracy also keeps me alert to the need for healthy 'I-Thou' relationships, and causes me to be watchful of communication that slides towards a reductionist 'I-It' stance to the self or others.

To start things off we arranged to conduct one-to-one and group interviews with a variety of trainers – some of whom were directly involved with the recent incident that sparked this consultancy plus those who had witnessed the event. As we expected cultural influences to come to light we contemplated management and personnel, departmental heads and others being drawn at some stage into the interview frame. From this sample we hoped to distinguish between custom-and-practice or cultural effects, and the unique influences that contributed to the diversity training incident that heralded our arrival. Informal observation and involvement with trainers and their department, we surmised, would also provide valuable insights into the feelings and experience of trainers and the wider training culture.

Between interviews we determined to collect papers pertaining to diversity training and its file of complaints; to review policy documentation and health and safety legislation; to compare our initial impressions with the emerging picture of events; to compare training here to that we had met elsewhere; to re-enter the field when necessary with newly formed working hypotheses; to meet together regularly in order to distil, evaluate and challenge our own evaluations. In this way we planned to immerse ourselves within the field, to examine our own biases and to reflect upon the 'how' as well as the 'what' of our consultancy processes. In this way, we interwove an emergent case study approach and a collaborative inquiry approach, which would feed our emerging ideas and hypotheses back to our interviewees and respondents for confirmation.

(Identification)

Life – What Happens When You've Planned for Everything Else

Gradually, as we pooled our respective interviews, a picture began to form. Diversity training had been embedded in a personal development programme originally introduced for the whole of the organisation, but became a core component in the syllabus for new recruits shortly after. Time pressures then reduced it from a week's course to a two-day block, and more lately as racial issues had begun to bite it had been extended to a three-day block. Diversity training was seemingly being used to purge racialism throughout the organisation, and was being delivered by a training team set up for this purpose.

Being a new organisational player and something of a 'spoilt infant' in the eyes of traditionalists, the experiential learning approach of the diversity training team was seen by many as 'too touchy-feely' for the service demands of recruits. Simply, it was counter-cultural. To complicate matters further, the diversity team were expected to work alongside their more traditional colleagues who provided basic training to new recruits. In this way the organisation had inadvertently brought two diverse cultures together to fight it out. When a training needs analysis identified a need for even more diversity training, class sizes had been increased and duration of the course had been increased to five days, thus placing ever more pressure on organisational resources, trainers and class dynamics alike. In this light, the critical incident that sparked off our consultancy appeared as a natural consequence of an ever-congested educational field creaking under the weight of racial tensions and cultural rehabilitation.

On our entry into the organisation four official complaints had been raised against the five-day personal development training, three as a result of one course. When two further complaints were raised by school trainers in other departments it was decided that the course would be 'risk-assessed' and so our consultancy began.

Documentation relating to diversity training was thorough and the course had been competently planned. For example, the aim of programme was clear and its learning objectives – some sixteen in number – were wide ranging (see **Table 1**). An exhaustive educational consultancy had identified an array of lesson plans, learning activities and evaluative tools for each day of the course which, if used as a facilitative guide, would suggest on paper a well-structured, focused, developmental and progressive learning experience.

For example:

> Day 1 – Lesson plans are suggested for: Orientation; Icebreaking; Course Context and Content; Personal Introductions; Classroom Contract; Johari's Window and Feedback; Demands of Disciplined Service – The Role of a Facilitator; Knowledge and Attitude Check (Part 1); Diversity Knowledge and Attitude Check; Personal Values.

In our consulting debriefing sessions we surfaced an awareness that although the integration of well-chosen objectives with excellently designed lesson plans and practical learning activities might intellectually suggest a clear and useful rationale, wherein trainer and participants alike may know 'what they are being invited to learn', 'how they might learn', and 'how they might evaluate their learning', nevertheless it was naïve to believe that emotions can be controlled by intellect. This said, the organisation had done its level best to provide a framework within which 'diversity' might be safely explored, but emotional content and personal and group attitudes are tricky things, and surfacing racial attitudes demands the facilitative ability to make chaos a friend, to be informed by the wisdom of insecurity, and to retain faith that the unfolding process will lead you somewhere fruitful and interesting in the end.

Simply, in experiential learning climates a facilitator needs to have the courage and experience to support others 'going through feelings' rather than to 'stepping around them', and has to 'experientially and intuitively know' the most appropriate level of 'challenge' versus 'support' if they are to effect a successful learning outcome. This is a high-level skill which demands a level of personal and relational sensitivity that goes beyond the remit of an average trainer. Trainers acting in this way, no matter how experienced, need ongoing 'shadow consultancy/supervision' – and even then there is no guarantee of success.

In the context of the host organisation and with its prevailing training culture the detailed lesson planning in evidence, no matter how excellent the quality, was insufficient to support experiential encounter in the hypersensitive area of diversity training.

Likewise, as facilitators ourselves, we realised that diversity training required a body of relational and group sensitivity that often lies beyond the scope of most trainer preparation, and much more time and attention needed to be invested in the preparation of the co-facilitator relationship than is usual in more conventional

Table 1 **The Aim and Learning Objectives of the Diversity Training Programme**

Aim:

'To develop the cognitive and affective understanding of diversity issues'.

Objectives:

- To understand the relationship between the context of the course and their role within the organisation
- To share personal information about each other and the facilitators
- To understand the role of feedback in assisting personal growth and developing personal awareness within diversity training
- To allow participants to understand their role within the organisation and as trainers
- To allow participants to establish their cognitive and affective position to diversity issues
- To understand how personal values may influence the behaviour of individuals, groups and organisations
- To understand the concept of culture and how it may influence the behaviour of individuals, groups and organisations
- To understand inter-group relations under conditions of equal and unequal power and the concept of a multi-cultural society
- To understand how individuals and groups may respond to being in a minority situation
- To understand the influence of culture on the communication process
- To understand the relationship between prejudice and discrimination and the factors that influence them
- To understand the concept of sexism and the effect it has on women, individually and organisationally
- To enable participants to understand the different aspects of racialism, how it has developed and behaviours associated with it
- To understand the concept and impact of 'pro' behaviour
- To understand the concepts of institutional discrimination and institutional racialism
- To identify possible post-course personal maintenance issues.

aspects of training.

Organisationally, everything had seemingly been done to fine tune and to plan their offering of diversity training to trainers, but then, life still happens when you've planned for everything else and unconscious process will always win out in the end.

Very quickly the following questions surfaced in our first trawl through the organisational literature:

- How, in the problematic critical event that occurred, might the teaching style and content have deviated to the degree that they departed from the written brief?

- In a co-facilitated session, how did the quality-control function of peer review and co-supervision seemingly fail to operate to the degree of defusing the events described?

- How might the trainers and the organisation best learn from events and put into place a procedure to better prevent/address subsequent similar crises should these arise?

- To what extent did the delivery of this module meet its stated aims and work within the scope of its written objectives?

Alerted to the above we began our interviews.

(Exploration)

Critical Incidents in Diversity Training – A Study of Conflict

Within our developing relationship with the interviewees, largely trainers and training managers themselves, we were surprised at the degree of emotional debriefing that naturally unfolded as we entered into dialogue. Indeed, after some five to ten minutes of orientation, during which respondents would often question us about our objectivity and solicit from us reassurances that we were truly external, and after we had assured them that we had control over our report and did not have an organisational axe to grind, the level of communication that unfolded appeared highly authentic and emotionally expressive; as if interviewees felt relieved to find an audience in which they could divest themselves of pent up hurts! What we thought were to be fact-finding interviews, rapidly transformed into emotional debriefings.

a) Participant perceptions of the recent problematic course

Even before participants of the last 'problematic' diversity training course entered the programme, its reputation – and that of the trainer involved – had seemingly gone before them:

'Rumours circulate when people get back from training and then others may have gone along with preconceived ideas – with a self-fulfilling prophesy of what it might be like. A trainer in one staff room has a relationship with a trainer in another staff room so they went out with a tarnished impression from day one. Experiences I think can sometimes get exaggerated.'

'Some trainers have got into the habit of being professional denouncers and this travels before them, is very damaging and does nothing but reinforce mistrust of change in this organisation.'

Add to the above rumour-mill scenario that some participants reported being put under pressure to attend the course, and a very negative entry attitude to training is fermented:

220

'I felt real pressure to go on this mandatory course. It was "do this course or you'll be back stacking shelves on the night shift at three o'clock in the morning" if I didn't do the course – which I took as a direct threat.'

Once upon the problematic diversity course, the worst expectations were seemingly realised as earlier agreements were dishonoured and expectations of the learning contract fell apart:

'One or two participants in my group had quite far to travel – from Kent so we tried to negotiate around time. We had an agreement but he reneged on the agreement, it's as if whatever you say doesn't matter, I'm in charge of this course you'll do what I say. When challenging he used 'you, you, you' and I challenged him. I said you've got to use we because you're part of this organisation. But he presented himself as detached from this nasty organisation, racist, homophobic, sexist.'

Indeed, contention and challenge without accompanying support seemed to be the order of the day:

'We were told that anyone who thinks racist thoughts has no place in this organisation. It was quite a hostile challenging thing to say early on. I got angry and I've never got angry for so long on a course. We were told that doing this course was a condition of doing the job and I really considered packing it in.'

'The tone of it all was kind of evangelical and that was insulting: you are sinners, you are the block and until you move on the organisation can't move on.'

'He made what I thought to be two bold statements: Don't ask me about my sexuality, or I'll ask you about yours and I'll expect you to tell me. And don't ask me to tell you what I did in bed with my partner last night or I'll ask you. I thought this is a very bizarre, very strange thing to say. By Thursday I thought he had some serious issues and was using the students on the course to exorcise his own personal demons. I thought we were there for his benefit. By this time I was also in a state, I was absolutely shattered mentally, depressed. It was almost this is how you are, what you are'.

'X (the trainer) got me so wound up asking me to explore my childhood. The impression was I would lose my job if I didn't explore my childhood.'

'He wouldn't accept any feedback. He said "I don't do feedback. Send me an email." So that's what I did. He didn't care.'

'He challenged the rescuing, slapped down participants and was bullying.' i.e. *'One civilian staff member was constantly being put down, with X saying he was fed up with group attempts to rescue each other. Colleagues were being bullied off the course. At this point I raised the questions around Health and Safety. He (the trainer in question) had personal issues and he wanted to use us as a way of exploring them'* (When asked what he perceived these issues to be he replied: *'trans-sexuality'*) *'You'll read in my report I challenged him over what Occupational Health input there was into the course.'*

'Everyone seemed to get on with each other. I don't know what they should have done. But the most vocal people were bullied off'.

'What worried me was that the person co-training with X seemed to support him all

the way and this person I knew was higher up in the management hierarchy.'

In light of the above experience, the reputation of diversity training in general seems to have suffered a severe setback:

'There's no inherent value in it; there are real dangers so why risk it. I have never come off any course feeling so het up and stressed – in seventeen years in this job.'

'We need to stick to issues that affect us.'

'The course should be abandoned.'

'Five-day mandatory training is quite threatening. Give people the information as to why the training is happening; what it entails; what the safety mechanisms are to deal with issues as they arise; and ensure there is support before, during and after.'

Post-course, even after complaints were received, participants continued to feel unheard and undervalued as no further action nor debrief was forthcoming:

'And after I submitted my complaint, there was not a word from the diversity training team; no one came over to have a word to support or explain.'

As for being prepared for the job at hand:

'Some people maybe shouldn't be delivering training in diversity; they won't feel ready when it comes to them delivering the three-day training to twenty-two recruits in a classroom and I expect some will take annual leave.'

b) Participant perspectives of the problematic course and earlier courses

As for how the problematic course in question was more widely perceived within the tutorial community:

'There seemed to be problems with one trainer with an accusatory, confrontational style. There have been three courses with him that have been a problem. Someone at a supervisory level in the DTS should have rung alarm bells about this individual – and also consider the impact back at the basic training school to dispel myths and rumours. Certainly something needed to be done at an earlier stage.'

'There was no declared statement at the beginning offering people the option to sit out of any exercises. One participant on my course said they didn't wish to "talk about this any more" but they were happy to stay and listen and this was accepted.'

'Issues were raised over content; personal questions were asked and not managed well. From what I can gather, no health warning was given or support offered. There were personal issues towards one trainer. Participants were concerned about the mental welfare of a particular trainer'.

Indeed, one trainer appeared to have been instrumental in fielding the complaint process:

'Two individuals left the course last December and sought support from X and myself and from their line manager. A third individual stayed till the end. I advised all three to put their complaint in writing.'

Regarding how the facilitator on the problematic course had been perceived by trainers who experienced his facilitation in earlier programmes:

'X kept his interventions within normal boundaries. You could see what he was doing – he was asking one woman "what do you really mean by that". He did go round at the start of the morning to take any feedback from the previous day; there was no mandatory taking part – generally we did have control. The exercises were dire though. It went like a typical diversity lesson. One participant also asked what happens if personal issues come up, and X said he was a trained counsellor'.

'I did the course with X (the trainer of the course in question) and Y. On my five-day training course some people found it very difficult, but it worked well because it was a small group and a comfortable working environment, just twelve people and one trainer, and several people had difficulties on that course.'

'I'd heard before the course there were some concerns, so I went in massively in fear, but this was completely unfounded.'

Re earlier diversity courses in general:

'There's a tendency in diversity training – it was used also on my course – to be challenging. But you have to be very careful how you do it in the group, especially since they know each other before they come on the course'.

'Same ethos on ours (personally challenging culture) but from the beginning the guy running it said, that by the end of a course like this, you're often expected then to teach it, but he said, by the end of this you won't be responsible for anything else, or anybody's feelings. This really relaxed us and by the end we were exhausted by all the prejudices we realised we were bringing. It felt absolutely safe and no suspicion that it's gone anywhere else, and I can now sit quite openly in front of a group and talk about things quite openly, and if I find anything in myself then I feel safe enough to find out about it without feeling like the organisation is going to come down on me with an axe.'

'I learned how not to do it if nothing else. It's not a bad thing to have a reminder, but I learned nothing from it. This is a one- or two-day course that's got to fill a five-day slot. We spent half a day doing introductions.

'I was on a course that I absolutely loved and I really enjoyed it.'

As to their concerns and how the delivery of diversity training might be improved, participants of earlier programmes suggested the following changes:

'We would have liked the diversity trainers to come over and prepare the trainers; the participants said they would have liked to have known what to expect. Aims and Objectives were sent out after the first couple of courses. The IT staff also said they hadn't been briefed.'

'Creating a comfortable environment is the key. It's not good practice having one facilitator with twelve people.'

'Obviously raw emotions come to the surface. But I'm not always convinced that people saw the signs, and that the facilitators dealt both with individual and group dynamics. Particularly in groups of ten or more; with smaller numbers you could be switched on to what's going on in the group'.

'My course included community members who would be delivering the training and

that variety of backgrounds helped. This five-day training is never going to be enough to deliver the three-day training to recruits – I can't think of anyone who would relish delivering this training. You might have to deliver the training to classes of up to forty-four people'.

'I did the earlier three-week course. We're all individuals, and we all need to be monitored and treated differently. My group had time for feedback – very luxurious. Yes we could manage our own learning.'

'The ideal would have been for the foundation course to have stayed as it was. The five-day training should be voluntary for those trainers going into diversity.'

'As the foundation course has changed, we're launching people into the classroom before they've had the training to do it.'

c) The 'problematic' facilitator's perspective

'This organisation has quite a bullying culture. The structure has moved on but if you don't fit into the mould (the masochism) – you are bullied'.

Regarding his involvement with diversity training courses:

'At first I thought "Wow"; "Cutting Edge". In January 2003 I sat in as a participant-cum-observer on a course. A lot of people came from one staffing group. They seemed to have the same view "We all think this". It was very cognitive, I felt like an outsider. After the first three days people started asking: "Well – Why are we here? We know all this. It's a repeat of work we've done before". I thought – "Where are the building blocks to enable the group to do this?"'

'There is seen to be a "pink and fluffy culture" in the diversity team – we don't usually look at "feelings" in this organisation. If I am seen to be doing that then I am seen as "unusual". The course starts with getting to know each other (around our culture)'.

In terms of how he sees himself perceived as a trainer:

'People come for very cognitive stuff, to be led, but with me I think I am viewed as a "weird guy" – like "What agenda has he got?" I didn't get this feeling before – when I was doing other training but this time round I am getting it. I put that down to how trainers were trained. Were they able to acknowledge defence mechanisms? What happens when the process got tough? What about comfort zones; resilience. I don't believe trainers have given any thought to what is going on within groups. They have no awareness of group dynamics.'

As to what he found the most rewarding aspect of his work:

'What's been enjoyable for me are the words X thinks I'm a racist. When I hear this I know where people are coming from. The game's up. I can't hide anymore. I take pleasure in saying "But you have been sold a lie – it's not you – it's your education". However – they are scared because they feel I have found them out as a racist (or homophobic) but I wanted them to step back and see that it was not about guilt or blame but about truth and honesty. It's constructive dialogue.'

'I can understand why people don't disclose – because if you are racist – you are out!'

Re why the decision was made to put a stop the Personal Awareness Training:

'My view was – four people met – sat round a table and said "Let's get X". I think they felt "Why are we here?" "It's about them not us"; "It's gone too far"; "It's about political correctness!" Four statements were brought back. That's where the complaints come from. At that meeting a deal was struck.'

'A lot has been played out about how risky this course is – I'm sceptical about the motives of some people.'

Regarding the nature of the co-facilitator relationship upon the problematic last diversity course offering:

'I was co-facilitating with Y – who had not experienced the course before. We had only half a day together a few days before the course. We were both quite vulnerable. On the second day of the course I did values. They got into pairs. I got some resistance from two or three people. One woman said "Are you prepared to deal with the outcome of this?" Anyway – she left – didn't come back. It created quite a storm. This lasted all afternoon. On the third day I was challenged – an issue relating to being gay and paedophilia. He walked out. One person had a grievance on sexism. I touched a raw nerve. I did try to help but he was the one I felt was sabotaging the training. Somehow I didn't think he was aware of what he was doing and why.'

'It worked better on other training courses with an established partnership. With Z it works very well. Z and I have a good rapport. It's less "directive". We have similar ideas. The gender balance works. We debrief a lot. We explore a lot more. It felt safer.'

'Then there was another: "This has not been Risk assessed!" I asked him "Do you want to talk" he said "No". Then he walked out! We started with thirteen and in the end we ended up with eight. With this number – some very good work was done.'

X felt especially aggrieved with how the complaints procedure had been handled, the way senior training managers had decided to put diversity training on hold:

'After a meeting was held with the Head about the course and why people walked out, I felt "How does the sponsor hold their end – it's about developing people – so what do they have to say?" "Where is the Sponsor – now and later?" Where is the preparation? People come to the course defended and shocked.'

'My argument was: "This is personal awareness – of course it's about you – but we are here to hear the dynamics of racism etc. – but it must also be about me". People felt they were forced onto the course – yet again.'

d) Perceptions of the co-facilitator of the last 'problematic' course

'It was a nightmare, horrendous. I felt frightened, physically angry and let down. I had an overwhelming desire to collude with the group and I'm a robust trainer! When you are sitting there with your notes on your lap – you want to hide!'

'They (the participants) said – "we're afraid" – well I've got news for you – "I'm frightened too!"'

'On Wednesday afternoon there was a road to Damascus turnaround. The question was put "Why are we here?" As trainers we are supposed to have an unconditionally positive regard to everyone in the room – I struggled with maintaining that!'

'We tried entering into a "Learning Contract" with them – they said "No" – that was too juvenile and they were not going to do it'.

'At the end of the day – we drove home together and in the car we just swore, swore and swore at each other (out loud) – this was the only way we could cope with the next day. "Is it me? Is it real?" We concluded it wasn't us.'

'How much of it was the organisation – they (participants) are happy to blame the organisation for not preparing them and they could be doing something else. Even with the exercise on "The Shield" where they are asked to draw something that would explain their culture – why you are here – they did not engage. In their view they had been ordered to be here. This course is compulsory and they were not happy with that.'

In relation to what was the main problem of the course:

'My gut feeling is they are frightened people who do not have the level of understanding to deal with the course. In their minds – they are seen as racists, sexist and homophobic – and can be sacked at any time!'

'I think the organisation has a lot to answer for. I was thinking the same thing X was thinking but he actually said it. His actual words were: "You don't have to be at the course if you don't want to be – go!" X said this and the organisation did not have the courage to back him. There was no service level agreement. No clearly defined outcomes and no expectations. We were doing it blind. We had no client sponsor for this one. We couldn't go back to the sponsors and say – this has happened – what are you doing about it? i.e. Role play exercise – they were saying "It made me feel silly" and "this makes me feel insecure". If we can't pass that stage – it's just not going to work! So there are clearly design issues. Yes it's a well thought through product. It gives opportunities to discuss but the group was not ready for it?'

e) Experienced trainer's perceptions of diversity training

'Best experiences are where people are prepared to engage and look at themselves and their own prejudices – where there is a good partnership relationship with your fellow trainer. It is good when you get comments like "this was good – it really made me think – I really enjoyed it "'.

'I first delivered a course on my own and was with X in February. But to be honest it was just as difficult. There was a storm half way through. Participants would say "Well if you had told me that before that would have helped". I have delivered between six to eight courses.'

'The best for me was when there were no basic trainers – when the participants were from a more person-aware culture. When the course is not mandatory it works so much better!'

'Worst – in course number four, the participants devised a plan (in my opinion) and devalued the course.'

'On day two one of them said "Okay we have had our debriefing and we have made a decision we don't need this". My colleague said "Okay we will join you for a debriefing at the end of the day". They said "No we are not doing that!" There was open hostility. My colleague got sworn at. The only emotion being shown was anger. There were open tactics to just rubbish the course. There had been anger looking at race, resentment discussing gender. It was OK to look at sexuality (two people in the group were gay). By the end of Day three we managed a good course (five students had left but the remainder were very satisfied). But we had to invest a great deal of energy to get to that stage.'

'Some people said they felt uncomfortable. Some people were saying that it was a particular trainer. I was aware of people walking out on courses. I have also been aware of some people bad mouthing a particular trainer X'.

'I think going in "too deep" was a problem. Some participants did not understand the methodology. I think we should go by the book because when we don't – sometimes it goes wrong.'

Regarding the way forward:

'Quite frankly I don't want to do anymore of these courses. I don't feel I can make a massive difference any more. You invest so much energy and there is no appreciation. In our department the cost is not recalled. I know I am a good trainer – I can't be going through this'.

'We really must also think about what we are doing with trainers from basic training. They have a big workload – constantly under pressure. They have to deal with a huge intake – brand new recruits – that long eighteen weeks – non-stop activities – no break – then five days training a week. As trainers we need to appreciate this. When we as trainers start appreciating them as real people – then they will respond! Also – the managers – they refer to the new recruits as "kids" and "boys and girls". But some are in their forties! Some have left their own businesses to do this job. Attitudes must change. There should be more respect from Managers.'

In terms of their own first experience of the diversity course:

'A very horrible experience, antagonistic, difficult; participants were rude, unco-operative. The first course I sat in as a participant, they did not allow me to join in. In fact they threw me out! The five-day course is just dreadful. I do not want any more courses to go ahead'.

'I think they felt they were being told they were not doing their jobs properly. There was a huge storm at about Wednesday of the course. The message as to why they were there had not been sold to them. The management (Chief Instructor) had not sold what the course was about. My view is it did not help that the course was here – at head office. If they were held "away" it may have made a big difference.'

'The fact that they had no choice; they felt they were being told they were deficient. People were made to feel bad. We were "sent in to tell them how to do their jobs". For them, the diversity trainers were from "another planet". "They used loads of big words and tried to put us down – but we are not going to let them! We will not co-operate" Yes it was seen as "them or us"'.

227

Re positives arising from the course:

'On the plus side, actually, a few came to us quietly at the end of the course and said "I quite enjoyed it"'.

'On one course, one of the black officers in one of the discussion groups said that he had never ever revealed "this" before – but it took him a week to do so – and he felt good that he had revealed it – so we do get somewhere!'

f) A senior training manager's perspective of what went wrong

'As far as I am aware, the knowledge base was low (e.g. race, gender etc. – so it went right over their heads. The training concerns centred mostly about a particular trainer – X. Some of the students said "this is too risky". My trainers were coming in to train the recruit school you see. This was about the effect my trainers were having – not the content.'

'One course went from thirteen to eight – but X is an experienced trainer. They saw my trainers as experts but this was very superficial training – like the brown outer skin of an onion – the deeper you go – the more you feel the effect.'

Re the complaints against identified trainers:

'I would say X might have been "clumsy" – he goes for the jugular. X and Z are full time trainers (twenty-six years and thirteen years in training). Members of basic training may have targeted them – I don't know. Yes they could have been personally targeted. But I would say Z is the typical organisational man who tells you like it is! But if you have lost the ability to relate to people then that's not on! But the course – how can you have "A time in your life where you felt vulnerable" on the first day! That's too soon. That could be the root of the problem – Who knows? But "skills" as a trainer – that is so important – let things go for now and again, he knows I'm coming back for him! So – they walked out on X's class – but he wanted to get rid of them just as much as they wanted to get rid of him!'

'There were four written complaints, but one lady said "this is the best thing since sliced bread!" Another says "It's total rubbish!" Quite frankly I can't see the courses "damaging someone's person – it's not dangerous". But there are some that would say "it's your fault that you are a Muslim and have to pray" – Do you see what I mean? But maybe there is something Ofsted missed – yes we had Ofsted done on it!'

Re the way forward:

'This course is not assessed. You can leave it being a racist or a homophobe!'

'There are fifty to sixty trainers to train. There are 170 basic manager trainers. There are a good six or seven courses left. I think they should have this training after six months as part of their Personal Development Plan as they need to experience things first.'

g) A Staff Development Officer's Perspective

Re the course:

'I have not participated – I have not delivered the training but I deal with the fall out – as a Staff Development Officer – so many new recruits come to me and say

"I cannot cope – I need help". We have had a number of people coming to us to talk to us about what "went on" on the diversity training course – we give confidential advice.'

Re the present situation:

'I think people are relieved that it came to a head – the diversity trainers have been out of control for too long. Who does X think he is? This course, it had to break. It was unforgivable what happened. Why are diversity trainers messing about in people's heads? Participants are told "think about a happy experience but don't use 'he' or 'she'". What about the ones that may have recently had bad experiences e.g. bereavement, divorce, loss of a child. Some will say "if I don't co-operate I am seen as obstructive". Where is your quality assurance? Where are the safeguards?'

'I really question the validity of the Personal Awareness course. You need to be so careful – there are "life skills" deaths – we need safeguards – we have to think about how people will cope'.

'There are those participants who would not be happy with the training but they would just sit there and lie. I accept we all need to learn but we are scaring people'.

A Field Emerges – Participants' Perspectives of the Last Course

Outside of the formal interviews a good deal of informal information comes our way. Having immersed ourselves within the field, collected numerous reports both past and present, spoken informally over coffee and soaked in our interviewees' world-views while experiencing at first hand the organisational culture, we, the consultancy team begin to sense wider forces at play within the system.

We see in reports relating to the last Personal Development Course a good deal of anger, irritation, vulnerability and hurt. All this was still apparent in the interviews and had lost little of its emotional steam, to the extent that some respondents said how helpful it was to talk about these events and to express their feelings in our interviews and focus groups. Our interviews here functioned like an overdue debrief, as participants said they hadn't felt listened to nor been able to reflect sufficiently with others upon what had transpired. As a process for the efficient and effective debriefing of trainers and learners post course does not appear to be in evidence, this should be rectified before training recommences.

Expectations of what to expect, the formation of ground rules, the negotiation of learning contracts, the sharing of trainer objectives and a transparency of trainer intentions and motives – criteria of excellence in facilitative practice – all seemed to be absent, and the learner's entry into the course and its experiential process seems to have suffered as a consequence of this. Contracting seems to require especial attention here.

Participants seem to have ended up feeling insignificant and disempowered, and if this was intentional – as a sort of experiential learning strategy so as to create a personal taste of being socially isolated – it didn't work, for its educational purpose wasn't made clear and there was no debrief nor reinforcement of learning. If, conversely, the challenging style adopted by trainers was not driven by educational intent, but was an expression of their personal stress due to the mandatory nature of the course and the context of a trapped audience, it could be suggested to amount to institutionalised bullying and borders upon an abuse of tutorial power.

229

There is also an acknowledgement that an experiential mode of facilitation is not suited for all and will scare some trainers off. This draws into question the present course's usefulness in preparing trainers. Indeed, at one level it seems counter-productive as many trainers are put off the subject by the group dynamics that attend the experiential method of teaching employed.

A substantial portion of trainees felt emotionally exposed and retaliated with anger, and attributed the behaviour of X as a central reason for this. There appears to be a lack of orientation to the course and its content, no negotiation and no clarity re the facilitator's expectation or of the courses learning intentions.

It would appear that learner preparation and contracting before the Personal Development Course is essential if they are to be encouraged to buy into the process, that is to say, if they are to feel less done-to and coerced into what is perceived to be a personally destabilising and threatening course. Indeed, learners appear to come to the course already sensitised to being labelled racialist and homophobic. Note how the negative effect of the rumour mill may contribute to this.

One could speculate that feeling prejudged and assumed guilty, and aggrieved to be labelled in this way, individuals may end up harbouring a sense of injustice when they meet a similar response within training from fellow peers. Add to this that trainers tend for the most part to represent the more enlightened developmental edge of the organisation and it is little wonder they feel especially resentful to be tarred with a racialist brush.

So How Were Earlier Diversity Courses Perceived?

We learn from reports that X has delivered effective Personal Development Courses when supported by a co-facilitator with whom rapport born of earlier experience was already developed. In the case reported, the Training Group felt empowered and supported, even when participants were in part resistive to the course and its content. It appears that that when participants feel empowered and listened to by trainers and are orientated into the learning culture and its intentions, they are empowered by challenge rather than diminished by it.

In general, trainers appear resistive and resentful to Personal Development training, seemingly because of the emotional address of personal issues and a foreboding that they will be under attack and 'have to bare all'; this expectation now seems to have entered the organisational culture and individual pre-course expectation. We might speculate that professionals who have to present a 'tough exterior' in order to deal with difficult work situations and whose managerial ethos supports the same, would naturally feel resistive and unprepared to bare their soul, especially upon a course whose content is counter-cultural.

If trainers are expected in the training culture described to teach large classes of up to forty-four recruits, the experiential approach modelled by trainers seems of little relevance to real-life practice, the more so as intimate challenge is inappropriate to short duration large groups. This said, it is to be noted that smaller class sizes seem to reap better results, and that the preparation of trainers, and indeed the training of recruits, upon courses which address personal change rather than skill transfer, work better in groups of eight and below.

Pre-course preparation again seems to be an arising and most important need, especially as rumour, reports of earlier negative results and the fear of emotional breakdown now colour the learner's expectations of the course.

What Do Personal Development Trainers Think?

Historically, X seems to suggest that institutionalised bullying is part and parcel of the organisational culture, and so believes there is a pressing need for diversity training and personal development.

Again, he suggests that smaller-sized classes run more effectively.

X seems to be following the training model that he was trained to employ, but strives to make it more relevant and real, to bring the subject alive. He observes that his approach is counter-cultural, but implies it needs to be this way if he is to address feelings or to redress bigotry. He also recognises that because of his association with a more challenging style of teaching he is perceived as different and possibly singled out because of this.

X observes that he and his co-facilitator on the last course had little time to prepare, were seemingly thrown in together and as a consequence experienced a considerable degree of vulnerability.

We learn that trainer X's reputation may have gone before him to the extent that groups come primed – and are possibly encouraged by others – to resist him. From a group dynamic perspective, attacking the facilitator is a common ploy members unconsciously employ in order to avoid contacting their own fears.

As the reputation of the Personal Development Course seems to go before it, we might speculate that the group entered highly charged and on the lookout for slights, and that when the first women walked out a self-fulfilling prophecy was acted out. X recognises his part in this dynamic and admits to the last course as touching a nerve.

We learn from the reports of trainers that the demands of Personal Development training is, at a personal level very high, and occasions a good deal of emotional cost.

The wider culture of the organisation is seen to contribute to the problem, as recognition of the supports that experiential learning requires appears to go unrecognised.

Due to the stress and strain of being enrolled as cultural change agents for the organisation and working with an experiential mode of delivery, tutorial partnerships forged between co-facilitators appear to be an essential ingredient of building trainer support, especially when cohorts of learners come ready to sabotage the training and seek to avoid an address of their own vulnerability.

The question must be asked, in light of the strain of teaching Personal Development and the resistance of learners to the programme, if an internal offering is really the best way forward, or if an outside agency should deliver Personal Development programmes? After all, if attitude change is desired which borders upon the therapeutic, it seems a very tall order indeed for trainers to be expected to do counter-cultural therapy within their own professional family. Then again, if internal delivery is to be adhered to, internal supports in the shape of time to build co-facilitator relationships, effective co-facilitator debriefs, ongoing peer and external supervision, plus opportunity to develop co-facilitator delivery by experienced partnered pairs is to be encouraged.

A cultural clash seems to be in evidence re the basic training and diversity training teams.

The workloads of both teams seem to squeeze the resources, personal and systemic, that might otherwise support the Personal Development Course. It needs to be recognised by the system, senior management especially, that the facilitation of attitude change via experiential learning requires much more personal preparation, supervision and debriefing time than conventional modes of training. Self selection of co-facilitators, and an appreciation of the need to put fewer learners through the process at any one time so as to enhance the necessary positive group dynamic, is also a must. Simply, there is a big difference between 'training' and 'facilitation', and if the present culture which is largely representative of a training mentality is to progress towards a facilitative one, senior managers will need to be educated to a differing mind-set. We therefore recommend that at the very least, senior ranks attend the Personal Development Course to experience and to understand its demands first hand.

To avoid going too deep too quickly, it seems advisable for trainers to follow the guidelines and style of their course documentation, which offers clear lesson plans along with appropriate learning activities, a guiding frame and suitable container for experiential inquiry. This is not to say that the more challenging approach should be discontinued, but rather that it be bedded within, and develop out from a foundation of cognitive clarity and learner orientation to the same.

What Do Managers Think?

Again, the cultural clash looms large between the tutorial teams for diversity and basic training, and has a negative effect all-round. This requires resolution for the sake of the training, the competitive group dynamic of the class, the trainers and the organisation in general.

Though we agree it feels right that the Personal Development Course remains un-assessed formally, student assessment of the programme should be built in and ongoing, especially as in the case of the last course, when there is a suggestion that the trainer may have over-stepped the appropriate boundary of ethical acceptability as the withholding of evaluations could be interpreted as an admission that something went badly wrong.

We also note the need for managers to monitor the quality assurance of programmes, more especially in the delivery of the Personal Development Course where there appears to be a break in training tradition, as in the documentation there is nothing to support the challenging approach adopted within the programme.

What Does the Personnel Manager Think?

Again, we hear how the Personal Development Programme occasions a good deal of emotional fallout. It may be suggested that, because of this, the diversity team and its trainers are perceived as different, to the extent that others feel they need to be pulled back into line.

A realistic caution is raised here, that personal development of the nature and degree seemingly practised on the course in question, needs to be tailored to the life and readiness of the individual learners involved. Preparation before such courses, contracting upon, clear ground rules and debriefing post learning activities and post the course itself are important safeguards here.

We are reminded that anyone or any group that raises the organisational shadow (all that the organisation would prefer to be kept under wraps) will be seen as problematic and distanced. This dynamic is exacerbated when people and groups do not share a common task or activity, have little contact and are permitted to remain out of dialogue.

(Resolution)

Review of the Initial Questions – A Further Step Towards Closure

In our consultancy debrief sessions we considered how best to present our report. Eventually we decided to include the above interview transcripts, our reflections on the same, plus the following overview along with the various recommendations we had surfaced together in plenary discussions. As the report was forming we emailed transcripts to each other, verified the material we had recorded from the interviews, circulated our accounts to interviewees for verification, re-drafted material and added further reflections and recommendations. As the issue was a complex one we decided to let complexity inform our report, and to encourage the client system to review the data and so see the evidence for our recommendations. What you are reading here, apart from the various asides and disguising of material, in the most part entered the report we submitted to our client.

> In regard to the wider territory of diversity training, several influences must be appreciated if we are to grasp the complex influences at play.
>
> Firstly we have the role of trainers upon the problematic course in question, did they go too far and too deep? Then again, if their brief is to change attitudes, a good deal of rattle and shaking of sensitivities may be appropriate, for are they not prepared in diversity training to train in this way? But attitude change requires a high degree of facilitative competence – and indeed therapeutic skill – over and above the more usual emotional demand placed on trainers and their training. This said, much can be done to support trainers and to support learners before, during and after course delivery.
>
> Secondly, we have the group dynamic, the tendency of individuals in groups to regress, and the larger the group the greater is the seduction to act out feelings as individuals find themselves fired up by the collective emotional energy of the group, which often causes individuals to be more raw and extreme than they would normally be. In this regard would it not be wise to have two facilitators and smaller sized groups?
>
> Thirdly we have the parent-child dynamic of the teacher-learner relationship that can re-create our earlier struggles with authority, being played out in a culture where individuals often feel at the mercy of authority, and who naturally enough nurse a desire to knock authority off its perch whenever they can; being an Aunt Sally comes with the territory

of being a trainer. In these terms, the more trainers negotiate ground rules, build a safe non-blaming culture and work as peers alongside their trainees, share our intentions and work to clear agendas, the better.

Fourthly we have the mandatory nature of the Personal Development course and the participant's sense of being a trapped audience forced to undergo yet another change process, even as other pressures of the job are crowding in and will await their return to normal duties. Tutors must therefore be accorded sufficient time to build an efficient and trusting co-facilitative relationship, and trainees need to be supported before and after diversity training.

Fifthly we have the rivalry and culture clash of two training teams with differing values who have fallen into a competitive 'us and them' mentality where 'us' are OK and 'them' are far from OK. If this rift is to be healed, sufficient common ground and purpose to establish a more wholesome dialogue will have to be found.

Sixthly we have an organisation which is endeavouring to re-create itself while under the watchful eyes of politicians, the tabloids and sceptical public opinion, who service providers in the public eye to be social workers and counsellors as well as custodians of professionalism and professional ethics. In this context, better we have ongoing peer supervision and debriefing sessions of trainers, and work-based peer review and action learning sets for trainees than mere immersion in an experiential workshop.

Seventhly we have a culture in transition, where 'the old school' and agents of change are struggling to understand and to live in superficial harmony with each other. Here dialogue needs to be fermented, not avoided, if both are to learn from the other.

Eighthly we have individuals who self-select to be action and task-centred, rather than to be in-depth self-reflectors alive to process; individuals who support themselves through strength and intellectual clarity rather than wallow in emotionality and doubt, who in diversity training are asked to step out of character. Diversity trainers need therefore to meet participants where they are now, appreciate difference and prejudice as an adaptive process, and build in the personal and group support necessary for experimentation. Indeed the existent course design and its suggested lesson plans go a long way to providing cognitive clarity and safety.

We share the above to prevent the reader falling into the trap of believing there is a simple one-dimensional solution.

A huge task is being asked of trainers, namely, to weed out racialist attitudes and to remedy the same. Education is often seen to be the universal panacea of all social ills; if we can just get people to understand why they must change, it is implied all will be well. But emotions are not logical and we grow to depend upon what is familiar. Nevertheless, busy trainers are being expected to spearhead change and to act as change agents. It is hard enough to change basic cognitive behaviour; it is yet even harder to change attitudes, and harder even more to facilitate the same in your own profession, yet trainers are being expected to almost act as the 'thought police' of the organisation. Is it any wonder, in this context, that trainers end up feeling under-resourced personally and professionally or that course participants resist being labelled as deviants.

Within the organisation individuals reported time and again that the way to survive was not by being open or trusting and sharing of your authentic emotions and inner beliefs, but rather by conforming to expectations and keeping your real self to yourself. Diversity training, in this context, came over as something of an elaborate game, where organisational success demanded compliance and a need to play 'the organisational game'.

Superficially the picture is relatively simple, either the trainer upon the problematic Personal Development Course went too far, too deep and too fast, or he is acting as required but without sufficient support. All this returns us to the initial questions of:

- How, in the problematic critical event that occurred, might the teaching style and content have deviated to the degree that they departed from the written brief?

- In a co-facilitated session, how did the quality-control function of peer review and co-supervision seemingly fail to operate to the degree of defusing the events described?

- How might the trainers and the organisation best learn from events and put into place a procedure to better prevent/address subsequent similar crises should these arise?

- How might the 'wider organisational culture' be adjusted to support trainers and learners upon Personal Development Courses, should these continue?

Our recommendations are to implement quality assurance and a more rigorous and wider ranging debriefing process; to integrate delivery with the aims, objectives and lesson plans; to release resources and to work to an optimum class size; to design a critical incident debriefing procedure – all address the above questions while suggesting a practical way forward.

Lastly, we recognise how public sector workers need to be skilful recipients of the public's projections of attitudes towards authority, so that they might perform the legitimate professional duties we license them to do. Personal development becomes an essential ingredient in this light, as it promotes an understanding of the psychodynamics of relationship.

Our recommendations are made with the above questions, Health and Safety suggestions and the aforementioned awareness in mind.

A Summary of Recommendations

We recommend that trainers return to the course documentation and that they structure experiential engagement, their delivery and intentions to promote personal learning around the aim and objectives herein stated, and thereby integrate personal challenge within the lesson plans and learning activities provided.

We recommend that time and resource be given to the preparation and to the development of an efficient co-facilitator relationship, and that staff of the diversity and basic training teams come together to 1) share their expectations of each other; 2) air their differences; 3) devise systems of delivery which better honour the practical needs of learners.

We recommend that Personal Development class sizes be kept at eight participants with two trainers delivering, so as to 1) allow the experiential experimentation that breeds excellence in teaching to continue; 2) to enact support for trainers; 3) to provide sufficient support for learners who are caused to reappraise their attitudes, beliefs and the emotions associated with personal development.

We recommend that trainers undergo regular quality assurance, that they debrief not just informally together, but formally with their senior managers and with a representation of other trainers in attendance, so that individual learning might be shared more widely within the trainer/training culture.

We recommend that learner evaluations of the course be given out routinely, that learners are prepared for the course prior to their attendance with a guiding rationale, aims and objectives, an overview of teaching methods and teacher intentions, plus sight of prospective ground rules they might further refine through negotiation, and that an opt-out clause (see **Figure C2**) be built into such rules to honour individual freedom and choice.

We also recommend that the diversity and basic training teams come together to form a critical incident procedure whereby any future trainees, should a similar classroom crisis occur, receive better support and a debriefing than would appear to have been the case this time.

We recommend that senior managers in the training division and elsewhere undergo personal development training so that they might appreciate demands of the course at first hand.

Immediate Recommendations

We recommend that as routine ground rules be negotiated with learners and that an opt-out clause (see **Figure C2** paragraph 5) be built in to such rules, so that the learning objectives and purpose of learning activities are clarified to learners prior to engagement. In this way, each learning activity in the manner of action research should evolve out of 1) plenary negotiation and planning, into 2) experimental learning activity, followed by 3) a debrief upon the outcome and learning, plus 4) a review of its practical usefulness in the training setting of recruits. If bullying is systemic in the service, a self-fulfilling prophecy or a mere fantasy, it is just as well that negotiation is integrated into training delivery in order to allay anxieties about the same.

We recommend that trainers return to the course documentation and that they structure their experiential engagement and intentions to promote personal learning around the aim and objectives herein stated, and hereby integrate personal challenge within the lesson plans and learning activities provided. We believe that without this integration, there is likely to be 'an experience' without a recognition of 'learning' or its 'practical usefulness', and a likelihood that crises similar to that of the last course will continue to emerge.

Figure C2 Guidelines for Team Inquiry

1) Share your reality and evidence with others:

Speak from the authority of your own experience, i.e. 'I think...'; 'I feel... '; 'I see and hear...'; 'I imagine...'; rather than generalise through such phrases as 'one thinks...'; 'people tend to...'; or by labelling others, i.e. 'you are...'.

2) Explore and question everything that happens:
Stay curious and sceptical, engage in ongoing exploration of the social events that arise and remain curious to the effects of these upon the behaviour of yourself and others.

3) Experiment and play with being different:
Risk opening yourself to others and reducing your guard; honour your own stuck-ness when this arises; experiment with being non-judgemental and tolerant of judgemental behaviour in others; be prepared to explore new ways of expressing and being you.

4) Respect yourself and others:
Do not leak confidential material beyond the group, nor share information you are privy to about others in the group without their consent; take responsibility for sharing or holding onto your own secrets.

5) Act on your beliefs:
Choose for yourself when to opt out of activities which appear wrong for you at the time; do not collude in situations that you feel are personally unhealthy for you.

6) Clarify the Intention behind your interventions:
Make it clear if you are attempting to support, intending to challenge, or merely seeking clarification.

7) Be here – now:
Endeavour to engage with what is happening in the moment, share how you are currently feeling and what you are thinking – right now!

We recommend that time and resources be given to the preparation and the development of an efficient co-facilitator relationship and that staff of both the School of Diversity and Recruitment come together to: 1) share their expectations of each other; 2) air their differences; 3) devise systems of delivery which honour the practical needs of both cultures. Without this we fear the existent split will grow to further hamper delivery, add still more negative fuel to the rumour mill, and will continue to cause delivery to wander further out of the zone of its practical usefulness.

We recommend that 'Training the Trainer' class sizes be kept at eight learners with two trainers delivering, so as to 1) allow the experiential experimentation that breeds excellence in teaching, 2) to provide sufficient support for learners who are caused to reappraise their attitudes, beliefs and the emotions associated with the same. Without this, we believe that training will stagnate rather than develop – perhaps in an effort to play safe, and that learners will be in danger of acting out familiar large group dynamics which subtract from development and learning.

We recommend that trainers debrief not just informally together, but formally with their senior managers and with a representation of other trainers in attendance, so that their learning might be shared more widely in the trainer/training culture. We believe this activity, especially if involving representatives of the diversity and basic training teams, will in the longer term go some way to opening a dialogue about the current projections of each team. These might then hopefully be resolved – although a good deal of resistance is to be expected in the short term.

We recommend that learner evaluations of the course be given out routinely, that learners are prepared for the course prior to their attendance with a guiding rationale, aims and objectives, teaching method and teacher intentions, plus sight of prospective ground rules they might further refine through negotiation. Omission of the above, we feel, did much to exacerbate recent events and contributed to the negative expectations of students.

We also recommend that the respective tutorial teams come together to form a critical incident procedure whereby any future trainees so affected will receive better support and a debriefing than would appear to have been the case this time. This we see as an important Health and Safety at work provision. It also provides one more activity where con-joint School activity might be facilitated.

We recommend that senior managers in the training division and elsewhere undergo personal development training so that that they might appreciate demands of the course at first hand. This we believe will fulfil a two-pronged process: it will add support to the premise that personal development is an important aspect of organisational preparation; it will provide opportunity for senior ranks to experientially engage with the issues and to better understand the demands this form of training provision demands.

A Long Term Recommendation

If in the unlikely occasion of having implemented the immediate recommend-ations, the respective tutorial teams still find themselves unable to deliver a Personal Development programme which supports trainers and learners alike, we recommend you put this element of your training to rest, deliver it alongside others more expert in the area, or offer it out to tender and give up all pretensions of developing an internal facilitative culture able to support more advanced levels of facilitation, stick to training and what you already do competently and well. This said, looking more widely afield, we believe whatever the training venue or educational organisation, should the recommendations suggested in this paper be heeded, experiential trainers and facilitators would be better prepared for experiential engagement and that training organisations and teams offering the same would be better able to support experiential learning and personal development.

Following the submission of our report we hear nothing. The consultancy that employed us was more than content with the report, but the organisation, we speculated, had not got the scapegoat it sought. In blame cultures scapegoats abound, solutions tend towards the swift and simple and the status quo holds sway.

On a workshop some eighteen months later I chanced to meet a trainer of the organisation concerned. He knew about the report, but it had never been discussed openly in his team, and its insights – he feared – had been swept under the institutional carpet!

Some Post-reading Reflective Triggers:

- I'm wondering how effective this study was in terms of honouring a holistic perspective that kept *Past – Future* and the qualities of **Figure 5** (5.3) in dialogue;

- In context of **Figure 6** (5.3) I'm considering how proficient this study was in locating and interweaving reality as intellectually constructed and sensed, plus influences of the moment with reality as felt and intuited;

- I wonder if I were to analyse this study in terms of the realities it supports *('sensory/physical'; 'social/cultural 'emotional/transferential'; 'imaginative/ projected'; 'intuitive/transpersonal')*, which would appear most influential (see 5.5); so here goes:

Thinking back over the above study I remember the visual impact the organisational site made on first meeting; the grounds like a large manorial park, the vastness of scale and the immense power this scene imaginatively stimulated for me. At a sensory/physical level the organisational space, functional concrete buildings, sports facilities and constant sensory bombardment of a busy organisation left me feeling physically exhausted at the end of the day. No doubt a similar dynamic was felt – in part – by those who worked here.

At the social/cultural level there was much emphasis within the organisation upon rules and roles. Procedures rather than initiative seemed to rule, and a tradition of macho male physicality prevailed; in fact tradition in all its forms was honoured along with systems of rank and social order. The 'world as it is conventionally taught to be' held much more sway here than the 'world as it was found and discovered' to be.

At an emotional/transferential level, within the one-to-one interviews there was often a palpable feeling of sadness, a sense of grief and loss, as if an emotional message of 'I do my very best and look what they do to me' was seemingly hanging in the air; a bit like a misunderstood teenager might feel towards a rejecting parent. Transferentially, the large grounds and emphasis on physical training with a sports track framing the boundary reminded me of a college of further education while portraying a youthful teenage feel. Was this a teenage culture at heart?

Although the social/cultural level is described in detail in the report, it was really the imaginative/projective level fuelled by emotional/transferential energies that hit us the hardest; the unseen energies that were coursing through the culture. Indeed, our hypotheses first began as little more than imaginative impressions until supported by sensory data or other external evidence.

Surprisingly, the transpersonal/spiritual level appeared to provide us with the best of clues. For instance, individuals within the consultancy team would intuitively arrive at the same summation independent of one another. At other times a sense of resonance with the environment would arise, as if 'the field' were informing us. This experience, qualitatively different to imaginative insight which we could recognise as coming essentially from within, seemed by contrast to be informing us from somewhere beyond ourselves. For instance, though we went through the motions of collecting information and circulating this along with our conclusions to our interviewees and the client system, intuitively, even before our entry into the organisation we playfully caught and described what had gone wrong in the organisation in our initial meeting as a consultancy team at Victoria Station! I wonder how often 'we know' something in this way, but because we lack confidence or a supporting logical rationale dismiss such wisdom as fancy. After all, what client would pay for consultancy at a distance? Organisational faith healing as it were!

Taking all the above levels of influence, I believe these come together as I begin to embody the organisational field; that is to say, when I see and hear and relate to a group or organisation in a sensate and physical way; when I'm informed and shaped by the socio-cultural milieu that prevails; when my emotional history resonates with current events; when I am imaginatively impacted; when I am sufficiently open and in flow with the holistic field that it intuitively speaks to me.

A good traveller leaves no track.

Lao Tse

Epilogue

(Post-contact)

So as this text draws to completion we glimpse the interplay of two experiential dimensions arrayed before us. In one we can appreciate a multi-layered model of experiential reality progressing from *sensate* to *transpersonal* phenomenon (**Figure 7**) – that journeys from the 'conscious and known' to the 'unconscious and unknown'. Complementing this multi-layered field from which we are suggested to co-construct reality, running through and within this, our experiential reality, is a developmental relationship travelling through phases of *orientation* to *resolution* which helps to signpost movement through time (Chapter 2); cycles of inquiry structure research movement here (Chapter 5). Within these simultaneously functioning dimensions, flowing into awareness and constellating around us is the 'now' – or unfolding gestalt of our existence (**Figure 6**); varying qualities of authenticity which enrich our contact and refine our awareness further cement these dimensions to our ongoing experience (Chapter 1). Taken together, these dimensions describe the 'how' and the 'what' of holistic inquiry (**Figures 3, 4** and **5**) and our ability to robustly contact the same is seen to dictate our research excellence (Chapters 3 and 4).

I hope you have found my propositions elucidating and thought-provoking. This said, I feel obliged to caution you that all my theories and speculations are in the final analysis senseless; that is to say, without anchor in your own senses or experience. *Climb over and above my suggestions, test them out and refine your own, for what works for me is unlikely to work for you.* Neither believe nor disbelieve in anything, merely encounter phenomena and observe how your own experiential truth and reality as a Gestalt-alerted practitioner-researcher speak to you.

> *Men do not understand how to see the invisible*
> *through the visible.*
> *They do not realise the arts they employ are*
> *reflections of their own natures.*
> *For all things are like and unlike, compatible and*
> *incompatible, communicating*
> *and non-communicating, intelligent and without*
> *intelligence. Each is a paradox.*
>
> **Hippocrates**

> *Be at peace and see a clear pattern running through*
> *your lives.*
> *Nothing is by chance.*
>
> **Eileen Caddy in Hayward 1990**

ITHACA

Keep Ithaca always in your mind.

Arriving there is what you're destined for

But don't hurry the journey at all.

Better if it lasts for years,

so you're old by the time you reach the island,

wealthy with all you've gained on the way,

not expecting Ithaca to make you rich.

Ithaca gave you the marvellous journey.

Without her you wouldn't have set out.

She has nothing left to give you now.

And if you find her poor, Ithaca won't have fooled you.

Wise as you will have become, so full of experience,

you'll have understood by then what these Ithacas mean.

Konstantinos P. Kavafis, Alexandria, Egypt 1911

References

Addison, R.B. (1989) 'Grounded interpersonal research: an investigation of physician socialisation'. In Parker, M.J. and R.B.Addison (eds) *Entering the circle: hermeneutic investigation in psychology.* SUNY Press, New York, USA.

Assagioli, R. (1976) *Psychosynthesis.* Penguin, New York, USA.

Barber, P. and J. Mulligan (1998) 'The Client-Consultant Relationship'. Chapter 4 in Sadler, P. (ed.) *The Management Consultancy Industry: Examples of Best Practice.* Kogan Page, London.

Barber, P. (1986) Unpublished field notes.

Barber, P. (1990a) Unpublished doctorate notes.

Barber, P. (1990b) 'The Facilitation of Personal and Professional Growth through Experiential Groupwork and Therapeutic Community Practice'. Doctoral thesis, Department of Educational Studies, University of Surrey, Guildford.

Barber, P. (1991/98) 'Caring: The Nature of a Therapeutic Relationship'. Chapter 5 in Jolly and Perry (eds) *Nursing: a Knowledge Base for Practice,* revised 2nd Edition, Edward Arnold.

Barber, P. (1992) 'An Exploration of Experiential Realities and Hidden Agendas in Group Encounter'. Chapter 4 in Mulligan, J. and C. Griffin (eds) *Empowerment through Experiential Learning.* Kogan Page, London.

Barber, P. (1994) *An Experiential Exploration of Stress in Group Settings.* Human Potential Research Group publication, University of Surrey, Guildford.

Barber, P. (1995) *The Trial and Tribulations of Pioneering Experiential Learning in Hong Kong: a reflection upon a workshop entitled 'Facilitating Change'.* Internal report, School of Educational Studies, University of Surrey, Guildford.

Barber, P. (1996a) Unpublished field notes.

Barber, P. (1996b) 'The Therapeutic "Educational" Community as an Agent of Change: Towards a Lewinian Model of Peer Learning. International'. *Journal of Therapeutic Communities and Supportive Organisations,* Vol.17 (8).

Barber, P. (1997a) 'Through the Eyes of a Client and Therapist: An Action Research Approach to Therapy (Part 1)'. *British Gestalt Journal,* Vol.6, No.1.

Barber, P. (1997b) 'Working Transparently with Transference: An Action Research Approach to Therapy (Part 2)'. *British Gestalt Journal,* Vol.6, No.2.

Barber, P. (1999a) 'The Therapeutic Educational Community as a Catalyst of Organisational Learning & Change'. *Therapeutic Communities: the International Journal for Therapeutic Communities and Supportive Organisations,* Vol.20.3.

Barber, P. (1999b) *Consultancy Relationships.* Management Consultancy Business School Publication, Chinor, Oxford.

Barber, P. (2000) *The Consultant and Change.* Module 7, MSc in Management Consultancy, School of Educational Studies, University of Surrey, Guildford.

Barber, P. (2001a) *The Consultant and the Process of Change.* Module 7, MSc in Management Consultancy. Management Consultancy Business School. School of Educational Studies, University of Surrey, Guildford.

Barber, P. (2001b) *The Practitioner-Researcher: An Educational Approach to the Facilitation of Social Inquiry within Groups and Organisations.* Module 9, MSc in Management Consultancy, School of Educational Studies, University of Surrey, Guildford.

Barber, P. (2002) *Researching Personally and Transpersonally: A Gestalt Approach to Facilitating Holistic Inquiry and Change in Groups and Organisations*. Work Based Learning, School of Educational Studies, University of Surrey, Guildford.

Beaumont, H. (1998) 'The Field of the Soul' (Interviewed by Judith Hemming). *British Gestalt Journal*, Vol.7, No.2.

Bion, W.R. (1960/68) *Experience in Groups*. Tavistock, London.

Black, T. and J. Holford (eds) (1999) *Introducing Qualitative Research: A Distance Learning Study Guide. School of Educational Studies*, University of Surrey, Guildford.

Blackham, H.J. (1968) *Humanism*. Pelican Original, Penguin Books Ltd, Middlesex.

Blumer, H. (1969) *Symbolic Interactionism: Perspective & Method*. Prentice Hall, New Jersey, USA.

Bly, R. (1988) *A Little Book on the Human Shadow*. Harper Collins, USA.

Boldt, L.G. (1993) *Zen and the Art of Making a Living: a Practical Guide to Creative Career Design*. Penguin Arkana, London & New York, USA.

Boud, D. and D. Walker (1998) 'Promoting Reflection in Professional Courses: the Challenge of Context'. *Studies in Higher Education*, 23 (2) pp.91–206.

Brammer, M.B., E.L. Shstrom, P.J. Abrego (1989) *Therapeutic Psychology: Fundamentals of Counselling and Psychotherapy*. Prentice Hall International Editions, London.

Buber, M. (1951) *I and Thou*. Scribner's Sons, New York, USA.

Burke, W.W. (1987) *Organisational Development: a Normative View*. Addison-Wesley, USA.

Bushe, G.R. (1998) 'Five Theories of Change Embedded in Appreciative Inquiry'. Presented at the 18th Annual World Congress of Organisational Development, Dublin, July 14–18 1998.

Byrne, D. (1961) 'Anxiety and Experimental Arousal of Affiliation Need'. *Journal of Abnormal Social Psychology*, 63, 660–2, 13.

Capra, F. (1991) *The Tao of Physics*. 3rd updated Edition, Shambhala, Collins, London.

Capra, F. (1997) *The Web of Life: a New Synthesis of Mind and Matter*. Flamingo, Harper-Collins, London.

Carr, W. and S. Kemmis (1986) *Becoming critical*. Falmer, London.

Chalmers, A.F. (1982) *What is this thing called science?* (2nd Edition) COMPLETE.

Clarkson, P. (1989) *Gestalt Counselling in Action*. Counselling in Action Series, Sage, London, pp.28–38.

Clarkson, P. (1991) 'Individuality and Commonality in Gestalt'. *British Gestalt Journal*, Vol.1, No.1.

Clarkson, P. (1993) '2,500 Years of Gestalt: from Heraclitus to the Big Bang'. *British Gestalt Journal*, Vol.1, No.1, pp.4–10.

Cohen, L. and L. Manion (1994) *Research Methods in Education* (4th Edition). Routledge, London.

Cooperrider, D.L. and S. Srivasta (1987) 'Appreciative Inquiry in Organisational Life'. In Pasmore, W. and R. Woodman (eds) *Research in Organisational Change and Development*. Vol.1, pp.129–169, Greenwich, CT: JAI Press, USA.

Cooperrider, D.L. (1990) 'Positive Image, Positive Action: The Affirmative Basis of Organizing'. In Srivasta, S. and D.L. Cooperrider (eds) *Appreciative Management and Leadership*. Jossey-Bass, London.

Critchley, B. and D. Casey (1989) 'Organizations Get Stuck Too'. *Leadership and Organizational Development Journal*, Vol.10, No.4.

244

Descartes, R. (1977) *The essential writings*. (Bion, J.J. trans.) Harper and Row, New York, USA.

Devall, B. and G. Sessions (1985) *Deep Ecology*. Peregrine Smith, Salt Lake City, USA.

Diesing, P. (1972) *Patterns of discovery in the social sciences*. Routledge and Kegan Paul, London.

Douglas, B. and C. Moustakas (1984) *Investigative Social Research: Individual and Team Field Research*. Sage, Beverley Hills, CA, USA

Elliot, J. (1992) 'Action Research: a Framework for Self-Evaluation in Schools'. Working Paper No.1, Teacher-Pupil Interaction and the Quality of Learning. London Schools Council Publication.

Flick, U. (1998) *An Introduction to Qualitative Research*. Sage, London.

Folkins, C.H. (1970) 'Temporal Factors and Cognitive Mediators of Stress Reaction'. *Journal of Personality and Social Psychology*, 14, 173–84, 13.

Fox, M. (1983) *Original Blessing*. Beaser and Co, New Mexico, USA.

Fox, W. (1990) *Toward a Transpersonal Ecology*. Shambhala, Boston, USA.

Frank, L.K. (1939) 'Time Perspectives'. *Journal of Social Philosophy*, 4, pp.293–312.

Frank, M. (1991) 'The Realisation of the Shadow in Dreams'. Chapter 6 in Zweig, C. and J. Abrams (eds) *Meeting the Shadow*. Jeremy Tarcher Inc., Los Angeles, USA.

Friedman, M. (1989) 'Dialogue, Philosophical Anthropology, and Gestalt Therapy. Based on a panel discussion on "Dialogical Gestalt", 11th Gestalt Conference', in *British Gestalt Journal*, 13, No.13, pp.7–40 1990. GPTI publication.

Fry, H. and H. Kolb (1979) 'Experiential Learning Theory and Learning Experiences in Liberal Arts Education'. In Brooks, S. and J. Althol (eds) *New Directions for Experiential Learning*. No.6, pp.79–82, Josey Bass, San Francisco, USA.

Gauthier, P. (1980) 'Psycho-education as a Re-education Model: Theoretical Foundations and Practical Implications'. Chapter 10 in Jansen, E. (ed.) (1980) *The Therapeutic Community*. Croom Helm Ltd, London.

Glaser, B. and A.L. Strauss (1967) *The discovery of grounded theory: strategies for qualitative research*. Adline, New York, USA.

Goffman, E. (1978) *The Presentation of Self in Everyday Life*. Pelican Books, London.

Goodlad, J. (1975) *The dynamics of educational change: towards responsive schools*. New York, USA.

Greenson, R. (1967) *The Technique and Practice of Psychoanalysis*. International Universities Press, New York, USA.

Haas, J. (1977) 'Learning Real Feelings: a Study of High Steel Worker's Reactions to Fear and Danger'. *Sociology of Work Occupations*, 4, 147–70. 13.

Harris, J.B. (1999) 'Gestalt Learning and Training'. *British Gestalt Journal*, Vol.8, No.2.

Hawkins, P. (1980) 'Between Scylla and Charybdis: Staff Training in Therapeutic Communities'. Chapter 13 in Jansen, E. (ed.) *The Therapeutic Community*. Croom Helm Ltd, London.

Hayward, S. and M. Cohen (1988) *Bag of Jewels*. In-Tune Books, Crows Nest, New South Wales, Australia.

Hayward, S. (1990) *A Guide for the Advanced Soul: a Book of Insight*. In-Tune Books, Crows Nest, New South Wales, Australia.

Heelas, P. (1987) 'Exegesis Methods and Aims'. In Clarke, P. (ed.) *The New Evangelists: Recruitment, Methods and Aims of New Religious Movements*. London Ethnographic pp.17–41.

Heidegger, M. (1977) *Basic writings*. Krell, D. (ed.) Harper and Row, New York, USA.

Heron, J. (1974) *The Concept of a Peer Learning Community*. Human Potential Research Project, University of Surrey, Guildford.

Heron, J. (1981) 'Experiential Research Methodology'. In Reason, P. and J. Rowen (eds) *Human Inquiry: A Sourcebook of New Paradigm Research*. Chichester, Wiley.

Heron, J. (1988) 'Impressions of the Other reality: a Collaborative Inquiry into Altered States of Consciousness'. Chapter 9 in *Human Inquiry in Action: Developments in New Paradigm Research*. Reason, P. (ed.) Sage, London.

Heron, J. (1989) *The Facilitator's Handbook*. Kogan Page, London.

Herrick, N.Q. and M. Maccoby (1975) 'Humanizing Work: a Priority Goal of the 1970s'. In Davis, L.E. and A.B. Cherns (eds) *The Quality of Working Life*, Vol.1. The Free Press, New York, USA.

Hinshelwood, B. (1987) *What Happens in Groups*. Free Association Books, London.

Hopkins, D. (1985) *A Teacher's Guide to Classroom Research*. Open University Press, Milton Keynes.

Huang, C.A. (1989) *Tai Ji: Beginner's Tai Ji Book*. Celestial Arts Press, Berkeley, CA, USA.

Hypocrates in Elliot-Binns, C. (1978) *Medicine: The Forgotten Art.* Pitman Medical Press.

I Ching, Wilhelm translation (1951) Routledge & Kegan Paul, London.

Jansen, E. (1980) *The Therapeutic Community*. Croom Helm Ltd, London.

Jones, M. (1952) *Social Psychiatry, a Study of Therapeutic Communities*. Tavistock, London.

Josephson, E. and M. Josephson (eds) (1972) *Man Alone: Alienation in Modern Society*. Dell Publishing Company, New York, USA.

Kahir (1977) edited by Bly, R. Beacon Press, Boston, USA.

Kavafis, K. (1911) webpage: http://kleidarotrypa.blogspot.com/2005/03/ithaca.html

Khan, M. (1983) *Hidden Selves*. Hogarth Press & The Institute of Group Analysis, London.

Knockelmanns, J.J. (ed.) (1967) *Phenomenology*. Garden City, Doubleday, New York, USA.

Kolb, D. and H. Fry (1975) 'Towards an Applied Theory of Experiential Learning'. In Cooper, G (ed.) *Theories of Group Processes*. Wiley, London.

Krathwohl, D.R., B.S. Bloom, B.B. Masia, *Taxonomy of Educational Objectives: The Classification of Educational Goals. Handbook 2: Affective Domain*. Appendix, pp.176–185, David McKay Co., London.

Kuhn, T. (1962) *The Structure of Scientific Revolutions*. University of Chicago Press, USA.

Kvale, S. (1992) *Psychology and Modernism*. Sage, London.

Leonard, G. (1978) *The Silent Pulse*. E.P. Dutton, New York, USA.

Lewin, K. (1946) 'Action research and minority problems'. *Journal of Social Issues*, 2. 34–36.

Lewin, K. (1952) *Field Theory in Social Science*. Tavistock, London.

Lincoln, Y.S. and E.G. Guba (1985) *Naturalistic Inquiry*. Newbury Park, London.

Loewenthal, D. (1996) 'The Postmodern Counsellor: some implications for Practice, Theory, Research and Professionalism'. *Counselling Psychology Quarterly*, Vol.8, No.4, pp.373–381.

Lorentz, L.A. (1991) 'Dimensions of Weather and Climate Attractors'. *Nature*, 353, pp.241–4.

Main, T.F. (1946) 'The Hospital as a Therapeutic Institution'. *Bulletin of the Menninger Clinic*, Vol.10, p.66.

Main, T.F. (1980) 'Some Basic Concepts in Therapeutic Community Work'. Chapter 1 in *The Therapeutic Community Outside the Hospital*. Jansen, E. (ed.), The Richmond Fellowship, Croom Helm, London.

Maslow, A. (1965) 'Cognition of Being in Peak Experience'. *Journal of Genetic Psychology*, 94, 43–66, USA.

Mead, M. (1928) *Coming of age in Samoa*. William C. Marrow, New York, USA.

Menzies, I (1960) *The Functioning of Social Systems as a Defence Against Anxiety*. Tavistock publication, pamphlet No.3, London.

Merton, R.K. (1968) *Social Theory and Social Structure*. The Free Press, New York, USA.

Miles, M.B. and A.M. Huberman (1984) *Qualitative Data Analysis: a Sourcebook of New Methods*. Sage, Newbury Park & London.

Mitroff, I.I. and R.H. Kilmann (1978) *Methodological Approaches to Social Science: Integrating Divergent Concepts and Theories*. Jossey-Bass, San Francisco, USA.

Mitroff, I.I. (1974) *The Subjective Side of Science: Philosophical Inquiry into the Psychology of Apollo Moon Scientists*. Elsevier, Amsterdam, Netherlands.

Morgan, G. (1997) *Images of Organisation*. Sage, London.

Moustakas, C. (1990) *Heuristic research: design, methodology and application*. Sage, Newbury Park.

Moustakas, C. (1994) *Phenomenological research methods*. Sage, London.

Mulligan, J. (1989–99) In conversation with the author.

Nixon, B. (1998) *Making a Difference: Strategies and Real Time Models to Transform your Organisation*. Gilmour Drummond Publishing, Cambridge.

O'Donohue, J. (1997) *Anam Cara: Spiritual Wisdom from the Celtic World*. Bantam Press, Transworld Publications, London.

Parlett, M. (1991) 'Reflections on Field Theory'. *British Gestalt Journal*, Vol.1, No.2, pp.69–81.

Parlett, M. (1993) 'Towards a more Lewinian Gestalt Therapy'. *British Gestalt Journal*, Vol.2, No.2, pp.11–4.

Pascale, R. (1991) *Managing on the Edge*. Penguin Books, London.

Patton, M.Q. (1995) *Qualitative Evaluation and Research Methods*. 2nd Edition, Sage, London.

Paul, D. and J. Lipham (1976) 'Strengthening facilitative environs'. In Lipham, J. and M. Froth (eds) *The principal and individually guided education*. Addison-Wesley, Reading, Massachusetts, USA.

Peck, S. (1993) *Meditations from the road*. Rider, London.

Pedler, M., J. Burgoyne, T. Boydell (1997) *The Learning Company: a Strategy for Sustainable Development*. 2nd Edition, The McGraw Hill Companies, London.

Peplau, H. (1952) *Interpersonal Relations in Nursing: A Conceptual Frame of Reference for Psychodynamic Nursing*. Putman & Sons, New York, USA.

Perls, F.S., R.E. Hefferline, E. Ralph, P. Goodman (1951) *Gestalt Therapy: Excitement and Growth in the Human Personality*. Reprinted 1972 by Souvenir Press, London.

Perls, F.S. (1969) *Gestalt Therapy Verbatim*. Real People Press, Moab, USA.

Perls, F.S. (1976) *The Gestalt Approach and Eye-Witness to Therapy*. Bantam, New York, USA.

Pines, M. (ed.) (1983) *The Evolution of Group Analysis*. Routledge and Kegan Paul, London.

Pollecoffe, M. (1998) MSc Thesis, Department of Educational Studies, University of Surrey, Guildford.

Polster, E. and M. Polster (1974) *Gestalt Therapy Integrated*. Vintage Books, New York, USA.

Polster, E. (1987) *Every Person's Life is Worth a Novel*. W.W. Norton, New York, USA.

Rapoport, R. (1960) *Community as Doctor*. Tavistock, London.

Rapoport, R. (1970) 'Three dilemmas in action research'. *Human Relations*, 23, pp.499-513.

Reason, P. and B. Goodwin (1999) 'Toward a Science of Qualities in Organisations: Lessons from Complexity Theory and Postmodern Biology. Concepts and Transformation'. *International Journal of Action Research and Organizational Renewal*, 4:3, pp.281-317.

Reason, P. (1981) 'Methodological Approaches to Social Science by Ian Mitroff and Ralph Kilman: An Appreciation'. Chapter 4 in Reason, P. and J. Rowen (eds) *Human Inquiry: A Sourcebook of New Paradigm Research*. John Wiley & Sons, Chichester.

Reason, P. (1988) 'Whole Person Medical Practice'. Chapter 5 in *Human Inquiry in Action: Developments in New Paradigm Research*. Reason, P. (ed.) Sage, London.

Reason, P. (1989) 'The co-operative inquiry group'. In *Human inquiry: developments in new paradigm research*. Reason, P. (ed.) Sage, London.

Reinharz, S. (1981) 'Implementing New Paradigm Research: a Model for Training and Practice'. In Reason, P. and J. Rowen (eds) *Human Inquiry: A Sourcebook of New Paradigm Research*. Wiley, Chichester.

Robson, C. (1983) *Experiment, design and statistics in psychology*. 2nd Edition, Penguin, London.

Robson, C. (1995) *Real World Research: a resource for Social Scientists & Practitioner-Researchers*. Oxford & Cambridge Press.

Rogers, C. (1967) *On Becoming a Person*. Constable, London.

Rogers, C. (1983) *Freedom to Learn for the Eighties*. Merril, Columbus, Ohio, USA.

Roszak, T. (1992) *The Voice of the Earth*. Simon & Schuster, New York, USA.

Rowen, J. (1981) 'A Dialectical Paradigm for Research'. In Reason, P. and J. Rowen (eds) Human Inquiry: *A Sourcebook of New Paradigm Research*. John Wiley & Sons, Chichester.

RSA (Royal Society of Arts) (1995) *Tomorrow's Company*. Copies available from RSA (T) 0171 839 1641.

Sadler, D.R. (1981) 'Intuitive Data Processing as a Potential Source of Bias in Educational Evaluation'. *Educational Evaluation and Policy Analysis*, 3, 25-31, 375.

Schwartz, P. and J. Lever (1976) 'Fear and Loathing in a College Mixer'. *Urban Life*, 4, 314-431, 13.

Scott, D. and R. Usher (1999) *Researching Education: Data, Methods and Theory in Educational Enquiry*. Cassell, London.

Shohet, R. (2005) 'The Work of Parker Palmer'. *Self and Society*, Vol.32 No.6, pp.37-41.

Smith, E.W.L. (1996) *Perlism, Gestalt therapy and the Concentration on Personal Process*.

Spradley, J.P. (1980) *Participant Observation*. Holt, Rinehart & Winston, New York, USA.

Staemmler, F.M. (1997) 'Cultivated Uncertainty: An Attitude for Gestalt Therapists'. *British Gestalt Journal*, Vol.6, No.1, pp.40-8.

Stapley, L.F. (1996) *The Personality of the Organization: a Psycho-Dynamic Explanation of Culture and Change*. Free Association Books, London.

Stevens, B. (1984) *Burst out Laughing*. Celestial Arts, Berkeley, USA.

Strauss, A.L. (1987) *Qualitative Analysis for Social Sciences*. Cambridge University Press, Cambridge.

Susman, C.I. and R.D. Evered (1978) 'An assessment of scientific merits of action research'. *Administrative Science Quarterly*, 23, 582-603. 60.

Suzuki, D.T. (1974) *Living by Zen*. First published 1950, Rider, London.

Tao Te Ching. Ta-Kao, C. translation (1976) Unwin Paperbacks, London.

Tosey, P. and J. Gregory (1998) 'The Peer Learning Community in Higher Education: Reflections on Practice'. *Innovations in Education and Training International*, 35, Issue 1.

Tuckman, B.W. (1965) 'Developmental Sequence in Small Groups'. *Psychological Bulletin*, 63.

Waitley, D. (1995) 'Empires of the Mind'. BCA, London and New York, USA.

Weick, K.E. (1985) 'Systematic Observational Methods'. In Lindzey, G. and E. Aronson (eds) *The Handbook of Social Psychology*. Vol.2, 2nd Edition, Addison-Wesley. Reading, Massachusetts, USA.

Wheelan, S.A., E.A. Pepitone, V. Abt (1990) *Advances in Field Theory*. Sage, London.

Whiteley, S. and J. Gordon (1979) *Group Approaches to Psychiatry*. Routledge & Kegan Paul, London.

Wilmot, J. (2005) 'Psychology for Teachers'. *Self and Society*, Vol.32 No.6, pp.31-6.

Winnicott, D.W. (1965) *The maturational processes and the facilitating environment: studies in the theory of emotional development*. Chapter 12, 'Ego distortion in terms of the true and false self'. Hogarth Press, London.

Woldt, A. and R.E. Ingersoll (1991) 'Where in the "Yang" has the "Yin" Gone in Gestalt Therapy?' *British Gestalt Journal*, Vol.1, No.2, pp.94-103.

Woldt, A.L. and S.M. Tolman (eds) (2005) *Gestalt Therapy: History, Theory and Practice*. Sage, California/London.

Yin, R.K. (1989) *Case study research: design and methods*. 2nd Edition, Sage, London.

Yontef, G. (1996) 'Gestalt Supervision'. *British Gestalt Journal*, Vol.5, No.2.

Zeisel, J. (1981) *Inquiry by Design: Tools for Environment-behaviour Research*. Cambridge University Press, Cambridge.

Zinker, J. (1978) *Creative Process in Gestalt Therapy*. Brunner Mazel, New York, USA.

Zweig, C. and J. Abrams (eds) (1991) *Meeting the Shadow*. Jeremy Tarcher Inc., Los Angeles, USA.

Index